FINDING GOD AMONG OUR NEIGHBORS

FINDING GOD AMONG OUR NEIGHBORS

AN INTERFAITH SYSTEMATIC THEOLOGY

KRISTIN JOHNSTON LARGEN

Fortress Press
Minneapolis

FINDING GOD AMONG OUR NEIGHBORS

An Interfaith Systematic Theology

Cover image: Peeling paint worn tree © iStockphoto.com / John_Woodcock
Cover design: Alisha Lofgren

Library of Congress Cataloging-in-Publication Data is available

Print ISBN: 978-0-8006-9933-8

eBook ISBN: 978-1-4514-3090-5

The paper used in this publication meets the minimum requirements of American National Standard for Information Sciences — Permanence of Paper for Printed Library Materials, ANSI Z329.48-1984.

Manufactured in the U.S.A.

This book was produced using PressBooks.com, and PDF rendering was done by PrinceXML.

To Betty, my mother, Bob and Priscilla, my father and stepmother, and Andrew, my brother: for your support and encouragement; and for showing me the meaning of faith and love in myriad ways, over and over again.

CONTENTS

Acknowledgements

I have a great many people to thank for their support and assistance during the research and writing of this book. First and foremost, I want to thank the ATS Lilly Theological Research Grants program, which awarded me a faculty fellowship in 2011–2012 that supported my sabbatical travel to Israel and Palestine, India, Japan, and Turkey in the spring of 2012. This practical experience proved invaluable in helping ground my understanding and presentation of the four world religions engaged in this text. My understanding of each was greatly enriched by firsthand conversation about, observation of, and participation in different religious beliefs and practices in these non-Christian contexts. I also want to thank the Lutheran Theological Seminary at Gettysburg for the generous eight-month sabbatical; and in particular, Dean Robin Steinke and President Michael Cooper-White for their strong advocacy of my work and its role in our seminary community.

Several people read and commented upon different drafts of different chapters, and their suggestions were of great assistance to me. Any errors or misrepresentations that remain are my responsibility alone. In particular, I want to thank Rabbi Carl Choper, Brooks Schramm, Richard Payne, and Zeyneb Sayilgan for their helpful comments.

Of the many, many people I met and spoke with in my travels, the following individuals warrant particular mention and thanks. While I was in Israel I had several insightful conversations about Judaism in general, and the history of Judaism in Israel in particular, with Dr. Ophir Yarden, Director of Educational Initiatives, Interreligious Coordinating Council of Israel. In addition, I was hosted at the Shabbat service at Kehilat Kol Haneshama, a Reformed synagogue, by Dr. Sarah Bernstein, Associate Director of the ICCI. She and her husband, Rabbi Michael Marmur, Ph.D., Vice President for Academic Affairs of Hebrew Union College, Jerusalem campus, welcomed me warmly to their home for the Shabbat meal, and the conversation around the table was lively and very interesting. I am deeply appreciative of their hospitality.

In Japan, the monastic community who hosted me at the Shingon temple in Koyasan was kind and gracious, including providing English translations for the recitations at the morning service. Kaori Kodama was an excellent guide to Koyasan: she took me all around the mountain, giving me an excellent introduction to the history and contemporary religious practices of the monastic communities and the many pilgrims who visit each year. There were two people in particular who facilitated my experience in Kyoto. First, Dr. Eisho Nasu, professor of Shin Buddhist studies at Ryukoku University, helped get me oriented to the university (including a much-treasured Internet connection!), the Monbou Kaikan, and the Nishi Hongwanji, the mother temple for Jodo Shinshu Buddhism. Second, Daisuke Sasaki, graduate student in the program for training priests at Ryukoku, toured me around a variety of temples in Kyoto. In particular, he guided me around Daitokuji, the headquarters of one school of Rinzai Zen. In addition to a fabulous multi-course traditional Zen meal at one of the temples in the complex, one of the monks at the temple where Daisuke lives invited us for a brief Zen service and then a formal tea ceremony. This was one of the highlights of my trip to Japan.

While I was in Istanbul, Dr. Faris Kaya hosted me at the Istanbul Foundation for Science and Culture and gave me an excellent introduction to the history and role of Islam in Turkey, and the work of Bediuzzaman Said Nursi. Hakan Gülerce, graduate student at Istanbul University, was extraordinarily gracious with his time and energy: he spent several days taking me through some of Istanbul's many mosques, and introducing me to Turkish coffee and the best baklava in the city. Also, he facilitated a meeting with Arzu Çerkez and Gülçin Kaya who took me to their *dershane*, where we had prayers, ate dinner, and then read from Nursi's works. All the women in the madrasah were very kind and welcoming to me. Finally, I spent a lovely day with Nazil Inal, who gave me a different, secular perspective on Istanbul.

Finally, Moses Penumaka was of great assistance to me both in planning my trip to India and offering support while I was there. During the trip, I was hosted and toured by a variety of people. In Chennai, my friend and colleague Monica Melanchthon, formerly of Gurukul Lutheran Theological College, graciously showed me around Chennai, including the San Thome Church and St. Thomas Mount Church, the Ramakrishna Mutt Temple, and the Kapaleeshwarar temple. In addition, Prasuna Nelevala invited me to St. Peter Paul's Lutheran Church in Naidupet, where I preached and celebrated International Women's Day with the newly consecrated bishop of South Andhra Lutheran Church, the Rt. Rev. Michael Benhur. His family hosted us for lunch after the service. Then, in Hyderabad, I stayed with John Devarapalli, his wife Shiphra, and their family—including David Onesimus and his sister Sowmya—who fed me very well and took me all over the city. They treated me like family, and I am grateful to them for their many kindnesses.

I also want to thank two groups of students at the Lutheran Theological Seminary at Gettysburg, with whom I tested out drafts of the manuscript. First, the members of "Doing Theology Interreligiously," fall 2012, read and commented upon several chapters, and together we worked out places of weakness and strength. They are: Benjamin S. Erzkus, Fritz E. Fowler, Christine Kirchner, Victoria A. Larson, J. Andrew McCaffery, Jane F. Mountain, M.D., Rudolf W. Smith, Felicia Swartz, Ron Valadez, Chasity L. Wiener, and Stephanie J. Zinn. Second, the students in the Introduction to Systematic Theology course, spring 2012, read the entire manuscript and made very helpful comments and critiques. Those students are: Jono Adams, Zachary Baer, Lamar S. Bailey, Patrick Ballard, Tristan Benson, Martha S. Boyd, Julie Bringman, Adam Buff, Erin M. Burns, Seanchai Dougherty, Robin Fero, Joseph Graumann Jr., Joshua W. Gyson, Pam Illick, Amy Krause, Ellen Lundie, Jan Martin, Jeff Martin, Barbara Oshlo, Christine Roe, James E. Smith, and Andrew Wagner. The book is better for their input and engagement.

Finally, I would like to thank my editors at Fortress Press, Will Bergkamp, Lisa Gruenisen, and Marissa Wold, for their support, good advice, and shepherding of the manuscript from start to finish. It was a great pleasure working with them.

Introduction

Imagine that you are building a house. The first things that need to be put in place are the basics: the foundation, the walls, the roof. Only once these core pieces are set is it possible to attend to the interior aspects of the house: bookshelves, kitchen cabinets, curtains. These decorative pieces are not essential to the construction of the home, but they certainly make it a nicer place to live.

This is the metaphor that I find helpful in describing the place of interreligious dialogue in much of contemporary Christian systematic theology. If you pick up any one-volume systematics written in the past few decades, it is typical to find one chapter on "Religious Pluralism" nestled somewhere toward the end—if it is there at all. The reason for this is that, typically, consideration of other religious traditions has been seen as "window dressing" for Christian theology: it is not essential to the task, but something that occurs alongside it—as a footnote or an aside. In other words, once the Christian "house" has been built, with all the right doctrines in all the right places, then one can engage in some interreligious exploration—if one has the time and the inclination to spruce the place up a bit.

This book is an attempt to do systematic theology in a new way, by considering interreligious engagement as part of the *foundation* of Christian theology, rather than its decoration. In the context of this book, what this means is that, for example, in the construction of a Christian doctrine of God, I include for consideration the concept of the goddess in Hinduism; and in the construction of a Christian understanding of the human person, I include for consideration Islam's belief in humanity's capacity to obey God. In this way, I am attempting to incorporate some general methods and commitments of comparative theology into the basic practice of Christian systematic theology itself, such that the task of defining and describing Christian doctrine includes *inherently* the task of interpreting that doctrine in conversation with specific practices and beliefs of non-Christian religious traditions.

The reason for this is twofold. First, by assuming that Christian theology can accomplish the task of observing, articulating, and proclaiming the work and presence of God in the world without any acknowledgment of that work and presence in non-Christian religions, we unnecessarily restrict the theological enterprise and we also exclude millions of people from the scope of God's self-revelation. Second, the human family is deeply and vastly

1

interconnected, with bonds of love, work, and play interweaving all of us together all around the globe. These bonds crisscross religious boundaries in all kinds of ways, and therefore, when Christian theology is trying to make sense of human life in the world and the relationship human beings have to God, it must recognize that what Christians confess about God, creation, and human beings crosses those boundaries, too—being both informed by and informing non-Christian religions.

I recognize that such work is not easy. For many students of theology, beginning this task for the first time, it is enough to try and get one's head around Augustine, Luther, Barth, Cone, and Ruether, let alone Muhammad and the Buddha. Quickly the task seems to spiral out of hand and out of control, and one is always in danger of losing one's way. This may be true, but frankly, it would be true without the addition of Muhammad and the Buddha; Christian theology is never anything but challenging, multifaceted, and dangerous: How could it be otherwise when we are venturing to name God, describe salvation, and envision the reign of God? So, while it cannot be denied that there are risks and challenges to this enterprise, I argue that the scales tip heavily on the side of reward; and there are three fruits in particular of this comparative work that make it of such critical importance for Christian theology.

First, in light of the interconnectedness of the human family mentioned above, it is incumbent upon Christian theology to engage non-Christian religious traditions for the sake of the neighbor, whom Christians are called both to refrain from bearing false witness against, and even more, to love. Second, Christian theology can and should expect to learn something about God in the course of that engagement, based on God's own universal self-revelation. Finally, Christian theology can and should expect that it will be stretched and challenged, but at the same time deepened and strengthened through this engagement, in ways that can transform and nurture the whole Christian community, empowering not only its witness to the gospel but also its relationships to non-Christian communities all over the world, with whom it must partner in the work of justice and peace. It is my hope that all three of these commitments are demonstrated in the chapters that follow.

INTRODUCTION TO PART ONE

There are two particular points of elaboration and explanation that are necessary by way of introduction to the first part of this book. The first relates to the specific audience for which this book is intended, and the second relates to the specific content of the chapters themselves.

The first four chapters consist of brief introductions to four major non-Christian world religions: Hinduism, Judaism, Buddhism, and Islam; and the choice of these four in particular requires a word of explanation. Certainly, the term "world religions" or "global religions" is not the category it used to be, in light of the unprecedented, rapid movement of both people and ideas in the twentieth and twenty-first centuries. Besides merely pointing to "religions that are practiced in the world," which would be its most general meaning, more specifically, the category of "world" religions refers to religious traditions that are not geographically bound: they transcend national, cultural, and physical barriers. Christianity, Buddhism, and Islam warrant the term because they are, inherently, "missionary" religions—that is, they actively welcome new adherents in new geographical locations: "In these traditions, the very core of their faith includes the notion that their religion is greater than any local group and cannot be confined to the cultural boundaries of any particular region."[1] Judaism and Hinduism belong to this category not because of an inherent transnational principle within each religion itself, but primarily because of migration and the establishment of diaspora populations all over the world. Four of these five are also the largest global religious traditions—Judaism is the exception. Certainly, other traditions could be considered: Sikhism likely would be the next logical choice. However, these four religious traditions, together with Christianity, are the ones typically named as the principal "world religions," and so they are the ones included here.

The introductions to these religions are intended specifically for Christians, particularly for Christians who are in seminary and preparing for careers in public ministry. Here is why that is important. Given my intended audience, I have chosen and organized the material for these chapters into categories that make sense for Christians, anticipating the questions Christians will ask, and the specific things Christians will want to know. What this means is that, basically, I am putting Hinduism into a Christian-shaped box, custom-fitting it for Christian eyes and minds. Inevitably, then, there will be distortions and omissions.

Think of it this way. Imagine that you have been asked to interview someone, to learn about who she is and what is significant in her life. The way you choose to do this is to ask her ten questions that you think are the most important, the most critical, the best, for getting to the heart of who she is. And, in the interview, that is what you do: you ask your questions, she answers them, and then you thank her and leave. Certainly there is no doubt you will have

---

1. *Global Religions: An Introduction*, ed. Mark Juergensmeyer (New York: Oxford University Press, 2003), 7.

received very important information, and certainly you will have a good picture of who she is. In that way, your interview will have been a success. However, think about what you have missed by not allowing *her* to narrate the story of her own life: allowing her to choose the topics of importance, allowing her to judge what is and is not significant, and allowing her to speak on the things that are most critical in her eyes. You may well miss some vital pieces of the puzzle, and you may distort other things by describing them out of context: giving some things too much attention, and giving other things too little.

So too, I fear, in the four chapters ahead. In order to be as clear as possible for a Christian audience, I have sacrificed some of each religion's own voice (I hope not too much), and I am telling their story in a way different from how they would tell it for themselves (continuing the metaphor). I say this to be honest up front: I am a Western Christian writing primarily for Western Christians, and this fact naturally affects the picture I am painting of these religions. Thus, it is not the same picture that an insider would paint. One's perspective always influences one's conclusions, and all scholars, particularly scholars of religion, must be transparent about that fact. It is my hope that the reader will seek out other sources of information, particularly texts and/or personal contacts from within these traditions, so that the unique voices of these religions might be heard on their own terms.

The second point of explanation relates to the content of these four chapters—specifically their brevity. Obviously in a book of this size and scope, there are serious and substantial limitations on the amount of detail, the number of differing facets, and the various exceptions to the rule that can be included. Some of this is actually quite fine: for those who are unfamiliar with these religious traditions, there is a limit to the amount of new information that can be accurately retained and processed in the grand scheme of this theological endeavor. Too much information is simply overwhelming and unhelpful. These chapters are meant to be stepping stones and entry points, nothing more.

However, the downside, of course, is that it has been impossible to describe at any length the nuances, subtleties, and intricacies of each tradition—to say nothing of the various subtraditions within each. These chapters use broad strokes, not detailed outlines; highways, not the back roads; and headlines, not marginalia. There is simply no way in these introductory chapters to do justice to the complexities of each religious tradition; thus I have not even tried.

Again, let me suggest an analogy. Imagine as a Christian you were asked to describe the Christian faith for someone entirely unfamiliar with it. Suddenly, you would find yourself in the unenviable position of having to describe and explain accurately not only mainline Protestantism, but also Roman

Catholicism, Eastern Orthodoxy, Pentecostal traditions, Seventh Day Adventists, etc. Somehow, you would have to create an umbrella under which these very different Christian groups could be located—to some degree at least. I hope it is clear that you would, by necessity, have to leave some individual particularities out, make use of generalizations, and privilege some traditions over others, based on your own particular Christian lens.

For example, as a Lutheran, when describing baptism, even though I can describe and explain "believer's baptism," my own theological understanding of baptism is rooted in infant baptism, and therefore my explanation of what baptism is, why Christians baptize, what baptism means in the life of an individual reflects that particular standpoint. This type of preferencing is unavoidable; and, inevitably, it will be in evidence in the following chapters, as my description of each religion necessarily reflects not only my own biases, but my academic and personal experiential background as well.

One final point of clarification needs mentioning here as well. Throughout the book, I have chosen not to use the diacritical marks needed to accurately transliterate foreign words into English, words from Arabic, Sanskrit, and Hebrew, for example. These marks are used to indicate pronunciation, vowel placement, and inflection, among other things. Obviously, they are very important for those who know the languages; however, for those who do not, they are meaningless and confusing; and because this book is not designed for specialists, I have chosen to omit them, primarily to avoid bogging down the general reader. Those who know the words in the original languages will mentally supply them, and those who do not will not miss them.

INTRODUCTION TO PART TWO

The second part of this book is where the heart of the comparative work occurs. As noted previously, the three chapters that make up Part Two demonstrate the core theological claim that I argue is essential for a faithful and relevant articulation of Christian theology in the twenty-first-century global context: Christian theology is strengthened and enhanced through the engagement with non-Christian religions. Basically, the argument is that "[Comparative theology] can in non-trivial ways be in harmony with traditional (doctrinal) theology";[2] and, even more, comparative theology actually can augment and deepen doctrinal theology.

---

2. Francis X. Clooney, S.J., *Comparative Theology: Deep Learning Across Religious Borders* (Malden, MA: Wiley-Blackwell, 2010), 111.

Seeking to demonstrate that claim, Part Two is comprised of three constructive theological chapters, each of which focuses on one central Christian theological locus—God, humanity, and creation—enriched by a vital comparative component. The chapters are laid out as follows. Each chapter elaborates the core claims Christian theology makes regarding each locus—the central assertions Christianity affirms about God, the human being, and creation. However, interspersed and alongside those claims, relevant and related doctrines from Buddhism, Hinduism, Judaism, and Islam are introduced. Through this juxtaposition, the chapters seek to nuance and deepen an understanding of Christian theology, helping the reader see familiar territory in new ways, and gain a fresh perspective on traditional faith claims.

In his book, *Comparative Theology: Deep Learning Across Religious Borders*, Francis Clooney writes: "If [comparative theology] does not disrespect doctrinal expressions of truth, neither does it merely repeat doctrinal statements as if nothing is learned from comparative reflection. Rarely, if ever, will comparative theology produce new truths, but it can make possible fresh insights into familiar and revered truths, and new ways of receiving those truths."[3] This, then, is the overarching goal of the book as a whole: creating for the Christian reader in particular the possibility of fresh insights, and new ways of understanding and articulating those insights—not only for one's own theological edification, but for the sake of the church as whole, and the presentation of the gospel.

In the pursuit of this goal, one deliberate choice has been made in constructing these three chapters: I intentionally have not drawn specific conclusions from the interreligious comparisons I present, in order to avoid telling the reader what she should think about this or that particular doctrine and its relationship to Christianity. Instead, I have left the specific interpretation to the reader, inviting her to make connections for herself. The simple reason for this is that I do not want readers to be limited or hindered by preestablished assumptions that prescribe what conclusions "should" be drawn. Instead, my hope is that readers will see connections I have not, thus contributing to the theological conversation in their own ways, from their own theological contexts and traditions. At the same time, however, to facilitate these connections, there are questions at the end of each chapter, inviting reflection on specific interreligious contrasts.

Finally, one last thing needs to be said. The principal theological conviction that grounds this particular book, and the comparative method that

3. Ibid., 112.

shapes it, is my belief that theology *matters*: it matters for one's individual life in the world, and it matters for the human community as a whole. It is my strong conviction that Christian theology can and should positively inform and transform the way Christians think and live, in such a way that not only are their lives richer and more meaningful, but also that they, in turn, through the power of the Holy Spirit, are inspired to create richer and more meaningful societies. But this can only happen if Christian theology meets people where they are, and speaks to the situations in which they find themselves.

James Cone, in *Risks of Faith*, recounts his struggle during his doctoral studies as he tried to bring his experiences as an African American in the civil rights movement into his theology courses. He writes, "When I asked my professors about what theology had to do with the black struggle for racial justice, they seemed surprised and uncomfortable with the question, not knowing what to say, and anxious to move on with the subject matter as they understood it. I was often told that theology and the struggle for racial justice were separate subjects."[4] This is untenable. If Christian theology has nothing to say about race, justice, and an ethical society—as though God has no interest in race, justice, and an ethical society—it renders itself irrelevant and relegates itself to the sidelines of human existence.

In the same way, I would argue that if Christian theology has nothing to say about the vast world of millions and millions of people with vibrant, diverse, passionately held religious beliefs and practices, it is hardly living up to its name as "God-talk." More is required of us. In addition to fidelity to the gospel and a healthy respect for the tradition, Christian theology also requires courage, daring, and innovation. It requires seeking God where God is found, loving the neighbor God has placed in front of us, and trusting always that God is with us, guiding us down paths as yet untrodden, where a marvelous future awaits. This is the spirit in which this book was written. I hope that it is also the spirit with which it is read.

4. James H. Cone, *Risks of Faith: The Emergence of a Black Theology of Liberation, 1968-1998* (Boston: Beacon, 1999), xiv.

PART I

Introductions to World Religions

1

A Brief Introduction to Hinduism

By design, I began writing this chapter in a particularly auspicious place: sitting on the roof of my hotel in Varanasi, India, looking out over the Ganges River.

Figure 1.1. On the banks of the Ganges, Varanasi, India, March 2012

The city of Varanasi (formerly called Benares) is one of the holiest cities in India, believed to have been founded by the god Shiva. It is sanctified by its proximity to the river Ganges, which is worshiped as a goddess who has the power both to purify sins and release a soul from the cycle of birth and death.

Millions and millions of pilgrims come here every year to bathe in the purifying waters, to die and be cremated on the banks of the river, and to worship in the temples scattered throughout the city. Though certainly touched by modernity, Varanasi continues to present an ancient face of Hinduism; and it was there, walking among sadhus, beggars, and pilgrims, that I began to think about how to introduce Hinduism to Christians. It is no easy task.

Of the five major world religions (Hinduism, Judaism, Buddhism, Christianity, and Islam), it is certainly the case that Hinduism is both the least known and the least experienced by most Americans. This state of ignorance cannot continue, however, as the Hindu population both in the United States and worldwide continues to grow. Hinduism is the third largest religion in the world, behind Christianity and Islam. The majority of Hindus are located in India (95 percent, according to one source[1]) and Nepal, a secular state though constitutionally Hindu, but Hinduism is on the rise in the United States as well, primarily due to immigration. According to the Hindu American Foundation, "From 1,700 people in 1900, the Hindu population in America grew to approximately 387,000 by 1980 and 1.1 million in 1997. As of 2008, the estimated U.S. population of Hindus of Indian origin is approximately 2.29 million (mainly of Indian and Indo-Caribbean descent). Estimates are that there may also be as many as 1 million practicing American Hindus, not of Indian origin, in the U.S.[2] In addition, the website for Diana Eck's well-regarded Pluralism Project (based at Harvard University) lists 723 Hindu temples and centers in the United States, and notes that there is a Hindu center and/or temple in every state, with the exception of Montana, Wyoming, North Dakota, South Dakota, and Vermont.[3]

HINDUISM: A WAY OF LIFE, NOT A CREED

Of all the major world religions discussed in this book, in my view, Hinduism is the most difficult for Christians to engage with and understand. Partly this is because the basic assumptions Christians make about what a religion is—the characteristics it has, the role it plays in one's life, and the questions it both asks and answers—simply do not fit Hinduism very well. Here is one example. Instinctively, when Christians begin to learn about another religious tradition, they want to know what the practitioners believe: their basic confessional statements, their unifying doctrines, etc. Frustratingly, however, Hinduism

---

1. Mark W. Muesse, *The Hindu Traditions* (Minneapolis: Fortress Press, 2011), 6.

2. http://www.hafsite.org/resources/hinduism_101/hinduism_demographics.

3. http://pluralism.org/directory/index/?sort=state%2Ccity%2Ctitle&tradition=Hindu.

not a belief system

simply does not have any of those things: rather, by definition, Hinduism is *not* a belief system. In fact, the Supreme Court of India, in the course of a ruling on a particular case, declared as one of its seven characteristics of a Hindu (listed in full later in the chapter): "In distinction from followers of other religions, one does not believe in a specific set of theological or philosophical conceptions."[4] Instead, as one Indian told me while we were touring the Taj Mahal, Hinduism is a "way of life." What does that mean?

Simply put, it means that Hinduism is more about how one conducts one's life than about what one holds to be true. That is, Hinduism is more about "orthopraxis," right actions, than "orthodoxy," right beliefs. Or, as Axel Michaels says, "Belief is secondary to behavior."[5] So, where what makes one a Christian is one's belief in Jesus Christ (and, correspondingly, baptism), what makes one a Hindu is being born and raised in a Hindu family and living one's life in accordance with specific religious customs, as expressed in a specific geographic, cultural, and familial context. One of the consequences of this is that Hinduism is not a missionary religion and does not actively seek converts. On the one hand, this is because many Hindus recognize other religious traditions as valid spiritual paths; and on the other, it is because many argue that only "Hindus by birth" are true Hindus. It also means that "Hinduism" as a whole is difficult, if not impossible to define. Let me explain.

The first thing that must be emphasized is that Hinduism is not one single religion, the way Christians understand the meaning of that term. Instead, it is more accurately seen as a medley of religious traditions that originated in India, best described not as "a monolithic entity but rather a conglomerate of religions that share certain traits in common."[6] As one scholar describes it: "What we label 'Hinduism' ranges from monotheism to polytheism, from monism to materialism and atheism; from nonviolent ethics to moral systems that see as imperative elaborate blood sacrifices to sustain the world; from critical, scholastic philosophical discussion to the cultivation of sublime, mystical, wordless inner experiences."[7]

Not surprisingly then, Mark Muesse opens his introductory textbook on Hinduism with the following sentence: "As strange as it may seem, most Hindus

---

4. Taken from *World Religions*, ed. Thomas Robinson and Hillary Rodrigues (Peabody, MA: Hendrickson, 2006), 175

5. Axel Michaels, *Hinduism: Past and Present*, trans. Barbara Harshav (Princeton: Princeton University Press, 2004), 14.

6. Steven Rosen, *Essential Hinduism* (Lanham, MD: Rowman & Littlefield, 2006), 17.

7. *World Religions Today*, ed. John L. Esposito, Darrell J. Fasching, and Todd Lewis, 3rd ed. (Oxford: Oxford University Press, 2008), 303–4.

do not think of themselves as practicing a religion called Hinduism."[8] Such a statement is unthinkable for Christians, who by definition self-identify with the religion that carries the name of the one they confess as God incarnate, savior, and lord. "Hinduism," however, is an umbrella category that was applied to a variety of traditions in India after the fact: the term didn't even exist until the late eighteenth/early nineteenth century, when the British coined it to categorize the religious traditions they were encountering in colonial India. The word *Hindu* has been around much longer, since the twelfth century or so, and was first used to describe the people living around the Indus River, now located in Pakistan. Over time, this whole region of India came to be called "Hindustan." However, what is important for our purposes is that, initially, the word *Hindu* did not have any particular religious significance. Instead, in the course of a few centuries, a purely geographic descriptor was morphed into a religious descriptor—and not by the people themselves, but by outsiders: hence the word itself has no inherently religious characteristics. In essence, then, the word *Hinduism* is a somewhat artificial designation, coined by scholars in the West to try to name and categorize Indian religion on the model of Christianity.[9]

For this reason, all definitions of Hinduism are long, complicated, and consume several pages of almost any introductory text. Here is part of the problem: "in India, we are dealing with various religions that belong to one geographically definable cultural space, influence one another, and sometimes overlap, but that often differ considerably from one another in their founders, holy writings, doctrine, divine worlds, rituals, languages, historical conditions, and supporters."[10] Even though Christianity comprises a wide variety of traditions and expressions, all Christians still ground their faith on the same historical figure—Jesus; the same text—the Bible; and to a large, though not universal extent, the same confession—the Nicene and/or Apostles' Creeds. Hinduism cannot claim any corresponding universal as a core principle of identity. In fact, when it comes right down to it, Judaism, Christianity, and Islam actually have more in common than many of the traditions subsumed under the category of Hinduism.[11]

Let me make that comparison explicit. Imagine that a scholar from the East had come to the Middle East around the tenth century, and determined

---

8. Muesse, *The Hindu Traditions*, 1.

9. Steven Rosen notes that the very concept of "Hinduism" as a world religion only developed with the British colonization of India in the nineteenth century. *Essential Hinduism*, 23.

10. Michaels, *Hinduism: Past and Present*, 17.

11. Ibid.

that Judaism, Christianity, and Islam were all variations of the same religion simply because they all were founded in the same general area, and they all had their roots in the same mythology, sharing similar stories, and similar ideas about the world, God, and humanity. An umbrella term might be created to categorize and group them together, based on simple geography: Jordanism or Euphratesism. To some degree, this is what happened in India; and now we are left with a word that is almost impossible to do without, and yet we must recognize that it does not carry the specificity of meaning once assumed. In light of this, many scholars would agree with the statement that, "Today without wanting to admit it, we know that Hinduism is nothing but an orchid cultivated by European scholarship. It is much too beautiful to be torn out, but it is a greenhouse plant: It does not exist in nature."[12]

HINDUISM'S ORIGINS

So how and when did Hinduism begin? While there is no shortage of historical scholars, sages, and teachers in Hinduism, there is no historical founder of the religion as a whole, no figure comparable to Jesus, the Buddha, Abraham, or Muhammad. As a consequence, no historical founder means that there is no firm date of origin of Hinduism, either. Scholars agree that Hinduism is the oldest living major religious tradition, but beyond that simple fact there is much debate, since it is clear that what we today call Hinduism is made up of different beliefs and practices that were handed down orally for millennia before they were finally written down. Thus, as the oral transmission of tradition is notoriously difficult to conclusively establish, there are wide variances even among scholars as to when certain texts, specific practices, and key doctrines originated. For example, the earliest known sacred texts of Hinduism, the Vedas, date back to at least 3000 bce, but some date them back even further, to 8000–6000 bce; and some Hindus themselves believe these texts to be of divine origin, and therefore timeless.

Related to this, it is also worth mentioning here that there is no designated religious hierarchy that determines official Hindu doctrine or practice. Thus there is no one who can speak for Hindus as a whole, and no single authority regarding what is "truly" Hindu or not. This means that many of the natural questions Christians might want ask about Hinduism—"What do Hindus believe about life after death?" "What do Hindus believe about abortion?" "What are the most important practices in Hinduism"—have no simple answer. You may well get ten different answers from ten different Hindus on each of

---

12. Quoted in Michaels, *Hinduism: Past & Present*, 12.

these questions. There simply is no one authority that establishes "orthodox" Hindu belief and practice. This is not to say, however, that there are no recognized general characteristics of Hinduism. For example, here is one list of principles that, by practitioner consensus, characterize one as "Hindu":

*Hindu
principles*

- Belief in the divinity of the Vedas
- Belief in one, all-pervasive Supreme Reality
- Belief in the cyclical nature of time
- Belief in karma
- Belief in reincarnation
- Belief in alternate realities with higher beings
- Belief in enlightened masters or gurus
- Belief in nonaggression and noninjury
- Belief that all revealed religions are essentially correct
- Belief that the living being is first and foremost a spiritual entity
- Belief in an "organic social system."[13]

A similar list comes from the Indian Supreme Court, which produced the following set of workable criteria as to what it means to be a Hindu:

*Supreme
court
criteria*

- The Vedas should be accepted and revered as the foundation of Hindu philosophy.
- One should have a spirit of tolerance, and recognize that the truth has many sides.
- One accepts belief in recurring cosmic cycles of creation, preservation, and dissolution.
- One accepts belief in reincarnation.
- One recognizes that there are numerous paths to truth and salvation.
- One recognizes that although the worship of idols may be deemed unnecessary, there may be many deities worthy of worship.
- In distinction from followers of other religions, one does not believe in a specific set of theological or philosophical conceptions.[14]

As should be clear from the emphasis on tolerating the different beliefs of others, respecting the pluriformity of truth, and recognizing the diversity of belief and practice, any talk of Hinduism as a whole needs to keep this internal multiplicity in mind at all times. All this has led one scholar to suggest the following metaphor: "If the essence of Hinduism could be summarized in a few words, those words might be 'structured diversity.' We might think of Hinduism as a

---

13. Rosen, *Essential Hinduism*, 18.

14. *World Religions*, ed. Robinson and Rodrigues, 175.

rainbow in which all the different colors are represented, but in which each of these colors has a very distinct place in the spectrum."[15]

DO HINDUS HAVE A BIBLE?

As I already noted, there is no single, authoritative text in Hinduism that functions like the Bible for Christians, or the Qur'an for Muslims. Instead, there are several different collections of texts, all grouped under two main categories. The first and most important is called *shruti* ("what is heard")—this is analogous to what Christians understand as divinely revealed scripture, and, like in Christianity, this category of texts, which includes the Vedas and the Upanishads, is the most authoritative. The second category is called *smrti* ("what is remembered")—for Christians, this is more like biblical and theological commentaries by the early church fathers, Vatican documents, etc. Their authority is secondary to *shruti*. Interestingly, however, it is the *smrti* texts that are more popular and widely read and actually have more practical importance for the daily life of a Hindu. I will say more about these writings, particularly the *Mahabharata* and the *Ramayana*, below.

First are the Vedas. They are the oldest Hindu sacred texts and have the most wide-ranging authority. They are believed to have been written anywhere from 1800 to 1200 bce, but the dating of these texts is very difficult. Certainly they existed in oral tradition long before they were written down, and even now, their power is derived in being spoken and heard, not by being read. According to tradition, their recitation can be properly performed only by Brahmins, the guardians of their secrets and power, who historically have used very complicated mnemonic techniques to ensure a perfect recitation every time of long, complicated sections of text.

In the narrowest sense of the term, "Veda" refers to the four *samhitas* ("collections") of sacred texts of ancient India. They are the oldest body of literature—not just religious texts—and "according to traditional belief, the Vedas have no authors and existed prior to this world's creation."[16] The most important of the Vedas and the most well known in the West is the *Rig Veda*, which comprises a large collection of hymns praising various gods and goddesses, and tells various stories of creation.[17] Again, speaking as broadly as

---

15. James Robinson, *Hinduism*, Religions of the World (New York: Chelsea House, 2004), 11.

16. Muesse, *The Hindu Traditions*, 42.

17. For an accessible introduction to the *Rig Veda*, see the Penguin Classics edition (September 2005), trans. Wendy Doniger, which contains 108 of the over 1,000 hymns that make up the collection.

possible, it is fair to say that the Vedas are the collection of writings held to be the basis of true belief and practice among most Hindus.

Upanishads Next are the Upanishads, which do not share the Vedas' focus on ritual and sacrifice but instead describe a more philosophical and theoretical approach to the practice of Hinduism.[18] They were written roughly between 800 and 400 bce, around the same time that the Buddha lived and taught, and Mahavira founded Jainism. It is not a coincidence that the key teachings of the Upanishads have certain important similarities to the teachings of both of these religious founders. The primary emphasis of the Upanishads is that the self (*atman*) is identical to the Ultimate ground of reality (*Brahman*), and the person who realizes this sacred truth (through disciplined practice and meditation) finds liberation (*moksha*) from the endless cycles of rebirth (*samsara*). In the Upanishads themselves, Brahman, the Ultimate Reality, is not personified or personalized; however, some later schools of Hindu thought did personalize this unified One Supreme Being, most typically as Shiva, Vishnu, or the Goddess.

The rest of the writings fall into the much larger and broader category of *smrti*. This category includes the two great Indian epics, the *Mahabharata* and the *Ramayana*. The *Mahabharata* is the oldest, and has existed in various forms for well over two thousand years. It is the longest epic poem in the world, and is said to have been written by the great sage Vyasa. However, it is clear that the epic as we have it today has been redacted by many hands over the centuries, so again, definitive determinations of both date and authorship elude scholars. The main plot narrative concerns the rivalry between two sets of paternal first cousins: the five sons of Pandu (the Pandavas), led by Yudhishthira; and the one hundred sons of blind King Dhritarashtra (he and his sons are called the Kauravas). However, within this overarching story, the reader finds elaborate asides on philosophy, ethics and politics, and other stories only tangentially related to the main characters.[19]

Bhagavad-Gita The most well-known portion of the *Mahabharata* is the *Bhagavad-Gita*, which is perhaps the most well-known and widely cited book in all of Hinduism. If any single text can be compared to the New Testament, it is this one; in fact, it is the second-most translated text in the world, after the Bible.[20] The story can be summarized quickly. After years of trickery, intrigue,

18. Here I would recommend the Oxford World's Classics edition (June 2008), trans. Patrick Olivelle, which contains twelve principal Upanishads.

19. A good introduction to the *Mahabharata* is R. K. Narayan's *The Mahabharata: A Shortened Modern Prose Version of the Indian Epic* (Chicago: University of Chicago Press, 2000).

20. *Modern Indian Interpreters of the Bhagavadgita*, ed. Robert N. Minor (Albany: State University of New York Press, 1986), 5.

and behind-the-scenes maneuvering, the Pandavas and the Kauravas found themselves on the brink of all-out war. The two massive armies faced off on the *Kurukshetra*, "Kuru's field," for what everyone knew would be the decisive battle for the entire Indian kingdom; and it was clear, even before the battle began, that the death-toll would be monstrous. At the very moment the battle is to commence, Arjuna, the Pandava champion, loses heart: looking out across the field of battle he sees cousins, friends, and mentors, and the thought of killing them overwhelms him. He sits down in his chariot, discouraged and refusing to fight. At this point, the god Krishna, who is acting as Arjuna's charioteer, preaches to him the most famous sermon in Hinduism, explaining to him why it is his duty to fight, and why fighting in the battle would be an act of great religious significance. In the course of this sermon, Krishna reveals his true self to Arjuna: Krishna himself is the one supreme reality—creator and destroyer of all. Arjuna then goes on to fight, helping his brothers win the war, and the kingdom.

The *Ramayana* is the other most important epic poem in Hinduism. In his book *Arrow of the Blue-skinned God*, Jonah Blank writes, "Imagine a story that was the *Odyssey*, *Romeo & Juliet*, the Bible, and a Hollywood blockbuster all rolled into one. Imagine a story that combined adventure and aphorism, romance and religion, fantasy and philosophy. Imagine a story that could make young children marvel, grown men weep, and old women dream. Such a story exists in India, and it is called the *Ramayana*."[21] Its earliest form is a Sanskrit poem attributed to the sage Valmiki, and scholars believe that it was composed sometime between 500 bce and 400 ce. However, as with other texts, Hindu tradition places the date of composition much earlier.

The story itself is about Prince Rama of Ayodhya and his wife Sita, her capture by the demon Ravenna, and her subsequent rescue by Rama, his brother Lakshmana, and their monkey helper Hanuman.[22] More broadly, however, the story models proper *dharma*—that is, the proper actions and behaviors one should exhibit to maintain or uphold one's place in the world, and support the proper functioning of the cosmos as a whole. Rama, Sita, and the other main characters all exemplify proper *dharma* through the way in which they live as a husband, a wife, a brother, a king, a son, and so forth. In all of their

---

21. Jonah Blank, *The Arrow of the Blue-skinned God: Retracing the Ramayana through India* (Boston: Houghton Mifflin, 1992), ix.

22. The Penguin Classics edition (August 2006), as told by R. K. Narayan, is a good first introduction to the text.

relationships, they demonstrate ideal social behavior. Thus, people today still model their own behavior on that of Rama and Sita.[23]

Figure 1.2. Images of Rama and Sita from the Hindu Temple and Cultural Center, Columbia, SC.

Finally, I want to mention the Puranas, a series of texts that describe specific gods in great detail, specifically Vishnu, Shiva, and Brahma, along with the way in which they are to be worshiped, and what rewards devotees can expect to receive from them. As with the other sacred texts in Hinduism, a date of composition for the Puranas is difficult to establish, given their long oral history. One scholar summarizes the problem this way: "On the whole, it is meaningless to speak of 'the date' of a Sanskrit *purana*, because many

23. This is, of course, problematic for women, as Sita's primary role is that of submissive wife; and there are many places in the epic in which feminists critique her role. See, for example, R. P. Goldman and S. J. Sutherland Goldman, "*Ramayana*," in *The Hindu World*, ed. Sushil Mittal and Gene Thursby (London: Routledge, 2004); and *Playing for Real: Hindu Role Models, Religion, and Gender*, ed. Jacqueline Suthren Hirst and Lynn Thomas (Oxford: Oxford University Press, 2004). I also recommend viewing the marvelous film "Sita Sings the Blues," available for free viewing or download at http://www.sitasingstheblues.com/.

generations of bards, etc., have been involved in the accumulation of material which at some stage has been given a name . . ."[24] While the list of Puranas is vast and varies widely, the major Puranas are typically listed at eighteen, and these books are subdivided into three sets of six books each, with each set corresponding to one of the three gods mentioned above, although many texts also are devoted to worship of the goddess.

DO HINDUS BELIEVE IN GOD?

Figure 1.3. A mass-produced image of the god Shiva. The Ganges River, personified as a goddess, descends to the earth, as Shiva first absorbs the weight of her descent in his hair.

Without a doubt, the answer to this question is "yes"—and more specifically, an emphatic, exuberant, multifaceted yes. But at the same time, that "yes" cannot at all be interpreted in the way Christians typically understand either the question

24. Freda Matchett, "The Puranas," in *The Blackwell Companion to Hinduism,* ed. Gavin Flood, (Oxford: Blackwell, 2003), 132.

or the answer. One scholar uses the lovely phrase, the "sheer exuberance of Hindu theism," and goes on to recognize that the characteristic "energy and inventiveness" Hindus display when it comes to Hindu theistic practice well may be "the greatest stumbling block for those outside the traditions. They often ask, Why do Hindus worship so many gods?"[25] I find this a succinct and clear way of stating the problem: there are so many different gods (or manifestations of the one universal reality), so many different ways of worshiping those gods, and such a lack of concern on the part of Hindus about which god is the best/highest, etc., that many Christians don't even recognize Hinduism as a theistic religion, instead seeing Hindus as simple idol worshipers. This could not be further from the truth.

Instead, it is fair to say that Hinduism encompasses a lush, expansive understanding of the divine—richer by far than the narrow, shallow range of conceptions, images, and language typically used for God in the Christian tradition. There is a simple, yet profound reason for that: "To Hindu ways of thinking, the ultimate reality is so far beyond our imagining, so complex, so utterly rich in potential, that a single image or even a mere handful of images will not do. If the absolute must be portrayed, then many, many images and symbols will be more successful than just one or a few."[26] Simply put, in Hinduism god is neither one nor many, but both; god is not male or female, but both; god is not formless or embodied, but both. Let me say more about that.

In order to appreciate a Hindu understanding of god, one must first move beyond the "either/or" of monotheism and polytheism: that is, one must let go of the idea that there are only two options—either people worship one god (monotheism) or they worship many gods (polytheism). Instead, in Hinduism, it is both/and: Hindus not only see no contradiction in believing that there is one god and believing that there are many gods, but for some, the tension between the one and the many actually generates deeper insight into the true nature of the divine than either one could produce on its own. There are different names for this "both/and," each of which has a slightly different connotation: *monolatry* is used to describe the worship of one greater god among many lesser gods; *kathenotheism* or *henotheism* is used to define the worship of different gods, but only one god at any given time (one god during one season or festival, for example, and another during a different time of the year); and finally, *polymorphic monotheism*, which refers to the worship of one

---

25. Muesse, *The Hindu Traditions*, 130.

26. Ibid., 132–33.

supreme god who reveals him/herself in many forms in different times and places in the world.[27]

Part of the reason for this complexity is that the histories of the various gods in Hinduism are long and intricate, and the depiction of many, if not all, the major deities has evolved over time, differing greatly depending on which sacred texts are being cited. This chronological diversity is accompanied by an equal geographical diversity: depending on where one is located, the actual worship of the different deities also varies—not only across the globe, but even from north to south India. Finally, as noted above, the theology that informs people's understanding of the various gods in Hinduism is polyvalent: some people believe that all gods are simply different faces of the same one Supreme Being; others reject all personified forms of this one; some are devoted to one god exclusively; and others worship many different gods simultaneously.

Naturally, then, Hinduism accommodates a vast assortment of dynamic and multifaceted concepts of god. For the most part, they can be categorized under two broad headings: *nirguna* Brahman, a formless, impersonal supreme reality without qualities or attributes—comparable in some general way to what Christians call an *apophatic* understanding of the Divine (God is limitless, immortal, formless, invisible, etc.); and *saguna* Brahman, the personified, personal form of the supreme reality—what Christians call a *kataphatic* understanding of the Divine (God is an all-loving father, a merciful judge, a gentle shepherd, etc.). Let me stress that these are not two different realities, but rather two different ways of perceiving the one true ultimate reality: the first is perhaps more the subject of philosophical and intellectual speculation and meditation; and the second is more the object of adoration, sacrifice, and devotion. However, in light of the fact that most, if not all, Hindus do worship some embodied, personal form of God, and certainly any visit to a Hindu home or temple bears this out, it is worth expanding on the notion of *saguna* Brahman, the idea of a personified god in Hinduism, using the god Vishnu as our example, one of the most important and widely venerated gods in Hinduism.

Unlike Christianity, which is grounded in a linear understanding of time, Hinduism has a cyclical understanding of time, in which the universe continually cycles into and out of existence, over many eons. In most descriptions of this process, instead of there being one single divinity behind it all, there are three: Brahma is the creator, the one who brings the universe into being; Shiva is the destroyer, the one who, at the right time, causes the universe to fall into nothingness; and during the in-between time stands Vishnu

27. Ibid., 25.

the preserver, the god who sustains the universe and protects it from evil while it is in existence. Together, these three gods make up what is sometimes (somewhat confusingly) called the Hindu "trinity," but the more accurate name in Hinduism is *trimurti*, which translates roughly as "three faces."

As should be expected, there are different understandings of what these gods represent and how they function. Some Hindus see all three gods as simply manifestations of one Supreme Being that is above all personification, but they still honor and worship the different manifestations individually as genuine representations of god—although it should be noted that today there is hardly any direct worship of Brahma alone. By contrast, both Shiva and Vishnu, as well as the goddess, who is personified with different names and in different forms, have millions of followers who worship him/her as the single supreme deity, the highest embodiment of the divine.

According to Steven Rosen, "two-thirds of the known Hindu world identifies themselves as Vaishnavas,"[28] that is, worshipers of Vishnu. Vaishnavas believe that Vishnu is the personal embodiment of the Divine—the highest form of the one supreme god himself who is the ground and source of all being. In terms of Hindu iconography and statuary, Vishnu always is depicted with dark skin—typically blue. He usually is shown with four arms, one holding a lotus flower, another holding a conch shell, another holding a disc or wheel, and the final arm holding a mace. Sometimes he is shown resting on the coils of a many-headed serpent, called *Sheshanaga*, and sometimes his consort, Lakshmi, is rubbing his feet—or sometimes she is sitting next to him. He also is depicted riding his "vehicle," the great eagle *Garuda.* Hinduism knows no prohibition against imaging the Divine, and in no other religion in the world is there such a profusion of depictions of the gods, in all manner of art forms, in all possible materials, from great stone statues to children's comic books.

One distinguishing aspect of Vishnu's mythology that makes him particularly interesting for many Christians is the doctrine of the *avatar. Avatara* is a Sanskrit word that refers to a divine incarnation (literally it means "one who descends"), and it is almost always associated with Vishnu. The word *incarnation* must be read and interpreted by Christians with care, however. Certainly, it is true that there are some general similarities with the concept of incarnation in Christianity, insofar as both refer to a divine decision to "come down" and dwell in and amidst creation. Nevertheless, there are many important differences as well, most notably the fact that unlike Jesus, whom Christian tradition affirms was truly fully divine *and* fully human, the *avatar* is more correctly viewed as

Vaish-navas

avatar

28. Rosen, *Essential Hinduism*, xvii.

a disguised appearance of the divine, something akin to the Greek god Zeus coming down from heaven cloaked as a mortal, but ready and willing to throw off his human camouflage in a moment's notice if the need arises. Further, while Jesus is believed to be the unique incarnation of God, Vishnu is believed to have many, many different *avatars*.

The purpose for this "divine descent" is also different in Hinduism, having nothing to do with a doctrine of sin or human alienation from God. Instead, Hindus believe that at various times in the endless cycles of history, Vishnu descends into the world in the form of some created being in order to save and preserve creation from a particular demonic force that is threatening the very existence of the cosmos. Tradition holds that there are ten primary *avatars* of Vishnu, the stories of which are told in elaborate detail both in the Puranas and in a variety of other sacred Hindu texts.

The ten are as follows: first, the fish, Matsya, who saved the world from a great flood; second, the tortoise, Kurma, who allowed the gods and demons to churn up valuable objects from the ocean of milk from a pivot resting on his back; and third, the boar, Varaha, who also rescued the earth from a flood by raising it up on one of his tusks. Fourth is the man-lion, Narasimha, who came to deliver the world from a terrible demon who had obtained from the gods a special boon that prohibited him from being killed by either a god, an animal, or a human—Narasimha was a combination of all these, and thus succeeded in destroying the demon. Fifth is the dwarf, Vamana, who confronted another demon who had conquered the entire universe. He begged the demon-king for just as much land as he could cover with three of his dwarf steps, and the king, scoffing at such a request, granted it; imagine his surprise when the dwarf covered the entire universe in his first two steps, placing his last step on the king's own head. Sixth is the man called "Rama with the axe," Parashurama, who was a hero that destroyed the entire *Kshatriya* class of warriors who were exploiting others.

The next two *avatars*, numbers seven and eight, are the most famous. First is Ramachandra—simply called Rama, the hero of the aforementioned *Ramayana*, who embodied in his person perfect obedience, dharma, filial love, and righteousness. He is still seen as the example *par excellence* for human conduct in Hinduism today. The eighth *avatar* is Krishna, who is not only viewed as the perfect and highest incarnation of Vishnu, but for many of his devotees, the relationship between Vishnu and Krishna is reversed, with Krishna being worshiped as the one supreme god and the source of all other incarnations, including Vishnu himself.[29] Finally, the last two *avatars* are ninth, the Buddha—in this way, Hinduism was able to enfold Buddhism as a whole under its large umbrella; and tenth, Kalki, the form of Vishnu who is still to come, and whose arrival will signal the end of the present age. It is a rare temple or home altar that does not contain an image of either Vishnu, his consort Lakshmi, who is herself the goddess of wealth, light, and fertility, or his *avatar* Krishna.

HOW DO HINDUS MARK TIME? SAMSKARAS AND FESTIVALS

One of the main practical functions of any religion is marking the passage of time—both for a people as a whole, and also for individuals: the ritual of the Jewish Bar/Bat Mitzvah and the Christian rite of Confirmation are two familiar examples. Hinduism is no different, and Hindu families practice a variety of *samskaras* to celebrate the various rites of passage in their life together. The number of *samskaras* varies widely, with the highest number being prescribed for Brahmin males, and the lowest number being performed by Dalit families with the fewest resources. These rites are performed by a Hindu priest, either at home or at a temple; and, at least in the United States, the fees for these services typically are listed on the temple websites.

As in Christianity, the most important of the *samskaras* are those related to birth, marriage, and death—although there are many other rites marking the healthy development of a child. In fact, many of these rites also are performed by Indian Christians, and they are considered ethnic customs rather than religious celebrations. In this case, Hindu prayers and offerings are replaced by Christian prayers and Bible readings. So, for example, many Christian families mark the *annaprashana,* the first solid food given to a baby, by inviting family and friends to the home and asking a pastor to provide a blessing. There is a *samskara* for the naming of a child, the child's first haircut, and the beginning of studies, just to name a few.

Of all the *samskaras*, however, marriage, *vivaha*, is one of the most important, celebrated lavishly over a period of days by Hindus and Indian Christians alike, with some common elements, and some regional variants. Arranged marriages still are common in India; by this I mean that the families of the two parties agree that a match would be harmonious, and then introduce

---

29. Edwin Bryant notes that "the Krishnaite theologies that emerged in the 16th century, initiated by influential teachers such as Vallabha and Chaitanya, find grounds to hold that it is not Krishna who is an incarnation of Vishnu but Vishnu who is a partial manifestation of Krishna. These sects extol Krishna as the supreme Absolute Truth from whom all other deities, including Vishnu, evolve, and the *Bhagavata Purana* is presented as the epistemological authority in this regard." "Krishna in the Tenth Book of the *Bhagavata Purana*," in *Krishna*, ed. Edwin F. Bryant (Oxford: Oxford University Press, 2007), 112.

the couple. In most situations it is more of a suggestion than a demand, though, as typically—at least in urban settings—the prospective couple is given time to get to know each other and agree to the match.

For Hindus, astrological charts are consulted, gifts are exchanged between families, a dowry is discussed (debate continues about whether the wedding jewelry—ostentatious and costly—is the bride's property or the groom's), offerings are made, and a sacred fire is circled by the couple either with seven steps or seven times. In addition, extravagant meals are prepared: for the immediate family, for relatives, for close friends, and finally, on the main day of the wedding itself, for a huge number of guests.[30] A wedding is the time for pulling out all the stops, and the family will celebrate to the absolute limit they can afford, including saris woven with gold thread, expensive gifts, and rich food. Here is one such example: "In 1995, the prime minister of Tamil Nadu, J. Jayalalitha, distributed more than ten million U.S. dollars for her stepson's wedding, which was attended by two hundred thousand guests serviced by six thousand cooks."[31]

After the wedding, the bride often will move in with her husband's parents where she is subject to her mother-in-law, and still today, multiple-generation homes are common. As an institution, marriage is, in practice, obligatory: divorce is rare, as is not having children and staying single. Marriage continues to be a foundational practice in Hindu families, and, in fact, this is true in most Indian families, Hindu or not.

The last important *samskara* to mention is the funeral. Cremation is the norm for Hindus, although certain categories of people, including *sadhus* and young children, typically are not cremated. As I mentioned previously, the Indian city of Varanasi is one of the most auspicious places to die and be cremated, and it is believed that dying here immediately liberates one's soul from the cycle of birth and death. Thus at two specific *ghats* (a series of steps leading down to the river) on the Ganges, cremations occur continually. The Manikarnika Ghat is the largest and the one where most cremations take place.

As you approach Manikarnika, the first thing you notice, after the smoke and the piles of burning embers, are the immense piles of wood: not only up against the buildings, but even in boats moored just off the shore. There are several places that have large scales where the wood is measured and purchased: different kinds of wood are more expensive than others, with sandalwood being the most expensive because of its fragrance. The wood is always purchased here,

---

30. For a table of events that make up the course of a Hindu wedding, see Michaels, *Hinduism: Past and Present*, 116–18.

31. Michaels, *Hinduism: Past and Present*, 119.

and then, after the haggling, the men who work the scales carry the wood down to the cremation area itself. The process of the cremation itself is polluting, as it involves contact with a dead body. Hence, it is only the "Doms," one particular Dalit caste, who manage the whole business of cremation, with the exception of firstborn sons and relatives who also take part in the specific rituals of the cremation itself. Women typically are not allowed to be involved in either the funeral procession or the cremation itself, although while I was in India I did see one woman, clearly grief-stricken, participating in the cremation of her husband, until family members finally, literally picked her up and carried her away.

Figure 1.4. *Wood being carried to a cremation, Varanasi, India, March 2012*

Once a person dies, she is anointed at home, and wrapped in layers of colorful cloth—mostly shades of orange, as this is the color associated with holiness in Hinduism—along with marigold garlands. Then, she is carried on a stretcher made of bamboo poles and straw through the streets, accompanied by chanting, singing, and drums, and brought down the stairs, straight to the Ganges. The body is submerged there, and certain rites are performed. Then, once the pyre is ready, the body is brought over to it, and all the cloths are stripped off, until the body is left wrapped in only a thin white sheet. The body is then placed on the pyre, and more wood is piled on top of it. At this point, a small pile of long grass is lit, and the oldest son (typically) circles the smoke around the head, and then circles the corpse with it as well. Finally, the lit grass is shoved under the pyre at the feet, where the wood then catches fire. It takes several hours for a body to burn, and even then, not all the bones are consumed. That which remains, larger bones as well as the ashes, is taken down and thrown in the Ganges. This whole rite is believed to free the soul from the body, and ensure a safe transition into either heaven, or the next life.

Finally, let me just briefly note that in addition to these *samskaras*, there are dozens upon dozens of Hindu festivals. Indeed, *The Oxford Dictionary of World Religions* writes that: "It is said that Hindus have a festival for every day of the year. That is a serious underestimate."[32] There are some Hindu festivals that are celebrated throughout the country, and many more that are primarily regional. They mark specific seasons, specific events in the lives of the different gods and goddesses, and specific concerns of life—wealth, health, fertility, etc. It is impossible to describe or even summarize them all, so let me just mention two that are perhaps the most well known in the United States. First is *Divali*, the festival of lights that falls somewhere in October or November. (Hinduism follows a primarily lunar calendar, like Judaism, so the specific dates of each festival vary from year to year.) Divali honors Lakshmi, the goddess of wealth and good fortune, and it lasts roughly four to five days. Families often visit the temple during this time and make offerings to her there, but they also worship her at home, perhaps even arranging a special place on their home altar for her. Doors are left open to welcome her into the house, and the whole period of celebration is a time of great joy, in which Hindus fill their houses with light.

The other main festival is called *Holi*, and it is lots of fun, celebrated with great abandon and gusto all over India—particularly in the north, in Indian communities in the West, and even on some Western college campuses. It inaugurates the coming of spring and is celebrated primarily by throwing colored paste and water on anyone who happens to be out walking around. It, too, is celebrated over a period of days.

Holi has a variety of myths and traditions behind it, two of which are worth mention here. The story is told that one day Krishna was complaining to his mother that his skin was dark while his beloved Radhu had such fine pale

32. "Festivals and Fasts: Hinduism," *The Oxford Dictionary of World Religions*, ed. John Bowker (Oxford: Oxford University Press, 1997), 342.

skin. His mother told him that if it bothered him, he should rub colored paste on her—playfully, of course—to darken her skin. This he did, and from this childish prank, a festival was born. Because of this legend, that Holi is celebrated with particular enthusiasm and verve around Mathura and Vrindivan—Krishna's birthplace and the place where he spent his childhood.

The more popular story, however, has to do with the triumph of good over evil. It is said that once there was a very wicked king (Indian mythology is full of wicked kings—foils for the good deeds of gods and their devotees) who demanded that everyone in the kingdom worship him. All obeyed him, save one, and the irony is that the one who defied his command was his own son, Prahlad, who was a great worshiper of Lord Narayana. This infuriated the king, who instructed his wicked sister, Holika, to take Prahlad onto her lap and step into a giant fire. The king knew that she had received a boon and would escape the fire unharmed, while Prahlad would be destroyed. She received just payment for her wickedness, however: unbeknownst to her, the boon was only valid if she entered a fire by herself—it was ineffective if she went in with another person. Thus she was immolated, but Prahlad, who chanted the name of Lord Narayana the whole time, came out unscathed. The festival thus takes its name from her name, Holika, and celebrates both the downfall of wickedness and also the faithfulness of devotion.

That story is recalled in the large piles of wood that are built at various points in cities and villages—sometimes right in the middle of the road. In them are placed small images of Holika and Prahlad. On the eve of the primary day of the festival, after much singing and dancing to Bollywood Holi songs played over loudspeakers, bonfires are lit and the whole pile is reduced to ashes. Holi is a particularly raucous celebration for boys of all ages, who can be seen wandering the streets covered in color, some carrying plastic water guns, purchased specifically for this holiday. Many shops simply close down, and most women stay indoors—at least this was the case in Varanasi, where I celebrated Holi in 2012. At my hotel, they encouraged us to stay indoors, and kept the door locked until around 4:00 p.m., when it was again safe to venture outside.

Figure 1.5. A woodpile with images of Holika and Prahlad, Varanasi, India, March 2012

WHAT DO HINDUS THINK ABOUT SALVATION?

In Hinduism there are what we might call penultimate spiritual goals as well as an ultimate spiritual goal, and Hindus strive after both, driven by two factors.

Hindus, like Buddhists, believe in a cyclical, rather than linear pattern of time and the universe. This means that they do not believe that the universe began at one discrete point of time and will end at another discrete point of time; instead, they believe that the universe cycles in and out of existence, through a series of eras, each of which has a different name and different characteristics. Along with the universe itself, all beings also cycle in and out of existence, from birth to death to rebirth: this is the doctrine of reincarnation.

The cycle of reincarnation is driven by *karma*. Literally, karma simply means "action," but in Hinduism, it has come to describe the belief that one's actions in the present have an unavoidable consequent effect on the destiny of the soul in the future. That is, the consequence of one's actions always boomerangs back onto the self—this is called "the fruiting of karma," and it is inevitable: "karma always returns to the agent who created it, no matter how long it takes."[33] In other words, in this lifetime you produce good karma or bad karma, and you will live out the ramifications of that karma in your next lifetime. Thus, one of the main soteriological goals of Hinduism is to produce good karma, which ensures a positive rebirth. The way to produce good karma is to act rightly; the question then becomes, how does one know what the "right actions" are? This is where the idea of *dharma* comes in.

Dharma refers to the proper duties/actions that are appropriate for one's caste. This means everyone's dharma is different, depending on gender, birth community, work, etc. There are a variety of texts that describe the different dharmas, and they each explain that every individual must do those actions fitting for his/her caste, and only those actions. Only in that way are people able to generate good karma. Meritorious actions, then, are not universal; ironically, if you are a Dalit, it is karmically more beneficial for you to do the actions appropriate for your caste, like carrying dead bodies and preparing cremations, even if they are not as ostensibly meritorious as the actions appropriate for a Brahmin; for example, learning Sanskrit and chanting sacred passages from the Vedas. Instead, it is believed that if you perform the actions appropriate to your station in life, you will continually move up the anthropological hierarchy in subsequent births, eventually being born as a Brahmin and attaining liberation, even if this takes many lifetimes.

With this cosmological and anthropological background in mind, let me describe the different means by which Hindus seek salvation—more typically called "liberation" in Hinduism. In *World Religions Today*, a popular college textbook, Hinduism is characterized with the phrase "myriad paths to

---

33. Muesse, *The Hindu Traditions*, 69.

salvation."[34] What this means is that there are many legitimate ways to seek liberation, and different ways that one might live one's life in pursuit of liberation. Indeed, one also might pursue some combination of paths, or at various stages in one's life pursue different paths. One is not better than another: they are different ways of attaining the same end. The first path is called *karma-marga* or *karma-yoga*, which represents the path of duty or action. As I said above, people who follow this spiritual path are concerned with the proper religious actions. This includes sacrifices and other ritual performances that honor various deities, and also individual or family rites that mark important life transitions. The second is called *jñana-marga* or *jñana-yoga*, which represents the path of knowledge. This is the path of realizing the truth of all existence—what is illusion and what is real. Typically it also includes physical and mental disciplines, such as physical austerities and meditation. The third is called *bhakti-marga* or *bhakti-yoga*, which represents the path of devotional participation.[35] This path has its roots in popular devotional movements, and is grounded in expressions of love to one's chosen manifestation of the divine, or to one's guru. In this form of Hindu practice, god's grace ameliorates the strict causality of one's own karma and can bring the devotee liberation. Again, one path is not necessarily better than another—although practitioners within each camp might argue the superior virtues of their path over and against the others. Instead, the particular way in which one chooses to live out one's faith often is determined by family, social status, personal disposition, and geographical location. What this means is that there are many different ways to live life as a "faithful" Hindu, and even within one lifetime, a person can choose radically different lifestyles.

How Do Hindus Pray?

One major difference between Hindus and Christians is that there is no weekly worship service, no set day or time in which a community is called to gather publically. Although most Hindus do visit temples regularly, or at least occasionally, praying and making offerings there, a "good" Hindu need never worship in public. Instead, all worship can be performed to icons in the home shrine, which is why the home is a very important place of worship in India.

The best word that describes and summarizes Hindu worship is *puja*. The word itself means respect, homage, or worship. Most—if not all—Hindus have

---

34. *World Religions Today*, ed. Esposito et al

35. Michaels, *Hinduism: Past and Present*, 24. Sometimes this list is described as various "yogas"—that is, disciplines, which often includes a fourth: *raja-yoga*, the way of mental focus and concentration. This is how the *Bhagavad-Gita* describes the various paths of salvation, for example.

small altars at home on which they place pictures and/or statues representing different deities, including those to whom the family is particularly devoted. (These are called *ishtadevatas*, one's personal god.) Each morning, one member of the family, usually the father or the mother, will perform a short puja at the altar. This may include saying prayers, lighting a lamp, burning incense, making offerings of fruit and flowers, and ringing a bell. The goal in this worship is to please the gods through all five senses—hence the incense, colored lights (this is the reason you often find Christmas lights hanging in American Hindu temples year round), bell and/or music, and food. The same thing happens in temples, although the rituals are much more elaborate there, and are done at various times throughout the day. This is because in a temple, the deity is believed to inhabit the images full-time, not just merely when invited to be present, which is what happens in a home puja: the deity is invoked, worshiped, and then the divine presence withdraws.

Figure 1.6. A modest home altar in Hyderabad, India, March 2012

By contrast, in the temple, a particular ritual involving the images has occurred called a *murti-puja*, which serves to invite the divinity down permanently into a particular image. This means that the image (the embodiment of the divine) must be tended to every day—morning, noon, and night. Priests live full-time at the temple in order to perform the daily pujas, which include waking, feeding, bathing, clothing, and worshiping these divinities. These services usually are open to the public (again, schedules of pujas in temples in the United States typically are posted on their websites), but whether or not anyone is there, the priest performs the rituals: the god is there, even if no one else is. In India, many temples even close for a few hours each afternoon, so that the deities may take a rest from their devotees.

After the priest performs the puja, on behalf of the god he returns to the people some of what they first brought as offerings—food, flowers, etc. This is called *prasad*, that is, grace, goodwill, or blessing. In this way, the things that were offered are then received back by the devotees as a blessing. So, for example, small morsels of food are eaten, flowers are worn in the hair, incense is wafted around one's body, holy water sipped, and colored powders are mixed with water and used to make a *tilak*, a mark in the center of the forehead above the eyes.

WHAT IS THE CASTE SYSTEM?

As the last point in this chapter, I want to briefly mention the caste system, since this is something many Christians have heard of, but often do not fully understand. The caste system refers to the different *varnas* in Indian society—*varna* means "color," and each caste is symbolized with a different color. These represent the four original classes of society. Traditionally in Hinduism the caste system is believed to be of divine origin, related to one particular creation story, told in the Vedas, in which the world is created through the dismemberment of the primordial man called *Purusha*. In the myth, he was ritually sacrificed, and from the pieces came the entire cosmos, including all human beings. One is born into one's caste, and caste identity is indelible and unchangeable.

Brahmins (white) are the highest caste: they are the priests and the teachers, the religious—though not the political—leaders of Hindu society, and they are said to have been created from the head or mouth of *Purusha*. The second caste is the warrior caste, called the *Kshatriyas* (red). These are the kings, the only caste allowed to rule, and they are said to have been created from the arms. The third caste is the merchant caste, the *Vaishyas* (yellow), the craftsmen, farmers, and traders of Hindu society, created from the thighs—note how we are moving down the body. Finally, the fourth caste is the worker caste, the *Shudras* (blue or black). They are the lowest caste, the peasants and servants, and they were created from the feet. Within each of these castes are thousands of subcategories, called *jatis*, or "birth communities" that specify rank and place in society more specifically, usually based on regional classifications.

Glaringly absent in this schema are the Dalits, the "outcastes"—so called because they fall outside of the caste system. They also were called "untouchables," referring to the fact that, in Hinduism, their very being is polluting, and therefore caste Hindus are not permitted even to touch them. Traditionally, Dalits have worked in ignominious, jobs dealing with the dead (like cremation, mentioned above), animal disposal, cleaning of human waste, and tanning leather. Historically, Dalits have suffered terrible discrimination: they were not allowed inside temples, they were not allowed to use common wells, and they even had to live outside the village boundaries. They could be killed without fear of punishment, and were considered less than human in many ways, practically, at least, if not theoretically. Thus it should come as no surprise that Dalits have converted en masse to both Buddhism and Christianity; today, roughly 95 percent of Indian Christians come from the Dalit castes.

Caste is so deeply woven into Indian society that even today it continues to play an important role in the daily lives of Hindus. It is true that the Indian constitution abolished untouchability—note, not caste in general—and made it illegal to disadvantage people because they were Dalits. However, in fact, caste discrimination is still alive and well in India, particularly in rural villages, where Dalit women especially continue to suffer persecution and violence. At the same time, though, particularly in the cities, economics trumps caste, and Dalits have access to both education and the lucrative occupations such education brings, including careers in engineering, medicine, and technology.

2

A Brief Introduction to Judaism

There is a famous Aesop's fable about a fox and a lion, which goes something like this. A lion and a fox both lived in a forest. At first, whenever the fox would see the lion, he became exceedingly frightened and ran away, hiding himself in the woods. However, as time went on, the fox grew more accustomed to the lion's presence, such that when the lion would pass by the fox would no longer run, but stand at a safe distance and watch. Finally, the fox ceased to be afraid of the lion at all; and when the lion came by again, the fox went right up to him, exchanging pleasantries and asking about the lion's family. When their conversation was over, the fox turned and walked away without any ceremony. The moral of this fable? "Familiarity breeds contempt."

I always think of this fable when talking with Christians about Judaism, because I think there is a similar dynamic going on here. Many Christians already presume they know more than they really do about Judaism: after all, we know their scriptures, we know their story, we know their God. That's most of it anyway, right? This attitude is, of course, not only patently false, but it's potentially dangerous as well. At best, it leads to a patronizing disinterest. At worst, it leads to supersessionism, persecution, and discrimination.

This is particularly problematic in light of the fact that, for centuries of Western European history, Christianity has been responsible for some of the most virulent negative stereotyping and persecution of the Jews. As just one small example, one may consider the depiction of Jews in Western European art. Norman Solomon writes,

> It is revealing and rather shocking, to look at the way Jews have been portrayed in Christian religious art, especially in the west. Prior to the twelfth century they have no physical features to distinguish them from other people. Then, suddenly, there is a change, and Europe's Jews acquire hooked noses, webbed feet, and other aspects of what was thought to be the physiognomy of the devil; even in the

twentieth century the folk belief persists in parts of Europe that Jews have horns.[1]

An occurrence like the Holocaust is unimaginable without this long and deep history of negative stereotypes. So, in light of all this, perhaps it would be most helpful for Christians to put aside what they think they know about Judaism, and approach this rich, complex religious tradition with fresh eyes and an open mind.

JEWS AND JUDAISM

First, a few statistics. As of August 24, 2012, the global population of Christians—the single largest religious group in the world—was estimated at 33.35 percent, of which roughly 17 percent are Roman Catholic, 6 percent are Protestant, and 4 percent are Orthodox. Muslims are the next largest religious group, making up roughly 22½ percent of the world's population. By comparison, the global Jewish population stands at roughly 0.2 percent, with the vast majority of the population living in the United States and Israel.[2] What this means is that of all the world's major religions, Judaism is by far the smallest, smaller even than the Sikh population, which stands at roughly 0.36 percent.[3] This simple fact must be kept in mind, as it affects the way many Jews see themselves and their religious tradition in relationship to the world, and also the way in which Judaism affects the political landscape, particularly in Israel.

In *Basic Judaism*, Rabbi Milton Steinberg notes that the word *Judaism* has two distinct and equally legitimate meanings. First, "Judaism" points to a multifaceted, complete civilization: the total history of the Jewish people that includes both sacred and secular elements. This history is on full and lavish display in the Israel Museum in Jerusalem, where one can see Torah ark doors from a synagogue in Krakow, decorations for Torah scrolls from Afghanistan, a bridal casket from northern Italy, a woven wool carpet from Kurdistan, and an amulet necklace from Yemen.[4] As these objects so beautifully illustrate, this definition of Judaism is not linked to one specific ethnic identity, nor does it have one single geographical location. Instead, it is as diverse and varied as the complex pattern of interwoven nationalities, cultures, and practices that comprise it. Perhaps the most important point to underscore here is that

---

1. Norman Solomon, *Judaism: A Very Short Introduction* (Oxford: Oxford University Press, 1996), 7.

2. https://www.cia.gov/library/publications/the-world-factbook/geos/xx.html.

3. Ibid.

4. All these items and more can be found on the museum's website: http://www.imj.org.il/imagine/galleries/judaicaE.asp.

Judaism is not a race—insofar as that term is even used any more. Instead, just like Christians, Jews come in all colors, all physical characteristics, and all nationalities.

Second, "Judaism" also describes the spiritual aspect of that civilization: Jewish religious practices and beliefs, which also are multivalent and complex. In describing the Jewish religion, Steinberg goes on to say that it is made up of no less than seven strands: doctrine, ethics, rites and customs, laws, a sacred literature, institutions, and the people Israel. This last strand, Steinberg argues, is the central strand around which the others are woven.[5] In light of that fact, then, one may well ask: Who are the "people Israel"? Or, more specifically and pointedly, "Who is a Jew?" This question is more complex than it may at first seem. One way to answer this question is by referring to the three major geographic and cultural groups that still serve as markers of identity today. It is important to remember that all of these communities share the same basic beliefs; however, there are some liturgical differences, as well as cultural and linguistic variations between them.

First is the *Ashkenazim*, a word first found in Gen. 10:3, which originally was used in the Middle Ages to describe the Jews living along the Rhine River in Germany and France. This led to the term *Ashkenaz* being used primarily to describe those Jews with German customs. However, it is important to note that there was a shift in the population of *Ashkenazi* Jews in the sixteenth century, as Poland in particular became the center of *Ashkenazi* Judaism, reflecting a new concentration of Judaism in Eastern Europe. Obviously, what this means is that the Holocaust, which will be discussed later in the chapter, affected primarily *Ashkenazi* Jews; and it was these communities that experienced that catastrophe most keenly.

Second is the *Sephardim*, which refers to those Jews who are the descendants of Spanish Jews, including those who fled during the expulsion of 1492 and settled in the Mediterranean areas. Finally, the smallest of the three groups—and in practice most closely aligned with the *Sephardim*—is the *Mizrahi*, which refers to those Jews who came from Persia, Ethiopia, and Yemen. This group comprises those Jews who remained in the Middle East and North Africa. However, these categories are not all-inclusive. There are other Jewish populations in other places who continue to assert their unique identity as well.

As an example of the complex identity questions facing Judaism in the twenty-first century, let me offer the example described in an article titled

5. Rabbi Milton Steinberg, *Basic Judaism* (San Diego: Harcourt Brace, 1975), 3–4.

"Newly Found Jews and the Politics of Recognition," by Stuart Charmé. He writes: ". . . both the process by which remote groups in Africa and Asia, such as the Abayudaya Jews of South Africa and the Mizo ('B'nei Menashe') Jews of northern India and Burma, start to recognize *themselves* as Jews—and the related process by which the established Jewish communities of Israel and the United States offer them recognition as Jews—are tied to complex political issues and agendas. They reflect how various Jewish constituencies define the essential characteristics of their own Jewish identities and understand the meaning of group identity in general."[6] The challenges facing these Jewish communities in Africa and Asia illustrate the complicated issues at play here, including assimilation and intermarriage, as well as differing cultural norms and varying interpretations of Jewish laws and traditions.

Technically, according to Jewish law, any child born of a Jewish mother is considered a Jew—this is what is meant by matrilineal descent; in addition, any person who formally converts is considered a Jew. However, in the past two centuries this definition has broadened somewhat. Currently, in two modern branches of Judaism, the Reform and Reconstructionist movements, patrilineal descent also is accepted. This means that if either parent is Jewish, and if the child is raised Jewish, the child may be considered Jewish. However, as other branches of Judaism, such as the Orthodox and Conservative movements, currently do not accept patrilineal descent, there continues to be significant controversy around who is in and who is out, so to speak. For example, Orthodox Judaism still requires that a child of a Jewish father and a non-Jewish mother—practicing or not—formally convert to Judaism if she wants to become a member of that specific Jewish community.

Perhaps it also would be helpful to mention here that, traditionally, Judaism is not a missionary religion: by that, I mean there is no inherent commandment or exhortation in Judaism (like Matthew 28 for Christians) to actively seek converts. At least part of the reason for this can be traced back to the Roman Empire. Once Christianity was declared the official religion in the early fourth century, "proselytizing by the Jews was forbidden on pain of death to both the convert and the one who converted him."[7] The seriousness and strength of this prohibition only increased over the centuries. This led to the custom of rabbis discouraging potential converts—not only in light of the potential danger, but also in order to test their conviction: taking on a life shaped by

---

6. Stuart Z. Charmé, "Newly Found Jews and the Politics of Recognition," *Journal of the American Academy of Religion* 80, no. 2 (June 2012): 388.

7. George Robinson, *Essential Judaism: A Complete Guide to Beliefs, Customs, and Rituals* (New York: Atria, 2001), 175.

the commandments is viewed as a serious commitment. Even today, in a more tolerant climate like the United States, while many rabbis do not follow the ancient practice of turning an inquirer away three times, it is still typical that when an applicant seeks to initiate the process of conversion, the rabbi often first counsels patience and further reflection, and only subsequently, when her sincerity and determination is established, is she accepted. What this means is that, still today, most Jews are born Jewish: Judaism is not a voluntary organization, like Christianity; it is passed down by biological descent.

Figure 2.1. Prayers are tucked into every nook and cranny in the Western Wall, Jerusalem. January 2012.

MODERN DENOMINATIONS WITHIN JUDAISM:
A NORTH AMERICAN OVERVIEW

Judaism today—in all its forms—is descended from Rabbinic Judaism, that is, the Judaism that emerged after the destruction of the second temple by the Romans in 70 ce.[8] This means that the Pharisees, who have a negative reputation in Christianity, are the ancestors of modern Judaism. The reason for this is simple: the Romans stamped out other Jewish groups, including the Essenes and the Zealots; and once the temple was destroyed, the Sadducees—already viewed

Pharisees

Rabbinic Judaism

with suspicion as being too cozy with Rome—were rendered irrelevant, as their base of authority had been destroyed. That left the Pharisees, the interpreters of Jewish law and scripture scholars, to step in and re-form the community around the Torah and the synagogue, instead of the temple.[9] From the first century ce up until the nineteenth century, there was basically only one way of being Jewish, and for the most part, by choice or not, it consisted of a life lived separated from the larger society.

With the growing secularization in nineteenth-century Western Europe, however, new possibilities came into being that allowed Jews to become more active participants in "secular" society, even while maintaining their "sacred" practices and beliefs. Different interpretations of Judaism itself developed that guided the interplay between these two worlds, the sacred and the secular. Over time, these differences resulted in the four main branches of Judaism that exist today, all of which share some core commonalities while at the same time exhibiting significant differences.

ORTHODOX JUDAISM

Orthodox Judaism is the modern term for what historically has been mainline Judaism: in other words, before the nineteenth century, Orthodox Judaism *was* Judaism, plain and simple. More stringently than other branches of Judaism, Orthodox Judaism is centered on the Torah; specifically, it is based on an understanding of the Torah as the unchangeable, inerrant revelation of God. As such, the Torah provides the unique guide for all aspects of one's daily life. Accordingly, Orthodox Jews meticulously observe Jewish law, that is, *halakhah* (literally "the way one walks"), which is based on an understanding that all 613 commandments have been revealed as the direct, immutable will of God.

What this means is that both beliefs and rituals—what one thinks and how one acts—are meticulously guarded and prescribed, and neither is negotiable.[10] For Orthodox Jews, then, fidelity demands continuity of tradition over time and

---

8. What is reflected in this section are categories and language typically used in the United States and Canada. However, it is worth noting that other language is used in other contexts. For example, in the United Kingdom, the main denominations of Judaism are Orthodox, Reform (which more closely resembles what is called Conservative Judaism in the United States), and Liberal Judaism. In Israel, typical categories include *Dati* (which means "religious"), *Hiloni* (which means "secular"), and *Masorti* (which means "traditional").

9. Robinson writes: "The importance of the Pharisees cannot be overemphasized: in the aftermath of the destruction of the Second Temple, it is only through the efforts of the rabbis, the heirs of the Pharisaic worldview, that Judaism was able to survive at all." *Essential Judaism*, 321.

10. *World Religions Today*, ed. John Esposito et al., 3rd ed. (Oxford: Oxford University Press, 2009), 79.

a corresponding rejection of change or evolution in the interpretation of God's law: today's Orthodox children continue to mirror in many ways the beliefs and rituals of their great-grandparents.

Figure 2.2. A Jewish man praying at the Western Wall, Jerusalem. January 2012.

However, at the same time, most Orthodox Jews do not reject secular education or jobs in the public sphere, demonstrating instead a positive attitude toward general participation in the life of the communities in which they live, as long as it does not conflict with or inhibit in any way one's observance of a Jewish way of life. The exception to this practice can be found in the scrupulously traditional strand of the Orthodox community known as the "Ultra-Orthodox." These groups seek to create an all-encompassing Jewish way of life, advocating complete separation not only from secular society but even from more modern forms of Judaism. Often—particularly in Israel—Ultra-Orthodox Jews are referred to as *haredim*, "those who tremble at the word of God," and their entire lives are lived with a palpable sense of God's presence and God's commandments. Ultra-Orthodox Judaism is, as its name suggests, the most rigid and conservative form of Judaism: "For the ultra-Orthodox, there cannot be many ways to keep the covenant—only one way. And that one way is all-encompassing."[11] There can be no compromise on any point of doctrine or practice; as such, it is almost impossible for Ultra-Orthodox Jews to live in anything but segregated neighborhoods, where everyone interprets Jewish law the same way: keeping kosher, celebrating the Sabbath, dressing modestly, etc.

Unlike the Amish, with whom they are sometimes compared, Ultra-Orthodox Jews do not reject technology outright: they use cell phones, they fly on airplanes, they use computers, etc. However, they do not, for the most part, have television sets, a quotidian piece of technology most of us take for granted. The reason for this apparent contradiction is that while technology itself is not prohibited, its use is subject to strict guidelines. When considering the use of any modern device, one central question must be answered: "Does this device support or hinder my faith?" So, for example, in some communities, if it is determined that one requires the Internet for one's work, a special permit from a rabbi is required.[12] Ultra-Orthodox Jews live primarily in the United States, Western Europe, and Israel, and they typically have large families, taking literally the command to "be fruitful and multiply." Many of the men engage in Torah study full-time, supported by other Jews and Jewish organizations.

Reform Judaism

As previously mentioned, for centuries and centuries, there were no denominations as such in Judaism—no such thing as "Orthodox

11. Ibid.

12. I am indebted to Ophir Yarden, Senior Lecturer in Jewish and Israel Studies, Brigham Young University, Jerusalem Center, for this information.

Judaism"—there was only Judaism; but in the eighteenth and nineteenth *Reform Judaism* centuries, this began to change. With the dawn of the Enlightenment, a new interpretation of Jewish custom and practice began, which came to be called "Reform Judaism." This tradition began in Germany, led by Moses *Mendelssohn* Mendelssohn in particular—specifically seeking to respond to the intellectual and religious climate created by the changing Enlightenment context. During the Enlightenment, there developed a more secular understanding of the world, a greater confidence in human reason, as demonstrated by science and economic developments, and a belief in universal values of equality and freedom. One of the consequences of these changes was that all over Western Europe, Jews began to be more accepted and integrated into society (this varied from country to country, of course), finally gaining citizenship in some countries.

All of these changes presented Jewish communities with a new urgent question: How were they to remain faithful to their Jewish identity and heritage while embracing their newfound freedoms and moving into a more active role in their communities? The name "Reform Judaism" thus came from the attempt to "reform" Jewish thought and practice in light of new scientific developments, political ideas, and modernism.

It is worth noting here that this very word "Reform" points to a fundamental difference between this branch of Judaism and Orthodoxy, which holds that the Torah is not "reformable" in any way, in any form. Instead, as described previously, in Orthodox Judaism, the Torah is immutable: it is the unchanging divine command of God. By contrast, Reform Judaism creates a space for reexamining the law by reinterpreting the whole concept of divine revelation, arguing that instead of being "authored" by God, the Torah was written by "divinely inspired" human authors. What this means is that the Torah—and more specifically the commandments therein—is regarded as instructional and inspirational, but not absolutely binding. What Reform Judaism emphasizes is the "rational ethic" that comes out of Judaism: that is, the obligation to the neighbor, the command to care for the world, and the injunction to offer hospitality and care to all in need. All other aspects of Judaism are open to negotiation. For Reform Judaism, the "essential unchanging core of Judaism is ethics, while all beliefs in supernatural phenomena and all traditional ritualistic requirements can be changed as needed."[13] For this reason, parallels have been made between Reform Judaism

---

13. *World Religions Today*, ed. Esposito et al., 79.

and Liberal Protestantism, as both focus on social ethics (a kind of "ethical monotheism"), and emphasize the rights and responsibilities of the individual.

Therefore, some of the changes that Reform Judaism instituted included the replacement of much of the Hebrew in the worship service with the vernacular, new prayer books, a modified, shortened liturgy, a relaxation or even elimination of kosher restrictions, and more flexibility in ritual dress. Contemporary Reform Judaism also is characterized by its staunch commitment to inclusive principles, including welcoming gays and lesbians and supporting women as rabbis, cantors, and synagogue presidents. In the United States, Reform leaders, under the direction of Rabbi Isaac Mayer Wise, established the Union of American Hebrew Congregations (UAHC) in 1873, which still functions as an umbrella organization for Reform Judaism in the U.S. today under the name "Union for Reform Judaism."[14]

The basic point to remember here is that Reform Judaism subscribes to an understanding of history in which there is progressive revelation, and corresponding change and development in both practice and belief. Therefore, it argues that Judaism itself should be viewed as a religion of change and development, such that it always can both shape and be shaped by the varying contexts in which it finds itself. Only in this way will Judaism not only survive, but also continue to be relevant and faithful in the modern world.

CONSERVATIVE JUDAISM

Any swing of the pendulum typically is followed by a backswing, if you will, a reaction calibrated to match a previous action; and so it was for Judaism in the latter half of the nineteenth century. Conservative Judaism was founded as a response to what were viewed as overly radical changes by Reform Judaism: it was believed that while change was needed, Reform Judaism had moved too far too quickly. The name, then, comes from the desire to "conserve" more of the tradition that Reform Judaism had eliminated.

In the United States one of the prime catalysts for the movement occurred at what has come to be known as the "trefa banquet." The banquet took place in 1883 at the Cincinnati Highland House, and its purpose was to honor the first graduating class of Hebrew Union College. Hebrew Union College (the first Jewish institute of higher education in North America and still in existence today) was founded in North America in 1875 by Reform Jews in order to train religious leaders to minister to the woefully underserved population of American Jews. At the celebratory banquet a variety of non-kosher food was

14. Their website is www.urj.org.

served, including shellfish, and this became one of the key steps leading to the decisive break between Reform and Conservative Judaism in the United States. This event led to the founding of Jewish Theological Seminary in New York in 1886.

In Conservative Judaism, the emphasis is on ritual practice, rather than specific doctrines, which are understood to be more fluid. Conservative Judaism, then, embraces both change and tradition: the slogan for Masorti Olami, the central organization for Conservative Judaism worldwide is, "Where Tradition and Modernity Meet." As one of their governing principles they emphasize "the importance of maintaining a centrist, dynamic Jewish practice based on *halacha* and *mitzvot*, grounded in Jewish knowledge and observance, reflecting a love of tradition; and embracing modernity and the positive aspects of change."[15] This "change" comes only cautiously, however, and with significant study and reflection. One of the distinguishing marks of Conservative Judaism, as opposed to Reform Judaism in particular, is its preservation of the *halakhic* process when deciding how traditional interpretation of Jewish law might be changed. In that process, rabbis consult sacred scriptures and commentaries, rabbinic codes of law, and also previous generations of rabbinical opinion, in order to craft a new reading for today.

As might be obvious by this point, Conservative Judaism has carved out for itself a central, fluid position between Reform and Orthodoxy. What this means in practice, then, is that there are many traditional practices that Conservative Judaism sees no need to adapt, such as traditional kosher observance and strict Sabbath adherence. However, the Committee on Jewish Law and Standards, which interprets Jewish law for Conservative Judaism as a whole, also continually weighs in with new interpretations of such issues as ordaining women rabbis, surrogacy and artificial insemination, and body piercing—which, by the way, is allowed, but only in moderation.

RECONSTRUCTIONIST JUDAISM

The Reconstructionist branch of Judaism is the youngest; and though it is by far the smallest of the four major denominations, it has been quite influential in the last century. It began in the United States in the early 1920s—the only major denomination of Judaism that originated in the New World. Still today, the vast majority of members are located in the United States, Canada, and the Caribbean, and it has only a limited presence in other parts of the world. Reconstructionist Judaism was founded by Rabbi Mordecai Kaplan, who began

---

15. http://www.masortiworld.org/molami/Mission_statement.

his career as an Orthodox rabbi, but went on to teach at the Conservative Jewish Theological Seminary for fifty-four years, during which time he founded the Society for the Advancement of Judaism, a synagogue in New York City, in 1922. There, with other likeminded Jews, he worked from within the Conservative movement in an attempt to "reconstruct" Judaism such that it might demonstrate greater relevance and practicality for American Jews. He did not seek to create a new branch of Judaism, but in the end, this was the result.

The fundamental shift in Reconstructionist Judaism is from God and the Torah to the people themselves. I cannot stress this enough: the emphasis in Reconstructionism is on community, and as such, it understands Judaism as an evolving response of the Jewish people to its encounter with God. What is important about Judaism is not that everyone believes the same things about divine revelation, miracles, and God (indeed, Kaplan advocated a form of religious naturalism that many would see as nontheistic), or that people follow Jewish law the same way. Instead, Reconstructionist Judaism sees the value of Judaism first and foremost as a cultural force uniting, supporting, and nurturing the Jewish people over time and space. As such, everything is open to debate and modification—all beliefs, all doctrines, all practices—according to the current needs of the Jewish community. Tradition is important, specifically in that it is a prime way of maintaining community, but it has only a voice, not a veto—and, as you might imagine, there are many different views about how much of a vote tradition should have in any specific decision about Jewish life.

In service of these ideas, Kaplan instituted several new practices that have spread broadly across much of the greater Jewish landscape. He was the first to recognize the cultural potential of having Jewish community centers and the spiritual potential of Jewish summer camps. In addition, he created the first *bat mitzvah* ceremony—his daughter was the first young woman to go through one, in 1922.[16] Reconstructionist Judaism maintains friendly relations with both Conservative and Reform Judaism; however, Orthodox religious authorities do not recognize its teachings.

While Kaplan had not intended to start a new branch of Judaism, in time it became clear that in order to promote and promulgate his vision, which he publicized in a variety of books—particularly *Judaism as a Civilization: Toward a Reconstruction of American-Jewish Life*, published in 1934—a new organization would be needed. Ultimately, three complementary institutions were founded: the Jewish Reconstructionist Federation in 1955, the Reconstructionist Rabbinical College in 1968, and the Reconstructionist Rabbinical Association

16. Robinson, *Essential Judaism*, 62.

in 1974.[17] Even earlier, however, there was a "Jewish Reconstructionist Foundation," which put out a "Reconstructionist Platform" in 1942, laying out the basic tenets of the faith. The following two give a good sense of the document as a whole: "All Jews should seek a conception of God which is free from superstition, and which is integrated with their general outlook on the universe"; and "Traditional forms of Jewish ritual observance should be maintained, if they are spiritually adequate or can be rendered adequate through reinterpretation."[18] This is about as far from Orthodox Judaism as one can travel.

UNDERSTANDING JEWISH SACRED TEXTS

As I said at the beginning of this chapter, many Christians make the mistake of assuming that Judaism shares the same understanding of sacred scripture as Christians—only without the New Testament. However, in fact, Judaism has its own interpretation of what constitutes "scripture" and how it is interpreted; some aspects overlap with Christianity, and others are quite different.

Let's begin with some definitions. When learning about Jewish scriptures, the most important word is *Torah*, which often is translated as "law," but more accurately means "teaching" or "instruction." As the authors of *The Jewish Study Bible* note, the word itself is derived from the root *y-r-h*, which means "'to shoot (an arrow),' and thus etymologically refers to that which 'hits the mark.'"[19] In its broadest meaning, the word *Torah* actually includes two different categories of writings: the written Torah, which points specifically to the first five books of the Hebrew scriptures—Genesis, Exodus, Leviticus, Numbers, and Deuteronomy, but includes by extension the entire Jewish Bible; and what is called the "oral Torah," the collection of instructions and interpretations traditionally said to have been given to Moses by God at Mount Sinai that has been transmitted orally ever since, down through the generations. This "oral Torah" provides explanation for how to interpret the written Torah, and therefore includes instruction for how to properly obey the commandments and live a faithful Jewish life. Over time, the amount of material contained in this oral transmission grew to be so great that it was deemed wise to write it down, creating a more permanent record. This occurred in the second/third centuries

[handwritten margin notes: Torah; written Torah; oral Torah]

---

17. On June 3, 2012, a restructuring of the movement took place, with the result that the Reconstructionist Rabbinical College is now the primary institution of Reconstructionist Judaism and the denomination has a new website: www.jewishrecon.org.

18. http://ufdc.ufl.edu/UF00072112/00001/10j.

19. *The Jewish Study Bible*, ed. Adele Berlin and Marc Zvi Brettler (Oxford: Oxford University Press, 2004), 1.

ce; and the resulting text is known as the *Mishnah*. More will be said about the *Mishnah* shortly, but first, let me say more about the Bible itself.

THE TANAKH

Taken as a whole, the *Tanakh* is the name of the Hebrew scriptures, what Christianity calls the Old Testament.[20] The name is an acronym for the three sections of scripture, *Torah*, *Nevi'im*, and *Kethuvim*, and a quick perusal of its table of contents reveals some differences between it and the Christian version. "Torah," also called the Pentateuch, includes the books of Genesis, Exodus, Leviticus, Numbers, and Deuteronomy. *Nevi'im*, or "prophets," includes the eight books of Joshua, Judges, Samuel, Kings, Isaiah, Jeremiah, Ezekiel, and "the Twelve." Notice that Samuel and Kings are each one book in the Hebrew scriptures, not divided into two books as they are in the Christian Bible; and also notice that what is one book in the *Tanakh*, "the Twelve," is divided into twelve individual books in the Christian Bible, each named for one of the prophets—Joel, Amos, Jonah, etc.[21]

Finally, *Kethuvim* is the name for "the writings," a motley collection of books, canonized last and used for a wide variety of purposes. This is the full list of books contained in this section: Psalms, Proverbs, Job, a group called "the five scrolls"—the five short books of the Song of Songs, Ruth, Lamentations, Ecclesiastes, and Esther, each of which is read for a specific Jewish holiday—and finally Daniel, Ezra-Nehemiah, and Chronicles. In Jewish tradition, Ezra and Nehemiah historically are viewed as one book, as is Chronicles.

THE ORAL TORAH

The Bible is the foundation of Jewish faith, but it does not stand alone. Instead, since at least the time of Ezra and the Jewish return from the Babylonian exile in the fifth century, there has been a vibrant, rich tradition of interpretation of the Torah, in order to help the Jewish people live faithfully according to its laws. So, for example, even though the Bible is clear that one should not work on the

---

20. Let me take a moment to note the obvious here: "Old Testament" can be viewed as a pejorative term by Jews, as it implies something that has been supplanted and superseded by the "New Testament." Many Christian scholars avoid the term altogether, using "Hebrews scriptures" or "Hebrew Bible" instead. The latter terms are preferable in Jewish-Christian conversations.

21. *The Jewish Study Bible*, and some others, follows the practice that was first instituted in the Septuagint (the Greek translation of the Hebrew scriptures) and divides both Samuel and Kings into two books, because of their length. It also treats individually each of the minor prophets (primarily because each book is treated separately in the rabbinic tradition), even though from early on they all were written on one scroll.

Sabbath, it says nothing about what constitutes work: Is cooking a meal work? What about mowing the lawn? It should be clear that this task of interpretation is ongoing, as new situations continually require fresh answers.

Originally, as the name suggests, this body of interpretation was oral, but in the decades following the fall of the second temple in 70 ce, it was determined that these legal rulings should be codified in writing, in order to better preserve both them and the Jewish people themselves, who, in the absence of a temple, now had to anchor themselves with parchment not stone. The scholars in charge of this work are called the *Tannaim*, the authors of what would become the Mishnah.

THE MISHNAH AND THE TALMUD

The scholar in charge of the daunting task of compiling the Mishnah was Judah Ha-Nasi, also called Judah the Prince, and he did his work over a period of roughly twenty years, from 200 to 220 ce. This resulting text became a document that could outlast the vagaries of history, and survive as a cornerstone of Jewish identity over time and space. Yet even more than that, it was a document of hope: "[I]t sent a message to the Jewish people in a time of darkness . . . the Mishnah presented Judaism as a faith and practice not bound by the fleeting passage of historical time. . . . Thus the Mishnah is a book of 'an eternal present.'"[22] The Mishnah is divided into six sections, or "orders," and sixty-three individual tractates, each of which contains detailed legal rulings—concise, terse, and orderly—governing a specific aspect of Jewish life: agricultural laws, Sabbath laws, laws of marriage, etc.

Once completed, the Mishnah exhibited both the classic strength and weakness of any written text: the strength is, of course, its permanence and authority; the weakness, however, is its inability to address any new situations or questions that might come up over time. Thus the rabbis' ongoing activity of interpretation now included not only the Bible itself, but this vast compilation of tradition and lore. The body of commentary/debate/discussion surrounding the Mishnah that developed is called the Gemara, composed from the early third century ce to the sixth century ce; and the resulting book containing both the Mishnah and the Gemara is the Talmud. Actually, to be more precise, there are two Talmuds, the Palestinian/Jerusalem Talmud, completed in roughly 400 ce, and the Babylonian Talmud, completed in roughly 500 ce. These two texts originated in the two main centers of Jewish scholarship at that time; of the two, it is the Babylonian Talmud that came to be considered the most authoritative.

22. Robinson, *Essential Judaism*, 323–24.

Commentary did not come to an end in the sixth century. Instead, generation after generation of rabbis and sages continued the work of interpretation for each new time and place; in particular, the various heads of the Jewish academies took upon themselves the task of writing responses to questions that came to them from Jewish communities all over the world. These eventually became the foundation of the rabbinic code of law. Additionally, a tradition of biblical and Talmudic commentary developed and blossomed, especially beginning with Rabbi Solomon ben Isaac, known as Rashi (1040–1105). Rashi was a French scholar who wrote an exhaustive commentary on the *Tanakh* and the Babylonian Talmud in the eleventh century. His influence is unmatched, and his commentary is considered to have special authority.

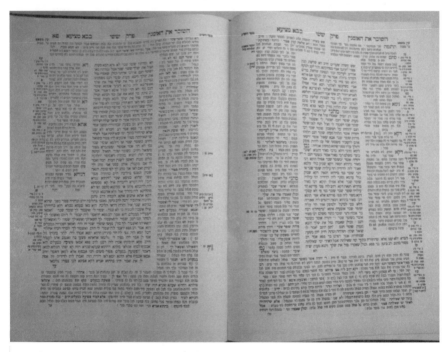

Figure 2.3. The Babylonian Talmud, tractate Baba Mezia, pp. 80b–81a [b. BM 80b–81a]

This authority is confirmed in the printed copies of the Talmud itself, once it was laid out after the invention of the printing press: when looking at any page of the Talmud, Rashi's commentary is always given pride of place, located on the side of the page closest to the binding, which means it is always in the middle of the opened book.[23] The last set of commentaries that must be mentioned is called the *Tosafot*, which means "additions" or "supplements." These authors (writing in the twelfth and thirteenth centuries) saw themselves as carrying on the work of Rashi, and clarifying his interpretations; these commentaries are printed on the outer margins of the pages of the Talmud—they are the columns of text closest to the edges of the pages. Even though the written Talmud is closed, interpretation continues, and Talmudic study is one of the most important, most sacred, most fulfilling religious activities a traditional or Orthodox Jew can undertake. Indeed, Judaism considers study a form of prayer.

WHAT DO JEWS BELIEVE?

Before discussing the central beliefs of Judaism, I want to elaborate on a generalization that I mentioned in the previous chapter, which involves a distinction between "orthopraxis," which means "right action" or "right practice," and "orthodoxy," "right belief" or "right doctrine." Obviously, in any religion, both of these things are important: every religion teaches certain specific beliefs, and every religion teaches certain specific practices. They go hand-in-hand. At the same time, however, it can be said fairly that many religions emphasize one more than the other: that is, for some religions, it is more important that you *act* a certain way; and in other religions, it is more important that you *believe* a certain way. Christianity, for example, is clearly a religion that emphasizes orthodoxy: generally speaking, you are a Christian if you believe in Jesus Christ and are baptized: they do go together but the one (belief) precedes the other (action), even when it is the parents or sponsors who confess the faith first. And, more importantly, once this public enactment of belief occurs, the person *is* a Christian, period; it doesn't matter how often you go to church—the Christmas/Easter attender is just as much a Christian as the weekly churchgoer; it doesn't matter how often you break the law—the thief is just as much a Christian as the police officer; and it doesn't matter how often you pray or read the Bible—the indolent is just as much a Christian as the dutiful. Now, obviously, actions are important in Christianity—in some denominations more than others—and certainly we do well to ask what good it does or what purpose it holds for an individual to say she is Christian when she never goes to church, never practices love of neighbor, never prays, etc. But the

---

23. This is a link to a picture of a page of the Talmud and explanation of how it is laid out: http://people.ucalgary.ca/~elsegal/TalmudPage.html. This is another good example: http://www.joshua-parker.net/portfolio/resourceguides/talmud_layout.pdf.

reality is, fundamentally, Christianity is a religion about creeds, doctrines, and confessions, and one's actions flow from one's beliefs, not the other way around.

In Judaism, by contrast, more emphasis is placed on how one acts. This certainly is true for Conservative, Reform, and Reconstructionist Jews, and many would argue that it is true for Orthodox Judaism as well. In general, Judaism assumes God's existence—it's hardly a topic of debate—and instead concerns itself with the relationship people have with God and how they respond to God's law. What this means is that the spectrum of what Jews believe is very broad; and Judaism in general is very tolerant of a wide variety of theological viewpoints. Having said all that, there still are, of course, some basic doctrines that help identify and define Judaism, some core principles that, for millennia, have undergirded and informed all other aspects of the tradition.

One can find many different lists of these principles, but still today the standard is that which was generated by one of Judaism's greatest minds, Moses Maimonides (also known as Rambam), a Spanish Jew who lived in the twelfth century. His thirteen principles of faith, first formulated in his *Commentary on the Mishnah* (written in 1160), is the most widely accepted list of Jewish beliefs. It reads as follows:

I believe with a perfect faith that:

1. The Creator is Author and Guide of everything that exists.
2. The Creator is One; His unity is unlike that of anything else; He is our God and exists eternally.
3. The Creator has no body or physical characteristics, and cannot be compared with anything that exists.
4. The Creator is first and last of all beings.
5. It is right to pray to the Creator, but to no other being.
6. All the words of the prophets are true.
7. The prophecy of Moses is true, and He was the father (that is, the greatest) of all prophets, both before and after him.
8. The Torah now in our possession is that given to Moses.
9. The Torah will not be changed, nor will the Creator give any other Torah.
10. The Creator knows the deeds and thoughts of people.
11. He rewards those who keep His commandments, and punishes those who disobey.
12. Though the Messiah delay, one must constantly expect His coming.
13. The dead will be resurrected.[24]

---

24. Solomon, *Judaism: A Very Short Introduction*, 136.

For Christians reading through that list, a few clarifications are in order. Clearly, there are many similarities: the belief in God's oneness (which, however, as stated here precludes Jesus' divinity), the belief that God created the world, the belief in the divine origin of the Hebrew Bible (although again, the idea of the New Testament as sacred scripture is ruled out), and also the belief in the resurrection of the dead. Yet, there also are some important differences.

Look at numbers eleven, twelve, and thirteen. Notice that there is a strong connection between this world and the next: the ramifications of our actions now on our future life with God; the importance of living rightly, in preparation for the expected coming of the Messiah; and the promise that our death does not end our relationship with God—there will be a resurrection. When trying to interpret these statements in a Jewish context, Christians should be aware that Judaism focuses much more on our lives here and now, and does not speculate much on the afterlife, beyond the confirmation that it exists. In fact, the whole idea of life after death is somewhat of a vague and unformulated concept in the *Tanakh* itself. While there are multiple mentions of an "underworld" of sorts in various books of the Hebrew Bible, it is only in Daniel where an unambiguous endorsement of life after death is found.[25]

Thus the most we can say for sure, then, is that heaven and hell—the way Christians understand them—don't really exist in Judaism. Instead of the concept of hell as a place of eternal torment and suffering, Judaism references the concept of *sheol*, a nebulous netherworld where souls descend after earthly existence. And instead of the concept of heaven, there are only scant metaphorical references to some sort of divine dwelling place, with one notable exception in Daniel, chapter twelve: "Many that sleep in the dust of the earth will awake, some to eternal life, others to reproaches, to everlasting abhorrence. And the knowledgeable will be radiant like the bright expanse of sky, and those who lead the many to righteousness will be like the stars forever and ever" (12:2-3). Here is what Jewish commentators say about those verses:

> The doctrine of resurrection and judgment probably came about during the persecutions of Antiochus IV as a means to effect justice as a time when pious people, the *knowledgeable*, were being martyred . . . . the resurrection here is not a metaphor for the rebirth of Israel, but individual resurrection for judgment. Whether bodily resurrection or some form of spiritual resurrection is intended is not stated. This is the only certain biblical reference to this doctrine, a doctrine that

25. *The Jewish Study Bible*, Isaiah 26, note 19, 834.

became central in Christian theology and remained a strong current in Judaism as well.[26]

The fluidity and ambiguity of this belief, both then and now, exemplifies a point I made about orthopraxic religions in general: "the afterlife is less central to Judaism than ethical behavior in this life."[27]

Finally, let me say a word about the concept of "messiah" in Judaism, a word that simply means "one who has been anointed." Obviously, Jews do not believe that Jesus is the messiah; and in fact, they reject the idea that the messiah is divine: in the few places in the Hebrew Bible where "messiah" is mentioned, it always refers to a human being, a king who comes to rule with great power: the Persian king Cyrus, for example. And, nowhere in the *Tanakh* is there mention of the messiah as a future king coming to inaugurate the reign of God—this belief only came later in rabbinic Judaism.[28] Instead, there is much more emphasis in Judaism on making the world ready for the messiah right now, rather than sitting around waiting for God to come and perfect the world. Jews believe that as part of their identity as God's chosen people, they have a special calling to participate in God's healing of the world and caring for the human community. In this way, humanity itself is able to bring the world closer to God's coming reign of peace and justice, making the time and day of the messiah's coming less important. A lovely Jewish poem sums it up this way:

If you will always assume
The person sitting next to you
Is the messiah
Waiting for some human kindness,
You will soon learn to weigh your words and watch your hands.
And if he so chooses
Not to reveal himself
In your time,
It will not matter.[29]

26. Ibid., Daniel 12, note 2-3, 1665. The authors also note in their commentary on Job 14:13-14 that "the notion of an afterlife, the resurrection of the dead, or a world to come where people are rewarded or punished for their deeds in this world, had not yet developed at the time that Job was written" [1523].

27. Robinson, *Essential Judaism*, 193.

28. *The Jewish Study Bible*, 2134.

29. Attributed to Danny Siegel, taken from a sermon by Rabbi Marc E. Berkson, http://ceebj.org/rabbis-sermons/next-year/.

JEWISH LIFE: MARKING TIME

As I was trying to find the right way to begin this section of the chapter, I kept returning to the title of a recent book on Judaism: *Judaism: A Way of Being*. This phrase points to what I already have mentioned: in many ways, being Jewish is much more about how one lives one's life in response to God, rather than what one thinks about God. And, exemplifying that point, in the first chapter of this book, the author, David Gelernter, lifts up the theme of "separation" as a way of understanding Jewish life. He argues that, in Jewish life, separation—that is, the activity of maintaining one's distinct and unique Jewish identity by following the elaborate and interwoven pattern of Jewish law—is what stands at the core of the faith, allowing one to choose life and participate in the twin pillars of holiness and beauty that support Judaism as a whole.[30]

Another way of explaining this is using the concept of harmony: "To act in harmony with the will of this God [of creation and history] is the highest goal of life. . . . The ideal of life is living in harmony with the will of God."[31] The "how" of this goal is answered by Jewish law, *halakhah*, commandments that govern every aspect of Jewish life, describing religious rituals that are meant to form one's life from beginning to end, from *Tishri* (the Jewish New Year) to *Elul*, from Sabbath to Sabbath. Here is how some of this looks in practice.

THE JEWISH CALENDAR

There are a few things to note about how time is calculated in Judaism. The first is that Judaism uses what it called a lunar-solar calendar: it is primarily lunar, but with some adjustments added in order to keep somewhat apace with the solar calendar. Without these adjustments, some years Passover, which the Torah says is a holiday of spring, would fall in April, and other years it would fall in August. In order to keep the fluctuation of holidays to a minimum, an additional month is added to the lunar calendar every two or three years. Also, the day is said to begin at sundown, rather than at sunup, and it ends at sundown the following day, so, the Sabbath begins Friday at sundown and ends Saturday after dark. The reason for this is that it follows the pattern narrated in the creation story in Genesis: ". . . and there was evening, and there was morning the first/second/third/etc. day."

Perhaps the most important thing to note about time, however, is the fact that Judaism emphasizes the holiness of *time*, rather than the holiness of place. As Abraham Joshua Heschel writes, "Judaism is a *religion of time* aiming at *the*

---

30. David Gelernter, *Judaism: A Way of Being* (New Haven: Yale University Press, 2009), 31.

31. *World Religions Today*, ed. Esposito et al., 76.

sanctification of time.[32] He goes on to note that in the Bible, the very first time the "distinguished word" *qadosh* (holy) is used, it is not to describe a place or a person, but rather a day: "And God blessed the seventh *day* and called it holy." What conclusion did Heschel draw from this? Before God sanctifies anything else, God creates *holiness in time*, or the Sabbath; and it is from the holiness of the Sabbath that all holiness in the world flows.[33] For this reason, the most important holy day in Judaism is not a specific "holiday" at all, but rather the weekly celebration of the Sabbath, the heart and soul of Jewish practice.

According to Heschel's famous description, the Sabbath belongs to that "realm of time where the goal is not to have but to be, not to own but to give, not to control but to share, not to subdue but to be in accord."[34] All the laws governing the Sabbath, then, are to further those ends, to establish a day of physical rest (the Sabbath is for the body as well as the soul) and spiritual renewal, and restore relationships with God, within the family, and within the community. It is for this reason that labor is prohibited on the Sabbath—doing business, shopping, doing housework, using electricity, etc.[35] These proscriptions, however, are seen as gifts, not punishments, for they set aside the sacred time in which life as is it intended can flourish, nurtured by prayer and contemplation, rest and reflection, laughter and joy. The life of every Jew, every Jewish family, and every Jewish community revolves around the Sabbath.

Judaism does have holidays, of course, the most sacred of which are called the "Days of Awe," the high holy days of Rosh Hashanah, which marks the New Year in Judaism, and Yom Kippur, which is the Day of Atonement. Yom Kippur is the culmination of the season, and it is a twenty-five-hour day of solemn prayer, repentance, and strict fasting. During that day, forgiveness is sought from God and from others for the transgressions of the past year, in order to purify and prepare oneself for the coming year.

---

32. Abraham Joshua Heschel, *The Sabbath* (New York: Farrar, Straus & Giroux, 2005), 8.

33. Ibid., 9.

34. Ibid., 3.

35. Specifically, what is prohibited is *melachah*, which refers to "creative" work—work that brings something new into being, changes something's character, or exercises control over one's environment. The key here is the reference back to God's creative work (the archetypal *melachah*) in creating the universe. Jews rest on the Sabbath to honor and emulate God's example.

Figure 2.4. Women praying at the Western Wall, Jerusalem. January 2012.

Another important set of holidays is the three pilgrimage festivals. The first is
Sukkot, which celebrates the fall harvest and recalls the journeys of the Hebrew
people. To commemorate this festival, families and communities typically build
a temporary outdoor shelter where one can eat, entertain guests, and sometimes
even sleep. The second is Shavu'ot, which celebrates both the harvest of the
first fruits and also the giving of the Torah at Mount Sinai. The third—the
one most familiar to Christians—is Passover, which commemorates the Exodus
event: the deliverance of the Hebrews out of slavery in Egypt. The major event
of Passover is the Seder, a special meal in which special foods are eaten, special
songs are sung, and a special book is used. This book is called the *haggadah*, and
it contains the passages from the Bible as well as rabbinic interpretation that
explains the significance of the celebration and describes the rituals that are to
be performed throughout the course of the evening.

Yet, the *haggadah* is not only about the past, but also about the present,
and so new books are written in new contexts, for new situations—like the
version written by American soldiers in 1945, for the Seder they celebrated
shortly after liberating Jews from the Nazi death camps.[36] The reason why
these emendations and changes are allowed—even encouraged—is simple: "In

every age, freedom must be renewed, reflecting the needs of particular places, issues and events. The *haggadah* gives Jews the opportunity to remember ancient slavery and celebrate historical redemption, while providing the framework for including the circumstances of the moment in the never-ending desire and quest for human freedom and dignity."[37] However, it also should be noted that Orthodoxy, and to a lesser extent, Conservative Judaism, holds to a set, traditional text.

THE LIFE CYCLE AND THE HOME

Harvey Goldberg notes that the Hebrew Bible is, above all else, the story of a relationship: the relationship between God, and the people God has made and chosen. What is particularly remarkable about this relationship—a relationship that is clearly not between equals—is that it takes the form of a covenant: "God and Israel agree to commit to each other."[38] The markers of this covenant can be found in all aspects of Jewish life, even on one's body, such that the whole of Jewish living is geared toward remembering that covenant and honoring that commitment. Circumcision for Jewish boys, for example, has been a standard practice since the covenant with Abraham was formed; and the passage into adulthood (in terms of religious responsibilities) occurs with a Bar or Bat/Bas Mitzvah ceremony. A Jewish home is immediately identified by the *mezuzah* on the doorpost, containing a small parchment inscribed with words from the Torah; and most Jewish kitchens include specific accommodations needed to keep the kosher laws, including not only special foods, but even in many cases two entire sets of dishes, pots, etc., one for meat products and one for dairy, as it is prohibited to eat these foods together. (This diligence is found outside the home, too, as many Jews go to great lengths to obey these dietary laws at all times, even when drinking coffee at Starbucks.[39]) Finally, upon death, one is quickly returned to God and to the earth, after the body is prepared and purified, dressed in white, and buried in a simple wooden coffin. There are

---

36. Rabbi Wayne Dosick, *Living Judaism: The Complete Guide to Jewish Belief, Tradition, and Practice* (New York: HarperCollins, 1995), 167–68.

37. Ibid.

38. Harvey E. Goldberg, "Judaism as a Religious System," in *The Cambridge Guide to Jewish History, Religion, and Culture*, ed. Judith R. Baskin and Kenneth Seeskin (Cambridge: Cambridge University Press, 2010), 289.

39. An article titled "Blending a Strong Interest in Kosher Ingredients with a Taste for Starbucks Coffee," discussed a young Orthodox Jew who runs a website helping other Jews know which Starbucks drinks are kosher. http://www.nytimes.com/2012/07/07/us/a-web-site-practices-coffee-kosherology.html?ref=us.

prescribed rituals of mourning; but even in grief, the *kaddish* is recited, which contains not psalms of lamentation but prayers of praise and thanksgiving: traditional Judaism expresses faith in God even in the worst of times.

Figure 2.5. Multiple Bar Mitzvah ceremonies at the Western Wall, Jerusalem. January 2012.

JEWS IN THE TWENTY-FIRST CENTURY: THE HOLOCAUST AND THE NATION OF ISRAEL

Any introduction to Judaism would be incomplete without a description of the two most important events for Judaism in the twentieth century, the two events that loom large over Judaism today, influencing widely and broadly its thought and practice. The first is the terrible event of the Holocaust; and the second is the historic creation of the nation of Israel and the subsequent challenges of identity, land, and diversity within Israel itself. In the few remaining pages, I can do no more than sketch a brief outline of both of these occurrences.

THE HOLOCAUST

The word *holocaust* comes from the Greek, and refers to "a sacrifice/offering totally consumed by fire." This is the word most commonly used to describe the systematic persecution and slaughter of the Jewish people under the Nazi regime. However, in Judaism, the term most often used is *shoah*, which is a biblical word that means "destruction" or "catastrophe." Many argue the latter term is preferable, for the following reasons: "few, if any, of the killers of the Jews during the Nazi era were seeking to propitiate divine power, many of those who were massacred would have rejected an attribution of religious meaning or purpose to their deaths, and burning is not how vast numbers of the victims either died or were disposed of. By virtue of being direct and unmetaphorical, 'the Shoah' avoids the sanctification of senseless killing that is implicit in the word 'holocaust.'"[40]

To properly understand the Holocaust, two underlying truths must be emphasized. First and foremost, as I mentioned earlier, what happened under the Nazi party is unthinkable without the larger culture of anti-Semitism that had existed throughout Western Europe for centuries. People were all too willing to accept Adolf Hitler's lies about the Jews in no small part because of the persistent, pervasive climate of suspicion and revulsion toward them that had deep roots in Western culture. Second, it cannot be stated strongly enough that anti-Semitism was a central component of Nazi ideology, and this is especially true when looking at Hitler himself. Peter Hayes writes, "Although the prominence of anti-Semitism in Nazi propaganda varied before and after 1933, Hitler's ideological fixation on Jews and the threat they supposedly posed to Germans and all humanity never wavered. This was the central theme of his first fervent public speeches in 1919–1920 and of his equally heated last will and testament in 1945."[41] Almost from the moment of his rise to power, the persecution began that was always inexorably headed toward genocide.

Here is just a brief account of some of the steps—both small and large—that led up to the horror that was the death camps. Just a few short months after becoming chancellor of Germany in 1933, Hitler declared a one-day boycott of Jewish businesses, on April 1st. Some of the signs posted read "German people, defend yourselves! Do not buy from Jews." This declaration was followed quickly by new laws that prohibited Jews from civil service and restricted the number of Jewish students at German high schools and universities. Then, in 1935, the Nuremberg Laws were passed, prohibiting intermarriage (to "protect German blood and German honor") and stripping Jews of their German citizenship.

---

40. Peter Hayes, "The Shoah and Its Legacies," in *The Cambridge Guide to Jewish History, Religion, and Culture*, 233.

41. Ibid., 237.

Jews were getting the message: "By the end of 1937 . . . nearly one-third of the German Jewish population had fled the country; some 60 percent of their businesses and 40–50 percent of their total wealth as of 1933 had become the property of other people or the German state."[42] Yet, far worse was to come. On November 9 and 10, 1938, what has come to be known as *Kristallnacht*—the night of broken glass—occurred. Gangs of Nazis ravaged Jewish neighborhoods, breaking the windows of Jewish businesses and homes, looting them when possible, and burning synagogues. When there was little public outcry, the Nazis were emboldened to intensify their persecution, and for this reason, some date the actual beginning of the events that came to be known as the Holocaust from this occurrence.

The next major phase in the Nazi extermination program was the establishment of the ghettos in 1939, first and foremost in Poland, but in other areas of Eastern Europe as well. In cities all over occupied Nazi territory, the Jews were forced into small areas of the city, and could be shot if found trying to leave. The ghettos were grossly overcrowded, and Jews died daily of starvation and disease. Most of the ghettos were located in major cities near rail lines, which facilitated the next and last step of the Nazi plan for the Jews, tellingly called "The Final Solution"—"the physical extinction of all Jews within [the Nazis'] reach."[43] This was accomplished by transporting millions of Jews to death camps, where they were gassed with systematic and shocking efficiency.

Unlike concentration camps, which were mostly located in Germany and used to incarcerate a variety of "undesirables," including Communists and those who were then called "homosexuals," the death camps were just that—places to exterminate as many Jews as possible, as quickly as possible. There were six main camps, all located in occupied Poland, and when it was all over, roughly 3 million Jews were killed in these camps—roughly half the number of Jews killed in the entire Holocaust.

There is no doubt that this is one of the most shameful periods in modern Christian history: the Nazis were, to large degree, unopposed by religious authorities, and only small pockets of resistance were formed, including the Pastors' Emergency League, founded by Martin Niemöller, and the Confessing Church movement, which produced the famous Barmen Declaration, written primarily by Swiss theologian Karl Barth in 1934. Instead, most Lutheran churches in Germany at least passively supported the Nazi party—some actively supported it— choosing to look the other way and keep silent. In a similar way, the Catholic Church as a whole, particularly its head, Pope Pius XII, also said

42. Ibid., 239.
43. Ibid., 246.

nothing, leaving individual dioceses and priests to make their own decisions about what, if anything, to do. It is a disgraceful fact that neither the Catholic nor the Protestant leadership officially protested Nazi treatment of the Jews at any point, with the result that only "rare and brave individuals and groups risked their lives to rescue Jews. . . . Thus, the Jews across occupied Europe saved in heroic fashion came to a rather small proportion, probably only 5–10 percent, of those who survived the war."[44]

This is not, of course, to denigrate or minimalize the efforts of those "righteous Gentiles" who did risk their own lives and the lives of their families to save as many Jews as they could; rather, it is to point out that, in the grand scheme of things, there was no massive mobilization of resistance, no large coordinated effort of subversion or sabotage. Instead, "At virtually every stage, the combination of German policy with the absence of escape routes from Europe and the widespread indifference or hostility of the surrounding populations meant that most Jews were confronted with 'choiceless choices' between immediate and delayed death."[45]

JEWISH THEOLOGICAL RESPONSES TO THE HOLOCAUST

The theological responses to the *Shoah* vary widely and come from a variety of sources: from different schools of thought within Judaism, and from different geographical locations. One of the best books that catalogues an excellent selection of these responses is titled *Wrestling with God: Jewish Theological Responses during and after the Holocaust.* I encourage the interested reader to consult this text for specific examples of all the responses I describe below.

To begin with, it is important to note that even while the Holocaust was taking place, Jewish rabbis and scholars were trying to make sense of this unimaginable disaster while still preserving one of the core bulwarks of their faith: the belief in a loving, just God who was active throughout history for the preservation of God's people. Early on, most of the responses originated from the Orthodox and Ultra-Orthodox communities, and while there were differences among them, they shared many primary convictions, including the following: the recognition that, at least initially, no response was possible—they simply did not have the language to describe an event like this; the belief that, even though God was sometimes hidden, God was not absent and was still active in history; a critique of increased secularization and assimilation on the part of the Jews; the power of repentance; and the significance of the suffering

primary convictions

44. Ibid., 250.
45. Ibid., 253.

of the pious.[46] Understandably, this group was most concerned to preserve the authority and veracity of the Torah, the goodness and power of God, and the need for continued fidelity to Jewish law. Unfortunately, this meant that sometimes Jews themselves were held to be responsible for the calamity, through their own indolence and lack of fidelity. Very different explanations would be offered by other Jewish communities.

One such community is the one that established itself in the new State of Israel after its formation in 1948. The Zionist ideology that had, at least in part, made the State of Israel a reality also complicated immensely the responses that came out of Israel. The problem originated in the creation of the "new Israeli Jew," over and against the "diaspora Jew"—that is, the Jew living outside Israel. These two stereotypes were set in opposition to one another:

> Zionism, as it was cultivated in Israel, essentially recognized the new Israeli Jew as the consummate negation of the "diaspora Jew," and nothing else. It characterized the diaspora Jew as passive, submissive, and wholly at the mercy of circumstances beyond his control. And then, almost stereotypically, it constructed the image of the modern Israeli as the total opposite of what it took to be the traditional image of the diaspora Jew.[47]

The new Israeli Jew was everything the "diaspora Jew" was not: confident, self-determining, and shaping history, rather than being subject to it.

Unfortunately, this created a climate of silence, shame, and alienation that marred the relationship between Holocaust survivors and those Jews who had settled earlier in Israel—most clearly exemplified in the inability to accept the victimization of European Jews, lauding those who resisted as martyrs, and challenging the others who were seen as "going like sheep to the slaughter."[48]

The final set of responses that must be mentioned is that which was generated by scholars in Europe and the United States, which contains the broadest spectrum of views that "range across the entire theological spectrum from those that are very traditional to those that conclude that the Holocaust proves God's nonexistence."[49] Steven Katz notes that there were two primary categories in which the responses fall: first, those that were based on biblical

---

46. *Wrestling with God: Jewish Theological Responses during and after the Holocaust*, ed. Steven T. Katz, Shlomo Biderman, and Gershon Greenberg (Oxford: Oxford University Press, 2007), 15–23.

47. Ibid., 207.

48. Ibid., 207–8.

49. Ibid., 355.

models; and second, those that were new theological constructions.[50] Some of the biblical models include: the *Akedah*, the binding of Isaac (with the Jews of the Holocaust being martyrs who willingly went to death to prove their faith in God); God's testing of Job; and the notion of *Hester Panim*, where God hides God's face for a time, in service of God's ultimate mercy.[51]

From a Christian theological point of view, however, particularly in a twenty-first-century North American context, perhaps the most interesting of all the different responses are those new theological constructions, each of which is innovative and provocative, challenging Christians and their concept of God as well. One construction is authored by Emil Fackenheim, arguing that, after Hitler "Jewish existence itself is a holy act"; and that a 614th commandment has come out of Auschwitz—the commandment to survive, not allowing Hitler "posthumous victories."[52] God was there in the Holocaust, and Jews are under a "sacred obligation" to survive and not despair of God's existence.[53]

Another concept, influenced by process theology, advocates a redefinition of God. Arthur Cohen, for example, argues that instead of investing God with purpose and agency in our lives, interrupting history with specific causal activity, we should better understand God as an immensity far greater than any historical event, the foundation of all existence and the reality awaiting us in the future. We can still love this God, though we cannot pray to God, nor can we have any expectation of an active relationship.[54]

A third idea comes from Richard Rubenstein, who starkly advocates the view that God is dead: that is the only honest response when faced with the reality of the Holocaust as a whole. There is no God, there is no covenant; and if there is to be any value in the world, humans must create it themselves. And, for that reason, it is all the more critical that the Jewish people survive,

---

50. Ibid.

51. Ibid., 355–58.

52. Ibid., 361.

53. I want to note here the interesting and well-documented response to Fackenheim, by the Catholic theologian Gregory Baum, who argued that Christians should no longer seek to convert Jews: "After Auschwitz the Christian churches no longer wish to convert the Jews. While they may not be sure of the theological grounds that dispense them from this mission, the churches have become aware that asking the Jews to become Christians is a spiritual way of blotting them out of existence and thus only reinforces the effects of the Holocaust." As cited by Hans Ucko in "Towards an Ethical Code of Conduct for Religious Conversations," *Current Dialogue* 50 (February 2008): http://www.oikoumene.org/en/programmes/interreligiousdialogue/current-dialogue/magazine/no-50-february-2008/towards-an-ethical-code-of-conduct-for-religious-conversions.html.

54. Ibid., 364.

sustaining meaning in and through the religious community alone, without any metaphysical speculation about God.[55] Finally, there is the response that comes from Elie Wiesel, among others, and that is the response of silence: "In the face of the abyss, the devouring of the Jewish people by the dark forces of evil incarnate, recourse to the God of mystery and the endorsement of human silence are not unworthy options."[56]

Let me conclude this section by pointing out that, during the Holocaust, the Jews were faced with unimaginable situations, put in untenable conditions, and forced to make the most monstrous choices. Even in these terrible circumstances, however, they turned to their rabbis, asking for guidance and seeking the best way to fulfill the law, in conditions explicitly designed to prevent them from doing just that. It is a powerful testimony to their continuing faith and their ongoing relationship with God that they did not give up or abandon their traditions, but rather wrestled both with the texts and with God to come to some solution. Norman Solomon recounts the following example, told by Rabbi Ephraim Oshry, a rabbi who survived a ghetto in Lithuania: He was asked,

> We Jews of the ghetto of Kovno . . . were enslaved by the Germans; we were worked to the bone night and day without rest; were starved and were paid nothing. The German enemy decreed our total annihilation. We were completely dispensable. Most would die. So was it proper to recite the customary blessings in the morning prayers thanking God "who has not made me a slave"? Oshry replied: "One of the earliest commentators on the prayers points out that this blessing was not formulated in order to praise God for our physical liberty but rather for our spiritual liberty. I therefore ruled that we might not skip or alter this blessing under any circumstances. On the contrary, despite our physical capacity, we were more obligated than ever to recite the blessings to show our enemies that as a people we were spiritually free.[57]

This strength of spirit survives still, and both was and remains one of the driving forces behind the creation and preservation of the nation of Israel.

---

55. Ibid., 365.
56. Ibid., 366.
57. Solomon, *Judaism: A Very Short Introduction*, 117.

THE STATE OF ISRAEL

Figure 2.6. The city of Jerusalem with its most recognizable landmark, the Dome of the Rock. January 2012.

The founding of the State of Israel is intimately bound up with the Holocaust and its aftermath. Certainly, Jews had longed for a homeland centuries earlier, and political Zionism—that is, "an organized Jewish nationalist movement dedicated to founding a Jewish state"[58]—had been active since the latter part of the 1800s. However, it was the terrible situation created by the Holocaust, including the hundreds of thousands of Jewish displaced persons languishing in refugee camps, that forced the issue. At that time, Great Britain controlled Palestine, and initially, they were reluctant to allow the survivors to relocate to Palestine. Nevertheless, in light of Britain's own losses in the war, fairly quickly Britain decided to relinquish control of Palestine to the United Nations, where the issue would be decided by a special committee.

After some negotiations, on November 29, 1947, the United Nations General Assembly voted to adopt what was called UNGA Resolution 181, which amounted to dividing the territory into a Jewish State and an Arab State,

58. Bernard Reich, "The Founding of Modern Israel and the Arab-Israeli Conflict," in the *Cambridge Guide to Jewish History, Religion, and Culture*, 258.

with Jerusalem set aside as an international zone: "In this way, the international system created Israel, within the territory of the Palestine mandate."[59] This decision was heavily criticized by both the Palestinian Arabs and the neighboring Arab states; and when the agreement took effect on May 14, 1948, Jewish communities worldwide reacted with great celebration, while the Arab world "greeted the declaration . . . with negative reactions ranging from dismay to outrage."[60] What is called the War of Independence began almost immediately following the declaration and did not end until 1949. Sadly, this was only the first in a series of wars that have shattered both sides and created a situation of such animosity and tension that it seems to be carved in stone. Although there have been positive moves in both directions and intermittent signs of hope, it is hard to feel optimistic in light of Shimon Peres's description of the whole peace process as "the art of the impossible."[61]

What else can be said? When trying to explain and understand the significance of Israel for the Jewish people, a good summary can be found in a line from the Midrash Tanhuma to Leviticus: "As the navel is in the middle of the person, so is Eretz Israel the navel of the world, as it is written, 'That dwell in the navel of the earth (Ezek. 38:12).'"[62] And while it certainly is possible to ask ten different Jews about the importance of Israel, and receive ten different answers, there is no doubt that both the land of Israel and the nation of Israel possess profound religious and political meaning for a vast majority of Jews of all denominations and nationalities. For many Jews, it is Israel that allows Jews to have a voice, to have a place, to have a civilization; it is Israel that guarantees the survival of the Jewish people, and allows Jewish customs and history to thrive and grow.

---

59. Ibid., 269.

60. Ibid., 271.

61. Ibid., 286.

62. As quoted in Philip S. Alexander, "Jerusalem as the *Omphalos* of the World," in *Jerusalem: Its Sanctity and Centrality to Judaism, Christianity, and Islam,* ed. Lee I. Levine (New York: Continuum, 1999), 114.

Figure 2.6. A view of the separation barrier, with the West Bank behind it, Jerusalem. January 2012.

Yet, at the same time, there are strident differences among Jews about how this significance and meaning are to be best supported and honored. Some argue against any humanly created state of Israel at all, believing that it could be seen as attempting to force God's hand. Some argue for the strongest possible Israeli state, in which all Palestinians should be expelled and all land brought under full Jewish control. And some argue for peaceful coexistence and equal cohabitation with Palestinians. These discussions and divisions affect not only Jews living in Israel, but Jews all over the world, all of whom have a vested interest in the outcome; and American Jews in particular are deeply drawn into the political ramifications of these arguments. For a land intimately bound up with key religious concepts of promise, covenant, and chosen-ness, there are no easy answers.

3

A Brief Introduction to Buddhism

In my experience, of all the major world religions, Christians tend to be the most positive, the most receptive toward Buddhism. I am sure there are a variety of reasons for this, but certainly one of the most important is that predominantly, the way in which Buddhism is understood and experienced in the West is as a philosophy—a way of life, rather than a competing religious tradition. Practices of mindfulness, meditation, simplicity, and nonviolence are easily and seamlessly incorporated into a Christian framework; and without a deity that demands worship, a single sacred text that demands fidelity, or a creed that requires adherence, it is no surprise that the phenomenon of "double-religious belonging"—when one person holds dual religious identities, claiming to be an adherent of two different religions simultaneously—seems to occur most with Christianity and Buddhism (rather than, for example, Christianity and Islam). This is not the place to either critically examine or challenge any of this, although I will say that there certainly are some misconceptions behind this easy familiarity Christians presume with Buddhism. Instead, what I hope to do in this chapter is provide a basic introduction to Buddhism, correcting some of the most common misconceptions so that Christians are better able to understand, appreciate, and critically engage with both Buddhists themselves and the religion as a whole.

Like all major world religious traditions, Buddhism is complex: rich, wide, and deep. Its doctrinal and institutional history spans two and a half millennia, and its tenets have been translated across multiple linguistic and cultural boundaries in its spread out of northeast India. Given this history, a comprehensive, detailed analysis is impossible in one short chapter, and I can do no more here than provide a general overview.

BUDDHISM'S ORIGINS

Like Christianity, Buddhism has a historical founder, Siddhartha Gautama, whose origins can be dated with approximate accuracy. The word *Buddha* actually means "awakened one"; thus Gautama was not born with this title, but rather achieved it in the course of his lifetime. The Buddha also is sometimes referred to as Shakyamuni, which means "sage of the Shakya clan."

The life of Siddhartha Gautama was deeply shaped by the Indian context into which he was born.[1] In his study on Buddhism, Donald Mitchell notes that "Gautama was born during a historical epoch when the Indian culture was open to his religious message of enlightenment, compassion, and peace."[2] The religious landscape of India at this time was fertile soil for a new religious teaching. In Hinduism, the recently composed Upanishads emphasized a move away from the ritual worship of different personal gods and presented a more contemplative path that focused on breaking the cycle of rebirth. One development within that movement saw this as being accomplished by the mystical union between the individual and an impersonal One, the spiritual reality called Brahman. These texts taught that through meditation and insight, one could realize the truth of this belief and attain liberation, *moksha*, from the endless cycles of suffering and death that characterize human existence in the world, known as *samsara*. This paradigm, in which the individual soul seeks release from the endless cycle of rebirths into a world characterized by change, decay, and illusion, was accepted not only by Hinduism but also by Buddhism and Jainism—both of which developed at this time in India. This move away from a focus on an established structure of ritual and rites, combined with the suspicion some people were feeling toward the priests, who were making a fine living from their participation in these rituals, led many people to leave the cities and reside in forests as "strivers," or *shramanas*—those who were seeking liberation and contentment beyond the temporary pleasures of the world. This world of religious and philosophical restlessness is the world into which Siddhartha Gautama was born.

WHO IS THE BUDDHA?

Let me start this section by noting that the Buddha is not a "god" in the Christian sense of the term—at least not entirely. The understanding one most

---

1. Buddhism actually began in India, a somewhat ironic fact given that in subsequent centuries it died out there completely, for reasons still debated by scholars. Thus the forms of Buddhism practiced in India today actually were reintroduced from other parts of Asia, beginning in the nineteenth century.

2. Donald W. Mitchell, *Buddhism* (Oxford: Oxford University Press, 2002), 9.

likely will encounter today is that the Buddha is seen as an awakened human being—no more, no less—one who saw through to the reality of existence and taught others how to escape the suffering in this life just as he did. The Buddha did not create the world nor does he save it; instead, he is a teacher of awakening. It is true that later schools of Buddhism did attribute salvific power to the Buddha (more will be said about that later), but even then, the Buddha was never believed to have created the universe, nor is he seen as the one singular omnipotent divine being, the way God is understood in Christianity. Rather, as Buddhism developed over time, the historical Buddha came to be seen as a particular embodiment of a universal nature that is present in all sentient life; a Buddhist thus can simultaneously venerate Gautama Buddha while seeking to realize that same Buddha nature abiding within herself.

In the beginning, however, there was the man, Siddhartha Gautama; and when we turn to the life of this historical figure, it should come as no surprise that many of the details of his birth and life are shrouded in mystery and controversy. In no small part this is because the first complete biographies of the Buddha were not written until hundreds of years after his death (compare this to Paul writing a mere thirty years after Jesus' death), and they include legends that were not part of earlier texts. Where the earliest texts give only fragmentary information about the Buddha himself, later biographies offer detailed accounts of every important moment in the Buddha's life, and not all of the details are the same in every biography. What follows, then, is a synthesis, one that represents the life narrative of the Buddha as many contemporary Buddhists understand it.

The Buddha was born sometime in the fifth century bce in Kosala, a former Indian state in the northeastern part of the country, at the foothills of the Himalayas; a region that now belongs to Nepal. He was born into a family of warriors and rulers—members of what has been traditionally called the Kshatriya caste—and all the early texts agree that he enjoyed a pampered existence in his youth.

Gautama was raised by his father and his stepmother, Mahaprajapati. It is said that his mother, Maya, died seven days after giving birth, and many different texts describe the auspicious nature of his birth. One of the most important of these concerns a dream his mother had while she was pregnant. One night, his mother fell asleep and dreamed that a white elephant, holding a white lotus flower in his trunk, entered her womb from the right side while she was sleeping. When Maya awoke the following day, she asked her advisors to explain the dream to her. They explained that the child she was carrying was a son and that, upon his birth, two divergent paths would stretch out before him. If he adopted the traditional life of a householder, marrying and having children, he would become a mighty ruler, a warrior who could possibly unite all of India into one great kingdom. If, however, he adopted the path of a religious teacher, he would become an awakened one who would teach the way of enlightenment and remove the veil of ignorance and suffering from the world.[3]

In response to this prediction, his father told the sages that he wanted his son to become a warrior. In order to facilitate this goal, the sages advised him to surround his son with every type of sensual pleasure and luxury and to hide from him anything that might discourage him from following a conventional path of life as a husband and father. Thus from the moment of his birth, Gautama's parents shielded him from all that is ugly in life, all that is tragic, all that is painful; surrounding him instead with beautiful women, rich foods, luxurious accommodations, and every sort of physical pleasure.

THE FOUR SIGHTS

Satiated in this life of luxury, Gautama grew up and married a woman named Yashodhara. Eventually they had a son, whom they named Rahula. This name means "fetter," which indicates that, despite his father's best efforts, Gautama was feeling torn between his ties to his family and his desire for religious awakening. This desire for a more religious life grew ever stronger in Gautama, and his dissatisfaction with the sensual pleasures of a wealthy householder grew as well. In the earliest sutras (Christians might think of sutras as sermons, the earliest of which were delivered by the Buddha; those that came later were written by his followers), the story of Gautama's leave-taking from his house is simple and straightforward: he shaved his hair and beard, and left his tearful family behind to practice an ascetic lifestyle. However, in later sutras, the story was elaborated into a larger narrative that is now called "The Four Sights." This story tells how Gautama finally was propelled to leave his home and begin his spiritual quest, which is called "The Great Renunciation."

It all began quite simply. One day, out on a chariot ride, Gautama went beyond the bounds that his father had marked off for him and he saw an old man. All signs of aging and decrepitude had been hidden from him up to this point in his life, so he was shocked and disturbed by what he saw. He asked the chariot driver who the man was and what had caused his miserable condition; Gautama was told that old age is the fate of every person and that no one can escape it. This was the first of the four sights, and it threw him into a deep melancholy.

---

3. *Buddhist Birth-Stories*, trans. Rhys Davids (Calcutta: Srishti, 1998), 150–51.

On a subsequent ride, he saw a severely diseased man, and he realized that no amount of power or wealth can keep disease away. This was the second sight, and it only intensified his misery. Sometime later, he went on a third chariot ride, and this time he saw a corpse for the first time in his life, and he realized that no matter how much pleasure or satisfaction one finds in one's life now, ultimately it will all end in death. This was the third sight. Finally, on the fourth and final chariot ride, he saw a religious hermit practicing meditation. When he asked who this person was and what he was doing, the chariot driver told Gautama that the hermit had left the physical pleasures of the householder's life in order to seek spiritual liberation from all the suffering and sorrow of the material world.

The stories say that this experience of the four sights as Gautama approached his thirtieth birthday created something of an existential crisis, a serious struggle between his attachment to his family and his desire for the wandering life of a religious ascetic. Ultimately, Gautama realized that the superficial pleasures he was enjoying in the palace were only passing and that they could not provide permanent happiness and peace. This is a lesson many Buddhists continue to apply to their own lives today: true contentment cannot be found by immersing oneself in the impermanent world of desire. Instead, release from the quest for permanence must be sought through the religious life of spiritual enlightenment. After Gautama came to this realization, he took leave of his family and set off on his spiritual quest, called "The Great Renunciation."

THE GREAT RENUNCIATION

After leaving home, Gautama first studied with a series of religious teachers, but he did not stay with any of them, quickly realizing that none of their practices led to ultimate enlightenment. He then began a program of severe physical austerities, joined by five other ascetics who were impressed with his discipline and drive. The images depicting the Buddha at this time in his life show him to be completely emaciated, and the stories recount that during this time, "his backbone became like a string of beads, and his buttocks became like the foot of a camel. Taking hold of his body from the front, he found he held it at the back."[4] He was said to have subsisted on only one sesame seed and one grain of rice per day.

For several years, Gautama and his five companions practiced together without any result, and he realized that severe asceticism was not the way to enlightenment—but, then, what was the way? Pondering this question, he

4. John Strong, *The Experience of Buddhism* (Belmont, CA: Wadsworth, 1995), 15.

remembered a time early on in his youth when he had attained a pleasant, transcendent state of awareness while sitting under a shady tree. He wondered if returning to that state of blissful contemplation might be the key to attaining enlightenment. Realizing that his body was too weak to support such a strenuous mental endeavor, he accepted some milk-rice (or yogurt, in some accounts) from a village girl, thereby abandoning his ascetic practice.

This act greatly disappointed the other five ascetics, and they left him to continue their own rigorous form of practice. For the religion that became Buddhism, however, this act had significant, lasting ramifications. As Richard Robinson and Willard Johnson write:

> Gautama's rejection of extreme austerities hinged on a critical moment when he realized that trying to gain liberation by escaping from the body through mortification was as ineffectual as attempting to escape through abstract absorptions. Caught at a dead end, he was able to open his mind to the possibility that physical pleasure of a nonsensual variety was not to be feared, and that it might form the basis for the liberating insight he sought. He went on to recognize that a healthy body is necessary for the development of discernment in order to understand the relationship of body to mind. In so doing, he took the first step on the Middle Way toward Awakening, a way that became central feature of the Dharma (or doctrine) he later taught.[5]

This "middle way" in Buddhism thus represents the path between the two extremes of self-denial and self-indulgence, between the sensual pleasures of the Buddha's youth and the self-mortification of his ascetic years.

5. Richard Robinson and Willard Johnson, *The Buddhist Religion* (Belmont, CA: Wadsworth, 1997), 14.

Figure 3.1. The Bodhi tree of Sarnath, planted in 1931, and taken from a cutting of the Sri Maha Bodhi tree of Anuradhapura, Sri Lanka, which is said to have been brought to Sri Lanka by Emperor Ashoka's daughter as a branch of the original Bodhi tree under which the Buddha attained enlightenment.

Thus fortified, Gautama then resolved to sit under what came to be called the Bodhi Tree, the Tree of Awakening, near Bodhgaya, vowing to remain there until he attained enlightenment. It would not, of course, be easy. It is said that Mara, the god of desire, could see the ramifications of Gautama's actions and realized that if he attained enlightenment, he would no longer be bound by craving and thus would no longer be under Mara's control. To prevent this from happening, Mara attempted to distract him from his meditation, attacking him with violent storms of mud, live coals, burning ashes, and rocks, all to no avail: Gautama continued his meditation undisturbed, turning the storms into showers of blossoms. Then Mara sent his three beautiful daughters—Lust, Thirst, and Discontent—to tempt him, but he remained unmoved. Finally, Mara gave up, and Gautama was free to continue his meditations.

Figure 3.2. A Statue of the Buddha at Senso-ji Temple, Tokyo. April 2012.

In the course of the night, the Buddha had three visions, each of which furthered him on the path from ignorance to awakening. In the first watch of the night, he had a vision of all his past lives, and he became aware of his personal identity as it had been formed through *samsara*, the endless cycle of birth and death. In the second watch of the night, he had a vision of the law of karma, or how beings come into being and then go out of being, rising into a more noble birth or falling into a lower birth as a result of their deeds. And in the third watch of the night, in the hours just before dawn, he became awakened. After he attained enlightenment, the Buddha then went back to his five ascetic companions, who were now residing at a park in Sarnath, near

Varanasi, India, and they became his first disciples. It is said that they also all attained enlightenment through his teaching.

Figure 3.3. The Dhamek Stupa, Sarnath, India, said to mark the place where the Buddha delivered his first sermon to his first five disciples. March 2012.

The Buddha lived and taught for eighty years, choosing for himself when it was time for him to end his life and attain final *nirvana*. He entered into final meditation peacefully, lying on his side, surrounded by all manner of animals, disciples, and even gods; and this scene of the Buddha passing into final *nirvana* is one of the most widely depicted in Buddhist art.

WHAT DO BUDDHISTS BELIEVE?

Perhaps the single most important difference between Buddhism and Christianity has to do with the role of belief. For many Christians, proper belief is necessary, if perhaps not sufficient in itself, for salvation. For Buddhists, proper belief is a preliminary, orienting step on the path to awakening, but the path is followed to its end by practice (specifically, mindfulness and meditation, which are discussed below). However, in order to provide an orientation to how Buddhists conceive of the world and the place of the religious person in it, let me turn first to the kinds of beliefs that Buddhists share.

While there are many important differences among Buddhists across time and space, the core of Buddhist belief can be found in the teachings of the Buddha's first sermon, which have come to be known as the Four Noble Truths. Together, these four assertions present the Buddha's interpretation of the dissatisfactory human condition and the means by which one can be released from it; and they are the heart of Buddhist doctrine and practice in every school of Buddhism across the globe.

THE FIRST NOBLE TRUTH: THE TRUTH OF SUFFERING

In the First Noble Truth, the Buddha makes a dramatic, comprehensive statement about the fundamental nature of human life: life the way it is normally lived is suffering, *dukkha*. However, by saying that all life is suffering, the Buddha does not intend to offer a pessimistic view of a horrible world from which one must escape in order to become awakened. Instead, what the Buddha is describing here is the fundamental and most basic consequence of a life lived in ignorance of how things really are.

It's like this. Typically, humans live their lives attempting to secure happiness for themselves by seeking impermanent things such as money, prestige, beauty, or skill. The reality is, however, that all things change; nothing has permanent, enduring substance. We grow old, people move, relationships fluctuate, our ideas and emotions shift and turn, and so we are constantly disappointed, constantly agitated, constantly unsatisfied. We strive continually after the next best thing, looking for that one final object or goal that will be "enough." However, all is in vain. Permanent happiness, says the Buddha, cannot be found by clinging to the physical and mental things of this world. Such fruitless grasping leads only to restlessness and dissatisfaction. Before we can progress on the path to enlightenment, we must realize this core truth of Buddhist teaching and recognize that the typical way of living—trying to secure a permanent end through transient means—can end only in unhappiness.

THE SECOND NOBLE TRUTH: THE TRUTH OF THE ORIGINATION OF SUFFERING

The Second Noble Truth points to the root cause of this suffering, and the reason why it continues. According to the Buddha, it is our desire that causes our suffering. Thus the Second Noble Truth states that the cause of our unhappiness and perpetual state of dissatisfaction with our lives is our craving or "thirst"—the many forms of desire that seek self-gratification in order to find happiness. The most easily recognizable form of this desire is our pursuit of sensual pleasures: the pleasures of food, drink, wealth, and sex. We eat too much, drink too much, spend too much, and exhaust ourselves seeking the perfect sexual partner, deluded into thinking that "one more" will be enough, and then we'll be content. Instead, however, the "one more" turns into another, and another, and another—each with a slight variation—but never do we say "enough."

One scholar describes it this way: "Pleasure is therefore compared to the relief felt when a heavy burden is shifted from one shoulder to another. After a while, the other shoulder will begin to hurt, at which point the burden will be shifted back."[6] Certain things may make us happy for a short while, but not for long; and surprisingly quickly, we find ourselves back in the grip of our familiar longing.

THE THIRD NOBLE TRUTH: THE TRUTH OF THE CESSATION OF SUFFERING

If these first two truths had been the extent of the Buddha's message, if the Buddha had taught only the negative symptoms of human life and offered no way of treating them, it is hardly conceivable that the Buddhist religion would have spread as it did, and developed so rapidly and widely. As it is, however, the diagnosis represents only half of the Buddha's first sermon; the second half is the cure. Thus the Third Noble Truth offers some hope, as it speaks of the true goal and aim of human life: the attainment of *nirvana*. This truth argues that the suffering of human existence is not inescapable and that, in fact, an end to such suffering is both possible and attainable. In this truth, then, the Buddha teaches that the cessation of suffering is brought about by a letting go

6. Donald Lopez, *The Story of Buddhism: A Concise Guide to Its History* (New York: HarperOne, 2002), 43.

of craving, a letting go of the thirst for more. This leads to the end of suffering; the realization of *nirvana*.

In Sanskrit, the word *nirvana* literally means "blowing out" or "extinguishing," and it traditionally referred to putting out a fire. For Christians in particular, the word *nirvana* has two common misconceptions associated with it, which must be dispelled. First, in Buddhism, *nirvana* is not a state of bliss, which is how the word is often used in common English parlance. *Nirvana* is explicitly not heaven; in fact, it is not a "place" at all to which one is delivered upon attaining enlightenment. That is, *nirvana* is not another realm opposed to and entirely distinct from this universe, or even from this life. While the teachings of various Buddhist schools differ somewhat on this last point, it is widely accepted by most Mahayana Buddhists at least that one realizes *nirvana* right in the midst of *samsara*; and that, when understood rightly, they are simply two different ways of looking at the same reality. I will say more about that shortly.

Second, *nirvana* is not annihilation, as though once one achieves *nirvana* one simply vanishes or ceases to exist. This is another common misunderstanding in the West, where *nirvana* also has been equated with nihilism and nothingness. When one attains enlightenment, it is not the self that is extinguished but, rather, the false understanding of the self, the delusion that the self is an independent, permanently existing entity. It is not the mere fact of one's existence that leads to suffering; rather, it is the distorted understanding of one's existence and the misguided attempts to secure and satisfy that existence that lead to suffering. Thus Buddhist practice is directed at correcting that distorted understanding and those misguided efforts, not at "destroying the self"—whatever that might mean. As Richard Payne notes, *nirvana* is the cessation of mistaken conceptions and misplaced affections,[7] not the annihilation of the self.

THE FOURTH NOBLE TRUTH: THE TRUTH OF THE EIGHTFOLD PATH

When looking at the example of the Buddha and his freedom from ignorance, and consequently his ability to act unmotivated by desires or cravings, one might well ask, "But how is this possible for me? How can I, too, attain such a state?" The "how" of *nirvana* is the subject of the Fourth Noble Truth. This

---

7. Richard K. Payne, "The Anti-Ritual Stance of Buddhist Modernism and Its Implication for the Relations between Buddhism and Psychotherapy" (paper presented at the conference "Deep Listening, Deep Hearing: Buddhism and Psychotherapy East and West," University of Oregon, Eugene, July 29–August 1, 2006).

truth teaches the means by which *nirvana* might be attained: the practice of the Eightfold Path. This path is the Buddha's "prescription," as it were, to cure the disease of suffering that plagues human existence, a path composed of eight elements that lead one along the way from suffering to enlightenment. The list of eight elements is not perfectly standardized and is sometimes translated with slight variations. Also, the list is not meant to be read sequentially, as though one should begin with the first and proceed to the last, crossing each one off as it is practiced. Instead, each element is to be pursued and practiced at the same time as all the others, so that one's mind and body are disciplined simultaneously, in all aspects. The eight elements are Right Understanding, Right Thoughts, Right Speech, Right Action, Right Livelihood, Right Effort, Right Mindfulness, and Right Concentration.

Very briefly, they are defined as follows. Right Understanding can be summarized as the knowledge of impermanence. In other words, it is the understanding of oneself as one really is. Right Thoughts are threefold: the thoughts of renunciation, which keep one from abandoning oneself to sensual pleasures; kind thoughts, which are opposed to ill will; and thoughts of harmlessness and peace, which keep one from acts of cruelty. Right Speech points to the act of refraining from falsehood, slandering, harsh words, and frivolous talk. Christians might here think of the commandment not to "bear false witness"—something similar is implied here. Right Action is about refraining from actions that injure others, such as killing, stealing, and promiscuity.

The element of Right Livelihood is very specific in that it describes five types of employment that all Buddhists should avoid: trade in deadly weapons, trade in animals for slaughter, trade in slavery, trade in intoxicants, and trade in poisons. One surely can think of many "respected" occupations that would fall into these categories, and one strength of this element is that it reminds Buddhists that every aspect of their lives, including their occupation, must conform to the Buddha's values. Simply put, Right Livelihood means earning one's living in a way that is not harmful to others.

Right Effort consists of the following four aspects: (1) the effort to rid oneself of the evil that already has arisen in one's previous births; (2) the effort to prevent the arising of new evil in one's current birth; (3) the effort to develop the good that already has arisen; and (4) the effort to cultivate the production of good that has not yet arisen. Buddhists believe that effort is needed to cultivate good conduct because humans are so easily distracted and tempted by what is easy and familiar—we keep making the same mistakes over and over, just because they are patterns we know.

Right Mindfulness is described as all encompassing, so it includes mindfulness with regard to every aspect of one's being: mindfulness about one's body, one's feelings and sensations, and one's thoughts. Finally, Right Concentration points to the gradual process of training the mind to focus on a single object and to remain fixed on that object without wavering. Buddhists believe that the consistent practice of meditation helps to develop a calm and concentrated mind, which is a necessary condition for attaining enlightenment. Another way Buddhists have described the purpose and function of the Eightfold Path is by organizing the eight elements into three "trainings": ethics (which includes action, speech, and livelihood), meditation (which includes effort, mindfulness, and concentration), and wisdom (which includes understanding and thought).

In all this, I want to emphasize that, in general, Buddhism teaches that the attainment of *nirvana* happens in the midst of one's ordinary life, rather than by escaping to an extraordinary reality: *nirvana* is achieving enlightenment in the here and now. A nice analogy that one reads occasionally in Buddhist literature points out that when a person enjoys the freedom of *nirvana* she is like a lotus flower that rises out of the muddy waters. Freed from the coating of mud that hid her true form, she is free to live unfettered as she really is. Notice that it is the same flower that was there all along; it is only the mud that has been removed to let the true nature of the flower show forth. So also with us. Once our cravings have been removed, our true enlightened nature is able to shine through clearly and we are able to see the world as it really is, and ourselves as we really are.

EXCURSUS: KARMA, TIME, AND THE UNIVERSE

At this point, it might help to say a few things about the Buddhist doctrine of karma and the role it plays in perpetuating human suffering. A Christian's understanding of karma can be hampered by the common usage of the term in the West: often, we say that it is "karma" when a person gets repaid in kind for his or her misdeed. So, for example, when a man leaves his wife for another woman who then leaves him for another man, that's karma. In Buddhism, however, karma refers to something much more complex than a simple one-to-one action/reaction relationship. Indeed, many Buddhists hold that karma is the driving force behind the cycle of rebirth, which characterizes all sentient life. According to karma theory, every action has a consequence—good actions generate good consequences, and bad actions generate bad consequences—and these consequences will come to fruition in either this life or a future life. Thus a life characterized by morally good acts will have positive consequences, which ultimately will lead to a higher rebirth, whereas bad acts will produce negative results, ultimately leading to a lower rebirth. If one is a human being, a life that has produced good karma will generate a future birth as a better human being—wealthier, happier, more prosperous—or perhaps as a god, in one of the heavenly realms of sensual pleasures. However, a life that has produced bad karma will generate a future birth as an animal or even a hell-being, consigned to the lowest realm of suffering and misery. Any individual's current birth, then, is explained by her past karma: she is either reaping the rewards of good karma or being punished for bad karma. While usually presented in terms of recurring lifetimes, this same dynamic works on the much shorter horizon of daily life as well.

Notice that this understanding of karma is undergirded by a cyclical understanding of time, and of the universe itself. In Buddhism, the universe has no beginning: it is eternal, while ever-changing. The way this is described in Indian Buddhism, for example, is that the universe is said to pass through four stages in unceasing cycles: creation, abiding, destruction, and nothingness. A new cycle of creation is said to begin when "the faint wind of past karma of beings" starts to blow in the nothingness.[8] Beings come into the world during the period of abiding. During the period of destruction, the physical universe is annihilated. Then, at the end of the period of nothingness, the cycle begins again.

The universe itself consists of six different realms, the highest being the best, and the lowest being the worse. The highest realm is the realm of the gods, typically described in utopian terms of beauty, fragrance, and abundance. Unlike Christianity, in Buddhism, the gods are still subject to karma and are not immortal. This realm, then, while paradisiacal, is not *nirvana*—that is, it is not the ultimate goal in Buddhism. While the gods live very long and enjoyable lives, they eventually will die, and, ironically enough, when they do, they often will be born into a lower realm, as typically they have squandered their fortuitous birth in the delight of sensual pleasures.

Below the realm of the gods is the realm of the demi-gods or titans; then the realm of humans. Many Buddhists view the human realm as the best possible realm in which to be born because there it is possible to be taught the Four Noble Truths and gain the knowledge one needs to attain enlightenment. Next is the realm of animals, then the realm of hungry ghosts, and finally, the lowest realm of hell-beings. Every being in *samsara* exists in one of these six realms, and a being's place in a certain realm is due to his or her past karma.

8. Lopez, *The Story of Buddhism*, 19.

It is important for Christians to understand that the ultimate goal in Buddhism is to escape this cycle of *samsara* altogether: this is what *nirvana* represents. That is, the object of Buddhist practice is to free oneself from the effects of karma entirely, not merely to generate good karma. However, as a penultimate goal, many Buddhists do focus on the production of good karma, and hence on achieving a positive rebirth. One simple reason for this is that one needs good karma to be born into a realm where one is able to hear the teachings of the Buddha and to practice them. Particularly in Theravada Buddhism, this distinction has been described as the difference between *nibbanic* and *kammatic* Buddhism, with the former being the Buddhism of the monastics, who have as their goal the attainment of *nirvana* (*nibbana*), and the latter being the Buddhism of the laity, who have the goal of creating good karma for a better rebirth, one in which it is possible to become a monk and pursue awakening.[9] Finally, it is also important to recognize that, in Buddhism, a good rebirth still leads to temporal happiness—just not to *nirvana*—and so, many Buddhists today also are concerned with generating good karma for its own sake, often by relieving the suffering of others.

THREE MAIN EXPRESSIONS OF BUDDHISM

There is no one monolithic Buddhism, just as there is no one monolithic Christianity—or any other religion, for that matter. Buddhism was influenced by the cultures and nations into which it spread, and thus, for example, Japanese Buddhism today has a unique character different from that of Tibetan Buddhism and so on. Furthermore, over time, as Buddhism developed and moved out from its origins in India, new interpretations of the Buddha's sermons were promulgated and new sutras were written. From our perspective in the twenty-first century, then, one can look back on the evolution of Buddhism as a whole and catalogue it generally into three different forms, keeping in mind that under each of these three broad categories many different particular schools exist.

THERAVADA BUDDHISM: THE WAY OF THE ELDERS

One major expression of Buddhism today is called Theravada Buddhism (or "foundational Buddhism"), which means "the way of the elders." Today, this form of Buddhism flourishes in South Asia, particularly in Sri Lanka, Cambodia, Laos, Burma, and Thailand. Sometimes in older books on Buddhism the term

9. See Melford Spiro, *Buddhism and Society: A Great Tradition and Its Burmese Vicissitudes*, 2nd ed. (Berkeley: University of California Press, 1982).

"Hinayana Buddhism" is used, but this nomenclature is to be avoided. It was developed after the rise of what are called the Mahayana schools, and where "Mahayana" means "greater vehicle," "Hinayana" means "lesser vehicle." Thus it is a derogatory term.

Several characteristics define this form of Buddhism. First is the use of the Pali language. The Theravada schools maintained a strict use of Pali as the language of liturgy and scholastic debates because they held that the Buddhist texts preserved in Pali were the most authentic and provided the most reliable record of his teachings. The Pali canon of the Buddha's teachings is still held in esteem by all schools of Buddhism today. Second is a special emphasis on morality and moral purification. In Theravada Buddhism, high moral standards are demanded of practitioners—the monks most particularly, but the laity as well. The morality that is advocated is not only external morality, that is, purity in action, but also inner morality, that is, purity of the mind.

The third important characteristic is the path of the arhat. An arhat is one who has attained the final stage of enlightenment, through *lifetimes* of strenuous, devoted practice. He (or more rarely, she) has, through his own efforts, followed the path of the Buddha faithfully and achieved *nirvana*. This path is long and rigorous, and only the most dedicated are able to walk it. Note that in these particular schools of Buddhism, the implication is that the Buddha himself, having attained enlightenment and entered final *nirvana*, is not able to offer any supernatural assistance. Each practitioner bears the sole responsibility for his or her own awakening.

Finally, monasticism is a very important component of Theravada Buddhism. The monks provide both moral and spiritual guidance to the laity, and a well-established and mutually beneficial pattern of interaction exists between the two. For example, in traditional Buddhist societies, the monasteries often had schools where the children could come for their education. Various images of the Buddha also were displayed in the monasteries, so that the laity could come and bring offerings of flowers, food, and incense in order to generate merit for themselves. The laity gave food to the monks, attended Dharma talks, and made monetary donations to the Sangha, all of which encouraged the laity in their pursuit of enlightenment. These acts brought them merit that would not only benefit them in this lifetime but also help them gain a more fortunate rebirth in the next. This relationship continues to be important today.

MAHAYANA BUDDHISM: THE PATH OF COMPASSIONATE ACTION

As Buddhism began to move into East Asia, certain changes in both doctrine and practice developed. The schools of Buddhism that incorporated these changes came to be grouped under the larger category of Mahayana Buddhism, and the new teachings represented in these schools comprise what is considered to be the second phase of the Buddha's teaching. It is worth noting, however, that the categories of Theravada and Mahayana were not mutually exclusive in the beginning, and that there still is some overlapping between them today. Mahayana Buddhism is the primary expression of Buddhism in Tibet, China, Korea, Japan, and Vietnam. Sometimes in older works, one sees this form of Buddhism referred to as "northern Buddhism."

new sutras One main source of these changes was new sutras of the Buddha that began to be promulgated around the first century ce. Most scholars agree that these new sutras did not actually date from the time of the Buddha. Instead, it is believed that they were written in Sanskrit from around the first century ce up until the eighth century. Nonetheless, they were accepted by many Buddhists as authentic, and they contain some of the most well-known and best-loved Buddhist texts in the world, including the Diamond Sutra and the Heart Sutra.

bodhi-sattva These new sutras of the Buddha extolled a new path, a path they claimed was superior to the path of the arhat promoted in Theravada Buddhism. The path these new sutras advocated is called the bodhisattva path. It differs from the path of the arhat in that it emphasizes taking many lifetimes to attain full Buddhahood in order to devote oneself to helping others attain awakening.

A bodhisattva is one who has vowed to dedicate his or her practice for the enlightenment of all sentient beings. Thus compassion is at the heart of the bodhisattva path. In this way, the path of the bodhisattva differs from the path of the arhat, in which one seeks purification and *nirvana* for oneself. Instead, the bodhisattva chooses to remain in the world of *samsara* in order to help others awaken, accumulating merit over countless lifetimes that can be transferred to needy sentient beings to help them attain awakening. According to Mahayana doctrine, there exists a plurality of bodhisattvas, including beginners who have just taken the bodhisattva vow as well as the vast array of celestial bodhisattvas who dwell in distant "Buddha-fields" and intervene in response to the petitions of living beings in distress. Shakyamuni Buddha remains the paradigmatic "bodhisattva," but as one among others. Human bodhisattvas might be compared to Christian saints, as both are people whose lives are marked by compassion and exemplary ethical behavior.

Figure 3.4. A statue of Kannon, the bodhisattva of compassion, Okunoin cemetery, Koyasan, Japan. April 2012.

In addition to the bodhisattva path, Mahayana Buddhism has several other unique characteristics. One of the most important is the concept of *upaya*, "skillful means." This doctrine points to the willingness of the Buddha to do anything, to appear anywhere at any time, in order to teach human beings the truth about reality, thereby leading them to enlightenment. We might think of it as the end justifying the means: whatever the Buddha does, even if it requires illusion, is justifiable as long as it promotes the goal of enlightenment.

According to some Mahayana Buddhist schools the Buddha is eternal, "a being who transcends all boundaries of time and space, an ever-abiding principle of truth and compassion that exists everywhere and within all beings."[10] In a manifestation of *upaya* he appeared in human form out of compassion, in order to teach human beings the truth about reality, and he entered final *nirvana* in order to motivate people in their own practice to follow him. But—and here is the important point—these were not historical events; instead, they were illusions, acts of *upaya* to facilitate the awakening of humanity.

Also important to note in Mahayana Buddhism is what might be called a more elaborate cosmology, a more complex view of the universe. In addition to the different realms of the universe I described previously, Mahayana Buddhism adds to this picture the existence of even higher realms, called "Buddha realms," in which different buddhas reside to help guide their disciples along the path to awakening. This change in cosmology relates to the bodhisattva path, one aspect of which is the belief that by following it, one can be reborn in one of the Buddha heavens, where one can continue to progress toward enlightenment under the guidance of the particular Buddha of that heaven. Naturally, this was seen as the most auspicious birth possible, one that has a much higher chance of success for the disciple. This is logical: the closer one is to a Buddha, the more likely it is that she will attain the goal of enlightenment.

VAJRAYANA BUDDHISM (TANTRIC BUDDHISM): AWAKENING IN THIS LIFE

Vajrayana Buddhism represents the last major development in Buddhist doctrine and practice. The word *Vajrayana* means the "diamond" or "thunderbolt" vehicle. Vajrayana is seen as a swift path to enlightenment, in contradistinction to the bodhisattva path or the path of an arhat. It teaches that it is possible to become awakened in one's current incarnation; it is not necessary to wait for an optimal rebirth. Enlightenment is attained through the development of specific practices and rituals. One important feature of many schools of Vajrayana that distinguishes them from the previously discussed forms of Buddhism is that a guru or teacher is needed to practice it correctly.

---

10. *The Lotus Sutra*, trans. Burton Watson (New York: Columbia University Press, 1993), xix.

The rituals are complex, one might even say dangerous, and thus a guru is needed in order to safeguard the disciple and ensure proper practice.

Vajrayana practice encourages a person to see that *nirvana* is *samsara*, that is, to see the sacred as identical with the secular rather than apart from it. To this end, it can involve the breaking of traditional Buddhist values and mores, and might include consuming alcohol and rejecting celibacy, for example. Through these practices, one becomes able to see the essence of *nirvana* in all reality, uniting the pure and the impure and dissolving all distinctions. However, it must be definitively stated that Vajrayana practice does not mean that anything goes—it is not a license to do whatever one wants! This is why a teacher is needed: to prevent excesses and to keep the disciple focused on his or her practice.

Doctrinally, Vajrayana espouses many of the same beliefs found in Mahayana Buddhism, such as the bodhisattva path and the role of cosmic Buddhas and bodhisattvas. This form of Buddhism is dominant in Tibet, where it is also characterized by the development of a rigorous monastic education, which lasts over a decade and includes the memorization of a copious canon of sacred texts. The debates over points of doctrine within the monastic communities are legendary and have the same drama and excitement as sporting events in the West. Tantric Buddhism is also represented in Japan in the tradition of Shingon Buddhism.

CENTRAL PRACTICES AND TEACHINGS OF BUDDHISM

I want to end this chapter with a brief description of several key doctrines and practices that characterize the majority of Buddhist schools experienced in the West. Since most of these are Mahayana schools, I am privileging that expression of Buddhism, with the rationale that if Western Christians seek out dialogue with Buddhists, or visit a Buddhist temple, it will most likely reflect what I am describing here. Please keep in mind that what follows omits much, and includes many generalizations. It is only a starting point, from which I hope Christians can build on through further reading and conversation of their own.

Figure 3.5. The Garan temple complex, the main temple complex founded by Kukai/Kobo Daishi, the founder of Shingon Buddhism, Koyasan. April 2012.

SUNYATA: THE CONCEPT OF EMPTINESS

The concept of *sunyata*, most often translated as "emptiness," is one of the most well-known Buddhist ideas in the world, and many would say that it is one of, if not the most important philosophical and religious concept in Mahayana Buddhism as a whole. It is difficult to give just one definition of *sunyata*, as the way in which it has been described by different Buddhist and non-Buddhist scholars throughout the tradition varies greatly. However, it is safe to say that for Buddhists, *sunyata* represents the true expression of existence, the state in which all things really "are." Further, and perhaps most importantly, an understanding of emptiness is the key to enlightenment, and the key to freeing oneself from suffering: it is the wisdom that leads to liberation. Without a proper understanding of *sunyata*, the world will never cease to delude and tempt the individual, and she will never be able to get beyond her simple sense perceptions and desires. Her suffering will never end, nor will she escape the karmic bonds that propel her through cycle after cycle of existence. Thus for anyone who seeks wisdom, the first and most important concept that must be grasped is emptiness.

So, what is it, exactly? The word itself points to the fact that everything that is, is "empty" of independent, eternal, autonomous substance and existence. Simply put, everything is constantly in flux, changing from moment to moment based on interaction with other beings; and in fact, all things actually are created through those interactions. Who "I" am as a person changes, sometimes radically, over time, depending on my circumstances, my relationships, my living context, my work, and so on. Thus I both am and am not the same person I was twenty years ago, and I both will be and will not be the same person twenty years out as I am today. Our lives change profoundly with illness, addiction, marriage, childbirth, wealth, poverty, depression, divorce, and so forth. Each year, each month, each day, even, I come into being anew, and this is true for all sentient life. This is the basic meaning of emptiness, *sunyata*. The experience of identity as continuous, as enduring over a lifetime, is the result of *karma*.

Here's another example. Perhaps all of us have experienced at one time or another the unsettling realization that no two people experience or even see the same event the same way: if ten people witness an accident, ten different accounts—sometimes with startling variance—will follow. The "true nature" of that event, then, is not frozen in time, permanently accessible and possessing the same meaning for everyone. Instead, its meaning and true nature are constituted by the participation of all the individuals involved, and may well change each time the story is told. Our own personal history, to say nothing of the history of our families, our communities, and our nations, bears this out, as the meaning and interpretation of the very same events can change radically from the perspective of ten years, fifty years, or one hundred years. This is the most basic meaning of the Buddhist concept of emptiness: not that the world itself doesn't really exist, but that lacking any permanent essence, its meaning and true nature are always evolving.

For Buddhists, understanding this central insight is the key to unlocking the door to *nirvana*. Once emptiness is truly understood, the root cause of suffering vanishes, and one is liberated from the cycle of fruitless grasping after people, things, and ideals—none of which have permanent existence, and thus certainly cannot satisfy one's desires. Let me offer another brief example by way of explanation. The Buddha taught that the primary cause of suffering is desire. Buddhists assert that because we do not understand the true nature of reality, we believe that having certain things—fame, money, power, or being certain things—a husband, a mother, a monk, or a CEO, will bring us permanent happiness. This is, of course, not the case, because the fact is, none of these things is static, and thus all of them change over time and can be removed or taken away overnight: fame is fleeting, money can be lost or stolen, power changes hands, and both jobs and relationships evolve and end. Buddhism appreciates that it is fruitless to try to possess happiness through the attainment of some external "thing" that will not, cannot last forever. This realization is at the heart of liberation.

PRATITYASAMUTPADA: THE DOCTRINE OF DEPENDENT ORIGINATION

The flip side of the doctrine of emptiness is the doctrine of dependent origination, or *pratityasamutpada*: they are simply two ways of describing the same reality. One of the most important Mahayana Buddhist thinkers, Nagarjuna, argues that there is no difference between understanding reality as "empty," and understanding it as "dependently arisen." What this means is that the mode of being in the world for any sentient being can be described in two equally accurate ways. Either one can say that all things exist in relationship to other things, and that those relationships are constitutive of their being. That is, nothing can exist on its own, independently: no man (or woman) is an island; nothing comes from nothing; every effect has a cause. There is a complex, vast interconnected matrix of being in which and out of which everything that is finds existence. That is the definition of *pratityasamutpada*.

Or, one can say that nothing exists fully independently, completely autonomously, exclusively in and of itself. Nothing that is possesses a static, permanent, unchangeable nature. Rather, everything is empty of independent, autonomous existence. That is the definition of *sunyata*. Either way, the same thing is asserted. Contrary to the traditional way of understanding phenomena in Western philosophy, in which independent entities are considered primary and the relationships between them only secondary, according to the doctrine of emptiness, relationships are primary for existence, and a permanent, autonomous, independent entity as such does not exist. Thus *pratityasamutpada* and *sunyata* are not two different things, but rather two ways of describing the same thing.

One of the best ways of illustrating this comes from a classic example that Nagarjuna employs, using the parent-child relationship.[11] He says that while a father and a son are two different people, they also only exist in relationship to each other: the very word "father" is a term of relationship, and (in the strictest definition) one cannot attain it independently, without having a child. A father cannot exist without a child, and a child only comes into existence with a father. The relationship creates the identity of each member of the relation, as it were, and the one cannot exist without the other.

This example is particularly revealing because it indicates the depth to which these relationships are fundamental to our being. The relationship a father has to his child profoundly changes his entire life. It is not just something added on to his "true self," which makes only a superficial change, in the way that a coat of paint merely makes the outside of the house look nicer, but doesn't alter the floor plan or the foundation. Rather, the very "selfhood" of a father is reconfigured and re-created by the event of having a child, so much so that he cannot conceive of himself outside that relationship. In just this way, says Nagarjuna, the entire world is interdependent and interrelated; we just fail to realize it.

MINDFULNESS

Given the fact that what is critical in Buddhism is realizing a new way of seeing reality, one of the most important Buddhist practices that one employs to attain enlightenment is mindfulness. Thich Nhat Hahn, a well-known Vietnamese Zen monk, describes mindfulness as "keeping one's consciousness alive to the present reality."[12] In his book, *The Miracle of Mindfulness*, he offers several concrete mundane examples of what this looks like in practice: it means eating with awareness and paying attention as food is tasted, chewed, and swallowed, rather than unconsciously inhaling a bag of popcorn while watching TV; it means being aware of the feel of the soap and the water and carefully handling every cup while washing dishes in the sink, rather than racing through the task carelessly while thinking about one's plans for the day; and finally, it means focusing one's full attention on one's partner or child when she or he is talking, rather than listening with one ear while reading a magazine. Most of us, I am sure, recognize ourselves in the "rather" clauses of those sentences. While

11. See Christian Lindtner, *Nagarjuniana: Studies in the Writings and Philosophy of Nāgārjuna* (Copenhagen: Akademisk, 1982), 41.

12. Thich Nhat Hanh, *The Miracle of Mindfulness*, revised edition, trans. Mobi Ho (Boston: Beacon, 1987), 11.

mindfulness is a concept we may know in theory, it is something we hardly ever take the time to practice.

The reason why mindfulness is such a central Buddhist practice is that ignorance lies at the heart of suffering—in particular, as we have seen, ignorance about the true nature of reality. Without the practice of mindfulness, our ignorance will continue, and we will keep on striving fruitlessly after false desires, blinded by a deluded sense of egoism. However, with discipline, concentration, and awareness, one is able to free oneself from these false delusions, and uncover what too often passes right by us unnoticed. In this way, one moves—either gradually or all at once—from ignorance to wisdom, from illusion to reality, from confusion to clarity; and also therefore, from anxiety to calm, from restlessness to peace, from perpetual dissatisfaction to contentment. This state of awareness and peace is the key to awakening, and one of the key practices through which this state is nurtured and developed is meditation.

MEDITATION

Many Christians, when they hear the word "meditation," think of closing their eyes, forgetting all the worries of the day, calming down, and relaxing. In many ways, then, meditation is looked upon as an "anti-practice"—more of a not-doing, not-thinking, not-rushing—rather than a disciplined practice with positive content in its own right. Further, many Christians also associate meditation with prayer, and think of meditation as another way of being in communication with God. While there is nothing inherently wrong with either of these interpretations from a Christian point of view, neither one is appropriate when trying to understand meditation in the Buddhist tradition. It is, therefore, necessary for Christians to put aside any preconceived notions of what meditation is or is not, and learn about the practice anew from a Buddhist perspective.

Meditation has been called the "heartbeat" of Buddhism, and few would dispute that the various practices of meditation are foundational to the Buddhist life. Meditation involves wisdom and compassion, the two central components of the path of enlightenment, and it is a primary means by which one shakes the hold of ignorance, greed, and anger. The goal of meditation—its "end"—is the realization of *nirvana*, but that in itself does not tell the whole story. Instead, the practice itself, the "means," if you will, is also an important component of the goal: the change in one's engagement with the world, and one's understanding of reality and oneself. In other words, the practice of meditation results in both intellectual understanding of truth and also the experiential realization of that truth for oneself in one's own life.

Many people are not aware that there is not one single Buddhist description of a definitive, universal form of meditation for all Buddhists in all times and places. Instead, there exist in Buddhism a wide variety of texts that offer a corresponding variety of forms of meditation. Different practices are suggested based on one's character and on the particular state of one's religious development. The texts recognize that meditation is a technical skill to be learned, practiced, and developed, akin to learning to play the piano; and for almost no one is the practice natural and innate. Much like the beginning pianist starts by playing scales, so also the novice begins by practicing an awareness of her breath, which is much harder than one might imagine. It is also important to recognize that many of the texts that discuss meditation emphasize one's physical condition, including one's posture for example, recognizing that the mind and the body do not work independently, and that the state of the latter affects the state of the former, either for good or for ill.

Through this deceptively difficult practice, one experiences one's true nature, which is also called "Buddha-nature," and develops the ability to express this nature not only while in sitting meditation, but also while engaged in the daily activities of one's life. In this way, the practice itself is an end in itself, and not simply the means to something else; and thus meditation itself becomes an experience of *nirvana*.

CONCLUSION: DOUBLE-RELIGIOUS BELONGING

"I take refuge in the Buddha, I take refuge in the Dharma, I take refuge in the Sangha." With these words and little else, one declares oneself a Buddhist, and begins the path to enlightenment. Yet, with Buddhism in the United States at least, perhaps one more thing needs to be said, which brings us back to the words with which I began this chapter, and the concept of "double-religious belonging." As I noted earlier, this phenomenon refers to the practice of understanding oneself to be simultaneously participating in two religious traditions: actively participating in the rituals of both, adhering to the beliefs of both, and defining one's self-identity in the symbols of both. While this practice does not work well with all religious traditions, for some Christians at least, it seems to work well with Buddhism.

Paul Knitter describes one example of this, using his own personal narrative as a lens through which to see how this dual-religious identity functions in the real world. Knitter, a self-described "Buddhist Christian" rather than a "Christian Buddhist"—it makes a difference which word is the adjective and which is the noun—writes, "Buddhism has enabled me to make sense of my Christian faith so that I can maintain my intellectual integrity and affirm what

I see as true and good in my culture; but at the same time, it has aided me to carry out my prophetic-religious responsibility and challenge what I see as false and harmful in my culture."[13] He acknowledges that some may see this as "spiritual sleeping around,"[14] but insists that his practice of Buddhism actually has deepened and strengthened his appreciation and understanding of the Christian faith. It is an interesting and provocative argument, and may well lead one to ask, "But why Buddhism?"

I would argue that one of the factors contributing to the phenomenon of double-religious belonging is that Buddhism, even with the threefold refuge, does not have any expectation of exclusive adherence. Indeed, it is only among the Abrahamic religions that one finds this expectation. In an important sense then, for Buddhists, one's personal identity is determined not by holding specific doctrinal beliefs, but rather by doing things that other Buddhists do. This is particularly reflective of the experience of many Buddhist converts in the United States today. Typically, there is no sudden conversion experience—and no defining trope of one in the tradition, in contrast to Paul's conversion on the road to Damascus, for example. Instead, most convert Buddhists are curious, and the more they learn the more the ideas that constitute the tradition make sense for them. Thus from the Buddhist side of the sense of double-belonging, no conflict is created. Mark Heim describes it this way: ". . . the 'success' of Buddhist teaching generally is measured more by the extent to which people have adopted its practices or realized its desired qualities than by the purity of affiliation."[15] Therefore, there is no notion that participating in the Mass is in any way "wrong," or "bad karma," for example.

It remains an open question, however, if the same thing can be said from the Christian side, and double religious belonging is certainly still a controversial practice in most Christian circles. However, somewhat ironically I would say, some Christian churches incorporate Buddhist meditation techniques into their prayer practices, but only as a "technology" as it were, without the doctrinal claims behind it, as a way to facilitate introspective silent prayer—using as a "mantra" something like, "Jesus remember me," or "Come, Lord Jesus." Such practices are not seen as entailing any additional faith commitments that would conflict with Christian teachings. The question legitimately can be asked, however, whether such practices are respectful to the

---

13. Paul F. Knitter, *Without Buddha I Could Not Be a Christian* (Oxford: Oneworld, 2009), xii.

14. Ibid., 213.

15. S. Mark Heim, "Mission Studies in an Age of Religious Pluralism," in *BTI Magazine* 11, no. 2 (Spring 2012): 20.

specific Buddhist traditions and contexts from which they are taken, and how helpful, in the long run, this sort of religious borrowing really is.

4

A Brief Introduction to Islam

SEEKING "TRUE" ISLAM

I began writing this chapter in Istanbul, sitting on my hotel balcony, looking out on the Blue Mosque and the Bosphorus beyond, as the sun set behind me. It seemed to me then, and still seems to me now, a particularly apt place to start this chapter, for several reasons. First, of course, is that Istanbul is an overwhelmingly Muslim city: 99 percent of all people in Turkey are Muslim, and though that percentage may be a bit lower in the cosmopolitan city of Istanbul, it's by not much. Yet, Turkey is also a secular state, and has been since Mustafa Kemal Atatürk abolished the Ottoman Empire and founded the Republic of Turkey in 1923, bringing it into the modern age.[1] Thus, in harmony with its strong Muslim foundation and character, Istanbul also possesses the feel of a modern European city, evidenced by its diversity, freedom, and tolerance.

Many Muslim women wear *hijab*—the headscarf, and some even wear *chador*—the full black covering that leaves only the face visible, but many also wear Western clothing and no head-covering of any kind. Alcohol is widely available, in spite of the fact that many Muslims don't drink. Mosques old and new pepper the city, and are always bustling, especially during daily prayer times, but visitors of all kinds are welcome; and the most famous mosques manage to be both active places of worship and active sites of tourism simultaneously. In short, Istanbul is a wonderful place to celebrate Islam's rich tradition, and its important place in the world today—its past and its present; and even more, it is a particularly helpful place to begin to dispel the myths about Islam that are all too prevalent among Christians.

---

1. It should be noted, however, that the imams are regulated and paid for by the government.

Figure 4.1. The Blue Mosque, Istanbul. May 2012.

In his short introduction to Islam, John Kaltner writes:

> No religion in recent times has labored under more stereotypes than Islam. Ask a non-Muslim for a description of the "typical" Muslim, and he or she will probably respond with one or more stock characterizations, the most common being a veiled woman, a bearded cleric, a desert dweller, and a suicide bomber. If you were to inquire further and ask for practices with which Islam is associated, the list would undoubtedly include such things as polygamy, amputation of limbs, terrorist activities, and anti-Western demonstrations.[2]

And, both in the United States and abroad, the consequences of these negative and misinformed stereotypes have been deadly—both literally and figuratively, as Muslim individuals and mosques have been attacked, discriminated against, and vilified. Christians, I would argue, have a particular responsibility to speak out against this kind of prejudice, not only because Christians and Muslims are cousins—fellow "people of the book"—and not only because of Jesus' command to love one's neighbor, but especially because of the commandment not to bear false witness.

---

2. John Kaltner, *Islam: What Non-Muslims Should Know* (Minneapolis: Fortress Press, 2003), 1.

NOT BEARING FALSE WITNESS

In Martin Luther's explanation of this commandment in his Large Catechism, he writes:

> Now we have the summary and substance of this commandment: No one shall use the tongue to harm a neighbor, whether friend or foe. No one shall say anything evil of a neighbor, whether true or false, unless it is done with proper authority or for that person's improvement. Rather, we should use our tongue to speak only the best about all people, to cover the sins and infirmities of our neighbors, to justify their actions, and to cloak and veil them with our own honor.[3]

Now, it must be noted, of course, that Luther himself did not extend his interpretation of this commandment to Muslims of his time, whom, admittedly, Luther knew only as a competing military power, laying siege to important cities in Europe. Luther called them "Turks" and criticized them strongly for their rejection of Jesus' divinity. Nonetheless, I would argue that it is possible—indeed even necessary—to interpret Luther's words more broadly and more generously in our diverse twenty-first-century context in order to include populations that Luther himself excoriated, such as the Jews. In this light, what is especially compelling in Luther's explication of this commandment is the part about using one's own honor and reputation to "cover" what is suspicious or mistrusted in another. A concrete example of this might be when a Christian church allows a Muslim congregation to use their space for meetings and/or worship. That act decisively communicates to the local community that the Christian church (usually above suspicion) trusts and values their Muslim brothers and sisters, which conveys upon them legitimacy and credibility.

Beyond this, however, at the very least, Christians should speak out whenever they hear misinformation and defamation being spread about Muslims. This requires not only some courage, but also some accurate knowledge, which means that it is incumbent upon Christians to learn something about Islam, so that when statements are made like: "All Muslims are terrorists," or "The Qur'an teaches violence and warfare," or "Mosques are just a cover for terrorist activity," Christians have the knowledge they need to both refute such falsehoods and provide a much-needed corrective. Here is Luther again:

---

3. *The Book of Concord: The Confessions of the Evangelical Lutheran Church*, ed. Robert Kolb and Timothy J. Wengert (Minneapolis: Fortress Press, 2000), 424.285.

Thus in our relations with one another all of us should veil whatever is dishonorable and weak in our neighbors, and do whatever we can to serve, assist, and promote their good name. On the other hand, we should prevent everything that may contribute to their disgrace. It is a particularly fine, noble virtue to put the best construction on all we may hear about our neighbors (as long as it is not an evil that is publicly known), and to defend them against the poisonous tongues of those who are busily trying to pry out and pounce on something to criticize in their neighbor, misconstruing and twisting things in the worst way . . . there is nothing around or in us that can do greater good or greater harm in temporal or spiritual matters than the tongue, although it is the smallest and weakest member.[4]

Anyone who has been on the receiving side of bullying or slander knows how powerful a weapon the tongue can be, and thus it is also a powerful show of solidarity to use one's words to stand with those who are being oppressed.

The Origins of Islam

Islam is the youngest of the major world religions, and as such, it is also the most well documented and historically verifiable. In fact, Muhammad, the founder of Islam—or rather, as taught in Islamic tradition, the messenger who called people back to the original faith—has been called "the first to live and preach in the full light of history."[5] For our information about Muhammad, we have not only the Qur'an, but also the *hadith*, the various reports of the sayings and deeds of Muhammad. These were collected and shared orally for roughly two hundred years after Muhammad's death, until they began to be written down and codified. Finally, there is also *sirah*, the religious biographies of Muhammad. These are similar to the gospel stories in that this biographical information is crafted to convey a particular theological message for followers of the tradition.

The story of Islam itself, then, begins with the story of one man, Muhammad ibn Abdullah, born in 570 ce in Mecca, which is located in the modern nation of Saudi Arabia. At that time, the Arabian Peninsula was dominated by a variety of polytheistic tribes, some of whom were nomadic and others of whom were settled, but all of whom often were divided by blood feuds and rivalries. One of these tribes was the Quraysh, dominant traders in the region and guardians of the main religious shrine in Mecca, the Ka'aba, home

---

4. Ibid., 424.288–425.291.

5. Caesar E. Farah, *Islam: Beliefs and Observances* (Hauppauge, NY: Barron's, 2003), 36.

to hundreds of deities and thus an important site of pilgrimage. This became an important part of their livelihood: "To encourage the flow of pilgrims and trade, the Qurayshites concluded pacts with various tribes securing the inviolability of transients and pilgrims. The Ka'bah and the area surrounding it were declared *haram* ('forbidden' i.e., to warfare); within a general mile radius from it no blood might be spilled."[6] It is interesting to note that the importance and role of the Ka'aba was maintained by Muhammad, even through the dramatic shift from polytheism to monotheism. More will be said about that shortly.

Muhammad was born into the Hashemite clan of this influential Quraysh tribe, but few details are known about his early life. One fact that is known—and is highly significant—is that he was orphaned early and raised first by his grandfather and then by an uncle, Abu Talib. The tradition notes that this part of Muhammad's own biography made him particularly sensitive to the needs of the marginalized and outcast, especially when he became a political leader and statesman. When he got older, he earned his living as a trader, and by all accounts he was widely considered to be wise and truthful: it is said that he was known by his people as *al-Amin* (the trustworthy one). In fact, it was this quality that led to Muhammad's first marriage, with a wealthy trader, Khadijah. She employed him to manage her caravans, and after seeing both his professional and personal excellence, she proposed to him and they were married, in 595 ce. At the time, Khadijah was forty, and Muhammad was twenty-five. By all accounts it was a happy marriage, and Muhammad did not marry anyone else while she was alive. Together they had four daughters, and two sons who died in infancy.

It is said that Muhammad was also a spiritual man, and he was in the practice of withdrawing periodically to a cave in the mountains nearby to meditate and think in solitude. When he was forty (610 ce), while he was on one of these retreats on Mount Hira, the angel Gabriel visited Muhammad for the first time, and he received what would be the first of many revelations over the course of his lifetime. Gabriel instructed Muhammad to "[r]ead [or 'recite'] in the name of your Lord who created. . . ."[7] Muhammad was distressed by this event, and he didn't know what to make of it, seriously considering that perhaps he had been possessed by a *jinn*—an evil spirit. He told Khadijah right away, and she calmed him, assuring him that he was of sound mind. He also was reassured by Khadijah's cousin, Waraqah, who was a Christian and thus familiar with the stories of God's communications with prophets from both Jewish and Christian

6. Farah, *Islam*, 31.

7. *Al-Qur'an: A Contemporary Translation by Ahmed Ali* (Princeton: Princeton University Press, 1993), 96:1.

scripture. He then told Muhammad that he would not be believed, and would be persecuted. This quickly proved to be true. Khadijah, however, believed that her husband was a prophet sent from God, and she became his first disciple. The date of this first revelation is still celebrated by Muslims today on the twenty-seventh night of Ramadan. It is called the "Night of Power," and every year many Muslims stay awake the entire night, in prayer.

Muhammad did not receive any further revelations right away, but shortly they began coming again; and all of these prophecies contained basically the same message (these are the Meccan *suras* found in the Qur'an). The people had turned away from the right worship of the one true God, and they needed to stop worshiping idols, and begin worshiping Allah alone.[8] In addition, they needed to begin living more ethical and socially responsible lives. When Muhammad began to share this message publicly he was criticized and ridiculed, particularly because he was threatening one of the major economic boons of the region: pilgrimages to the Ka'aba, which, remember, housed over 300 different idols, generating large sums of money for the Quraysh. In these early years, while there were a few notable converts, such as Ali, Muhammad's young cousin, Abu Bakr, and 'Uthman, most Meccans either ignored or actively persecuted Muhammad. However, the worst was yet to come.

Up to this point, Muhammad had been spared the foulest maltreatment thanks to the protection of his influential uncle Abu Talib; sadly, in 619 both Abu Talib and Khadijah died, leaving Muhammad grieving and bereft—and also very vulnerable to the powerful forces in Mecca who wanted him dead.

Around this time, another miraculous event occurred in the life of Muhammad. The angel Gabriel again visited Muhammad, but this time, he took him on what is called the "Night Journey." First, Muhammad flew to Jerusalem on a winged steed known as a *buraq*. From there, from the place now marked by the Dome of the Rock, Muhammad was taken on a mystical ascent up through the heavens into the presence of God. There, God gave Muhammad the final form of the daily prayers. It is primarily this event that makes Jerusalem holy to Muslims; and it, along with Mecca and Medina, are the three holiest cities of Islam.

8. Incidentally, it is worth mentioning that Christians in the Middle East and North Africa also call God "Allah."

Figure 4.2. The Dome of the Rock, Jerusalem. January 2012.

As the persecution of both Muhammad and his followers intensified, he began to search for a safer place where he and his followers, called "Muslims," might live in peace. (The word *Muslim* means "one who submits to the will of God," and both "Muslim" and "Islam" come from the same Arabic root *s-l-m*, which means "submission" or "peace.") At this time, some of the leaders of the city Yathrib came to Mecca and invited Muhammad to come to their city and serve as their leader. Several years before, a delegation had come to Mecca and been persuaded by Muhammad's preaching. They now felt they could use Muhammad's wisdom and influence in uniting the city and bringing a more peaceful way of life. They promised him that if he came, they would convert and establish an Islamic rule of life for the city. Muhammad agreed to leave Mecca, sneaking out and just narrowly avoiding an assassination attempt. He came to Yathrib in 622, which subsequently became known as Medina (*medinat al-Nabi* means "city of the Prophet"), and established a thriving theocracy. This migration is known in Islam as the *hijra*, and it is said to have inaugurated the birth of the Muslim faith; thus 622 ce is year 1 in the Islamic calendar.

It is important for Christians to note here that, with this event, Muhammad ceased to be simply a prophet, but also became a head of state. That is, from that time onward, he was both a religious and a political leader simultaneously. This meant that he could no longer live the traditional life of a prophet, speaking a word of proclamation and denunciation from the margins. Instead, he had political and civic responsibilities to the people of the city as a whole. In the course of his life in Medina, that necessitated making political alliances through a variety of marriages, and also going to war. One of the important ramifications of this aspect of Muhammad's life is that Islam has a model for what a society shaped along religious lines can and should look like, which is grounded in the very foundation of the faith; and thus many Muslims aspire to that type of society. This has caused some tensions within Islam itself, and raised questions about what it means to be a Muslim living in an explicitly secular Western nation, such as France, for example, and to some degree, the United States as well.[9]

While in Medina, Muhammad continued to receive revelations from God, but these revelations, recorded as the Medinan *suras* in the Qur'an, are of a more pragmatic nature, focused on solidifying Islamic society and establishing communal norms and rules of behavior. One author describes them this way: "more constitutional, that is, laying down the pattern of life for a settled community."[10] Muhammad had a long and successful governance in Medina, and his reputation contributed greatly to the rapid spread of Islam both during and after his death.

A few noteworthy episodes remain that deserve mention. First is the Battle of Badr. This battle, fought in 624, represents the decisive victory won by the Muslims against the Meccans. After Muhammad fled Mecca, hostilities between the two communities had continued, finally culminating in a military offensive from the Meccans. Even though the size of their forces was much smaller, the Medinans won the day, and the victory at Badr proved to be as significant psychologically and spiritually as militarily: "Muhammad had humbled the mighty of Mecca. Skeptical Bedouins flocked to the faith, the faithful were strengthened in their belief, and the disaffected had grounds for fear."[11]

Though they would be defeated by the Meccans a year later at the Battle of Uhud, ultimately the Muslims prevailed. After an aborted attempt at making a pilgrimage to Mecca and the Ka'aba in 628, which ended in a treaty giving the

---

9. For more on this topic, see Tariq Ramadan, *Western Muslims and the Future of Islam* (New York: Oxford University Press, 2004).

10. C. T. R. Hewer, *Understanding Islam: An Introduction* (Minneapolis: Fortress Press, 2006), 32.

11. Farah, *Islam*, 50. The importance of this battle is also evident in the fact that Egyptians used the name "Operation Badr" as a code for the 1973 war with Israel. (See the entry "Badr, Battle of," in John Esposito, *The Oxford Dictionary of Islam* [New York: Oxford University Press, 2003].)

Muslims recognition as a political power and calling a truce with the Meccans, Muhammad brought over 2,000 of his followers into Mecca the following year (629), and officially made the pilgrimage. It was the next year, however, in 630, that their victory was complete: Mecca finally officially surrendered to Muhammad, and thousands of Meccans formally converted to Islam. It was also during this year that Muhammad cleansed the Ka'aba of all its idols, and rededicated it to Allah alone. From 631 and onward, Islam spread rapidly throughout the Arabian Peninsula. Muhammad made his last pilgrimage in 632, the same year of his death, and it was during this time that he established the final form of the pilgrimage rites still performed today by millions of Muslims every year.

Muhammad is not worshiped in any way by Muslims, and in fact they would be horrified by the idea: worship is reserved for God alone. The obvious reason for this is that Muhammad was not divine, he was a man; not just any man, certainly, but still, only a man. Muhammad is considered the "seal" of the prophets—the last and the greatest among them; and he, like all the prophets, is considered to be sinless, by virtue of the purifying knowledge from God that he received.[12] Yet—and Islam is perfectly clear on this point—it would be idolatry and blasphemy to worship Muhammad in any way, regardless of how much one might desire to emulate his behavior.

However, it should be obvious that Muhammad continues to have deep and powerful significance long after his death. He is "like a jewel among stones," and is seen by Muslims as "the most perfect of all God's creatures."[13] For this reason, Christians might compare the guidance they seek for daily living in Jesus' own actions—exemplified in the "WWJD" bracelet trend from some years ago, to a Muslim gleaning practical wisdom from Muhammad's own words and deeds. Critical-care nurse Najah Bazzy describes it this way: "We live our lives through [Muhammad's] examples, but he's not God. . . . Our reverence is to God. And our reference is to [Muhammad]. So how I walk, and how I speak, and how I carry myself, and how I treat my husband, and how I treat my mother and my father, and how I behave as a sister and a daughter and a nurse and a friend and a neighbor, that's all prophet Muhammad in action."[14]

12. Hewer, *Understanding Islam: An Introduction*, 35.

13. Seyyed Hossein Nasr, *Islam: Religion, History, and Civilization* (New York: HarperSanFrancisco, 2003), 46.

14. Quoted in "Muhammad: Legacy of a Prophet," PBS film, copyright 2002, Kikim Media. See http://www.pbs.org/muhammad/film2.shtml.

ISLAM AFTER MUHAMMAD: THE PERIOD OF THE RIGHTLY GUIDED CALIPHS

There is not enough space in this chapter to detail all of the important periods in Islamic history and the influential empires that dominated them. However, I do want to briefly mention the period immediately following the death of Muhammad, since this is almost universally seen as the golden age of Muslim leadership and political expansion. This period also is important because it was during the final phase of this age that the division occurred between what came to be known as Shiite and Sunni Muslims: the two largest groups of Muslims in the world today. (Of the two, the Sunni is the largest group: roughly 80 percent of the world's Muslims are Sunni.)

Obviously, Muhammad's death was a huge blow to the budding Muslim community: he was not only their spiritual leader, but their political leader as well; and his death created an instant power vacuum and some critical questions about how the community would go forward. Muhammad had no surviving sons, and only one surviving daughter, who had married his cousin Ali, the son of Abu Talib. This left the question of who would become the next leader uncertain. There was also the problem that some of the different tribes felt that their allegiance was to Muhammad himself, not to Islam; and if Islam was to continue to grow, that attitude would have to be overcome.

In the midst of these challenges, however, one thing was always clear: there would not be another prophet. As I said earlier, Muslims believe that Muhammad is the "seal" of the prophets, which means that divine prophecy was completed in the revelations he received. Thus none who came after him would ever have his status or authority. Consequently, these subsequent leaders were called "caliphs," which is an Anglicized version of the Arabic word *khalifah*. The word means "successor" or "representative," and indicates that while they might "represent" the Prophet, they are not prophets themselves.

Of the many caliphs that came after Muhammad, the first four always are given privileged status. They all knew Muhammad personally; and the period in which the four of them ruled, sequentially, is called the age of the rightly guided caliphs (632–661). During this period, all of Arabia was conquered, as well as Egypt and modern-day Iraq and Iran, and the way was paved for two more centuries of rapid expansion, from North Africa all the way to Pakistan.

The first caliph was Abu Bakr al-Siddiq, who ruled from 632 to his death in 634. He was the father of one of Muhammad's wives, Aishah, and was elected by a group of Muslim community leaders. The second was Umar ibn al-Khattab, who ruled from 634 to 644. He is remembered fondly by Muslims for his sense of justice, and his caliphate is remembered primarily for its military prowess and the expansion of Islam. He was assassinated in 644. The third caliph was 'Uthman ibn Affan. He ruled from 644 to 656, when he, too, was murdered by dissenting Muslims. He was elected by a committee that was appointed by Umar on his deathbed, and it was during his caliphate that the text of the Qur'an was standardized and an authoritative version was written down. After his death, the first major split in Islam occurred, which still exists today.

The process of electing the previous three caliphs was basically a merit system: the idea was to choose the best, most qualified leader, not someone from a particular family or tribe. However, all along there had been a faction of Muslims who had disagreed with this system: they believed that authority (spiritual authority in particular) was derived from Muhammad himself; thus all subsequent rulers needed to come from Muhammad's family. In no small part, this idea came from a specific verse of the Qur'an, 33:33, which talks about the purity of the family of the prophet. This group of Muslims took that to mean that God had granted Muhammad and his family an exalted status, which in turn gave them and them alone the sole right to exercise both religious and political authority. In their view, the only legitimate successor to Muhammad was Ali, his son-in-law; and they therefore viewed the previous three caliphs as illegitimate. Ali's supporters were called *Shi'a Ali*, which means "the party of Ali." It is from this term that the name Shi'a/Shiite is derived.

So, when Ali ibn Abi Talib was chosen to be the fourth caliph, there seemed to be an opportunity for greater peace among the different Muslim groups, but it was not to be. He ruled from 656 to 661 until he was assassinated while praying in a mosque, and after his death, there continued to be much infighting, even as Islam continued its rapid expansion, shifting its capital first to Damascus, and then to Baghdad as the empire grew.

Continued tension remains today between Sunni and Shi'a Muslims, even though they agree on the most fundamental aspects of Islam. The main difference is their understanding of leadership: Shi'a Muslims call their leaders imams, and by virtue of their familial connection to Muhammad they are believed to be infallible in terms of their interpretation of the Qur'an and what constitutes a lawful way of life. For Shiites, "Imams are sinless guides of the community and possess both spiritual and political authority."[15] By contrast, Sunni Muslims tend to be more pragmatic when it comes to leadership, and generally do not insist on a special holiness or purity in their government officials. One time when this difference becomes of central importance is when a *fatwa* is issued. A *fatwa* is defined as an "authoritative legal opinion given by

---

15. Hewer, *Understanding Islam: An Introduction*, 39.

a mufti (legal scholar) in response to a question posed by an individual or a court of law."[16] In theory, a *fatwa* is not binding on any individual, nor is there any way of enforcing a particular *fatwa*. Indeed, you can often find conflicting *fatwas* issued on the same topic by scholars coming from different Islamic communities. However, when a Shiite imam issues a *fatwa*, it is considered binding by Shiites, and obedience is expected. The most well-known example of this is the *fatwa* that was issued in 1989 by the Ayatollah Khomeini of Iran against Salman Rushdie for his novel *The Satanic Verses*. Rushdie was in hiding for years following this *fatwa*.[17]

WHAT IS THE QUR'AN?

It is not surprising that when Christians are first learning about Islam, they use categories from their own tradition to try and understand new concepts and ideas found in Islam. So, for example, many Christians, when first hearing about Muhammad, assume he fills the same role for Muslims as Jesus does for Christians. And, correspondingly, when they read about the Qur'an,[18] they assume it is basically the "Muslim Bible." However, in fact, a much better parallel between the two faith traditions is the comparison between the Qur'an and Jesus, surprising as that may sound. Here's why.

In the same way that, for Christians, Jesus is considered the definitive revelation of the word of God (properly speaking, for mainline Protestants, the Bible is only secondarily the word of God, insofar as it has Christ as its center and reveals Christ), so the Qur'an is considered the definitive word of God for Muslims. Simply put, the Qur'an is the complete collection of all of the revelations Muhammad received from Gabriel—but that hardly tells the full story. Instead, when reading the Qur'an it is important for Christians to keep in mind that, for Muslims, the text we are reading is literally the voice of God.

Beginning in the ninth and tenth centuries ce, debates arose within the Muslim community of scholars regarding the nature of the Qur'an. One particularly heated debate concerned the issue of whether the Qur'an was the uncreated and eternal word of God or whether it was created in time. The issue was sparked by the idea that there is a "heavenly archetype"[19] of the Qur'an, a concept extrapolated from certain verses from the Qur'an that suggest the

---

16. Esposito, *The Oxford Dictionary of Islam*.

17. http://thelede.blogs.nytimes.com/2009/02/14/fatwa-on-rushdie-turns-20-still-in-force/.

18. In older textbooks especially you often see the English spelling "Koran." While this is also acceptable, "Qur'an" is a better transliteration of the Arabic.

19. John Kaltner, *Introducing the Qur'an for Today's Reader* (Minneapolis: Fortress Press, 2011), 12.

existence of a hidden copy of the book, preserved eternally in heaven with God. If this is so, the natural question that follows is whether "the Qur'an has existed with God from eternity and is therefore uncreated," or whether "it is not coeternal with God but a created entity that is dependent upon the divine will for its existence."[20] After much debate, the former view eventually came to dominate, although disputes continue today. This doctrine that the Qur'an is eternal and uncreated provides the foundation for the Qur'an/Jesus parallel. Gabriel Said Reynolds notes that "the prevailing Islamic tradition is that the Qur'an has always existed in heaven, along with God. . . . In this understanding, God did not 'inspire' Muhammad. He sent down a preexisting book to him. Thus the Islamic view of the revelation of the Qur'an is closer to the Christian view of the incarnation of the Word of God in Jesus than it is to the Christian view of the Bible."[21]

One of the other points here that must be emphasized is the privileged place Islam accords Arabic. Nasr writes, "The Quran is the central theophany of Islam, *the verbatim Word of God* revealed to the Prophet by the archangel Gabriel and transmitted by him in turn to his companions, who both memorized and recorded it."[22] An interesting, though entirely logical, consequence of this belief is the opposition to translating the Qur'an: if the direct speech of God was revealed in the Arabic language, then naturally, all other languages suffer by comparison, as none of them can be considered as holy, perfect, and unique as the one language spoken by God's own tongue, if you will. Reynolds explains it this way: "The idea of reading the Qur'an in translation, a practice that was almost nonexistent before modern times, is quite different. Muslims today might do so, but the point of doing so is only to gain some sense of the Scripture's meaning. . . . However, these translations are *not* the word of God. God spoke to Muhammad in Arabic."[23]

Lamin Sanneh has described well the difference here between Christianity and Islam in his book *Translating the Message.* He makes the argument that scriptural translation "is the vintage mark of Christianity, whereas for Islam universal adherence to a nontranslatable Arabic Qur'an remains its characteristic feature."[24] He notes that, since the Qur'an is the literal word of God, Arabic has

---

20. Ibid., 15.

21. Gabriel Said Reynolds, *The Emergence of Islam: Classical Traditions in Contemporary Perspective* (Minneapolis: Fortress Press, 2012), 96.

22. Nasr, *Islam: Religion, History, and Civilization*, 37, my emphasis.

23. Reynolds, *The Emergence of Islam*, 98.

24. Lamin Sanneh, *Translating the Message: The Missionary Impact on Culture* (Maryknoll, NY: Orbis, 1996), 211.

an elevated status as a "revealed language."[25] This means that while non-Arabic speakers may read a translation of the Qur'an in order to better understand its meaning, translations do not have the same weight and authority as the Arabic text. This is why it is important to pray in Arabic and recite verses from the Qur'an in Arabic, even if one doesn't understand the language.

Since the Arabic words are literally the word of God, reciting those words is considered spiritually beneficial; it is for this reason that the practice of memorizing the Qur'an is considered to be a deeply holy act (such a person is called a *hafiz*—literally, a "guardian/caretaker" of the Qur'an); and also why there are professional reciters, who often will be hired by large mosques to come and recite during holy days. The recitation of the Qur'an is extremely important and is considered to be a sacred act in and of itself; it is an act that invites listeners into the presence of God.

As I mentioned above, the recitation began in 610 ce, when the angel Gabriel appeared to Muhammad and commanded him to "recite." (This explains the name of the Qur'an: *al-qur'an* means "the recitation.") From that time forward, Gabriel would come to Muhammad at different times in his life and reveal different verses, all meant to call people back to fidelity to God. It is believed that, over time, Jews and Christians (considered "People of the Book") had gone astray, and the purpose of revealing the Qur'an to Muhammad was to restore right belief and practice to the faithful. This means that the Qur'an as we have it today was not revealed all at once, but rather over time, in bits and pieces, "according to the situation in which the Prophet found himself."[26] It was Gabriel himself who ensured that Muhammad had accurately memorized each *sura*, and also determined the order in which they were to be compiled.

During Muhammad's lifetime, no complete written copies of the Qur'an were made: instead, Muhammad memorized the *suras* and shared them with his followers, some of whom also memorized them. This meant that after the death of the Prophet, the complete text only existed orally, although there were some written pieces of parts of the recitation. During the caliphate of Abu Bakr, tradition recounts that the community determined that there needed to be a complete and authoritative written text. It is said that this was partly because during the military expansions of Islam, many of those who had memorized the Qur'an were killed, resulting in the fear that some of the revelation might be lost. Also, as Islam drew more and more followers who did not speak Arabic, concern grew that the purity of the original Arabic might be corrupted. So, Abu

25. Ibid., 212.

26. Reynolds, *The Emergence of Islam*, 100.

Bakr convened a council of scholars who used both written fragments and oral recitations to comprise one authoritative text. This text was further redacted by 'Uthman, the third caliph; when this version was complete, he had it bound and copied, and widely distributed. It is this text, called the "'Uthmanic recension" and created around 650 ce, that is considered to be the authoritative version.[27]

Theological issues aside, there are many differences between the Bible *qua* book, and the Qur'an, which are worth mentioning for a Christian audience, who might be confused when reading the Qur'an for the first time.[28] First, the Qur'an is not a historical narrative: that is, it does not tell a story that unfolds over time chronologically. Second, it is not organized thematically. Instead, there are 114 separate chapters, each of which is called a *sura*, and, with a few exceptions, they are organized from longest—actually *sura* 2, "The Cow"—to shortest, although the shortest *sura* is actually "Pre-eminence," *sura* 108. Third, the names by which each *sura* is designated do not reflect its primary emphasis or theme. Rather, as Reynolds observes, ". . . [the titles] appear simply to be labels by which one *sura* might be distinguished from others."[29]

The first *sura* of the Qur'an, called *al-Fatiha* (which means "the opening"), reads as follows: "All praise be to Allah, Lord of all the worlds, Most beneficent, ever-merciful, King of the Day of Judgment. You alone we worship, and to You alone we turn for help. Guide us (O Lord) to the path that is straight, the path of those you have blessed, not of those who have earned Your anger, nor those who have gone astray."[30] This *sura* is used to begin each of the five daily prayers, and is widely regarded as a concise articulation of what it means to be a Muslim, and particularly how one is to be in relationship to God. Hans Küng writes that "[s]ome classical and contemporary Muslim authors see in [this *sura*] the foundation, the sum and the quintessence of the Qur'an."[31]

Overall, one can detect one primary overarching theme in the Qur'an as a whole: the exhortation to repent and submit to the word and the will of God. To do this, the Qur'an emphasizes several key points that relate to God,

---

27. It is worth noting that scholars often have a different way of approaching the codification of the Qur'an, looking closely at the early texts still in existence and examining differences between the *scriptio defectiva*—the earliest, most basic script, and the different ways in which the full text of the Qur'an was established. See Reynolds, *The Emergence of Islam*, pp. 101–2.

28. See Michael Sells, *Approaching the Qur'an: The Early Revelations* (Ashland, OR: White Cloud, 1999) for more details regarding these distinctions.

29. Reynolds, *The Emergence of Islam*, 94.

30. *Al-Qur'an: A Contemporary Translation by Ahmed Ali.*

31. Hans Küng, *Islam: Past, Present and Future,* translated by John Bowden, (Oxford: Oneworld, 2009), 59.

humanity, and the relationship between them. First, God is the creator of the universe, and, as such, is its sovereign ruler. Only God is worthy of obedience, respect, and worship. Second, when creating humanity, God gave them reason, which includes the ability to know the difference between right and wrong, and to choose to follow God's will—or not. There is, therefore, no doctrine of original sin in Islam, nor is there an understanding of ontological, fundamental brokenness and alienation from God. Humans are capable of both knowing the good and doing it. (Incidentally, this is why Islam has prophets but no savior: a prophet is required to call people back to the right path; a savior is needed when people are entirely incapable of walking that path by themselves at all. More will be said about this shortly.)

Third, the life that one experiences now is transitory, and is, in some ways, a proving ground for life after death. Upon death, each individual will stand before God and be judged upon her actions and sentenced in the resurrection: right living and obedience to God will lead to eternal happiness with God in paradise; disobedience and unfaithfulness will lead to eternal punishment. To this end, there are repeated and extensive descriptions of both heaven and hell in a variety of *suras* in the Qur'an. Fourth and last, the Qur'an emphasizes that God repeatedly sent prophets to different people in different places all through time, each attempting to correct them when and where they had gone astray and call them back to right worship of the one true God. Finally, God sent Muhammad, the last and final prophet, and revealed to him the Qur'an—the peerless and complete revelation of God's divine word and law that now stands in perpetuity as the perfect, timeless guide for religious life. In these ways, the Qur'an attests to the unsurpassable nature of the authority of both Muhammad and the Qur'an itself, and lays out clearly and emphatically a way of life that facilitates a rich and meaningful existence, both in this life and the next.

WHAT DO MUSLIMS BELIEVE?

Unlike the wide variation among Christians regarding specific beliefs and practices, in both doctrine and practice Muslims are strongly uniform. However, at the same time, there are different cultural interpretations of Islam, such as women's dress for example, that result in different practices, and also different interpretations of Islamic law, which can reveal themselves in different political and/or legal systems. In spite of these differences, though, there are some foundational beliefs that are near-universally held, which serve as the bedrock on which the religion as a whole rests.

First and foremost is the belief in God, which in Islam is called *tawhid*, ~~tawhid~~ meaning "to acknowledge as one." This is, by general consensus, the heart of the Muslim faith, and it is commonly agreed that "Tawhid is the defining doctrine of Islam."[32] Islam is a religion of uncompromising monotheism: there is only one God, who has no helper, and no son. Obviously, this is where the key sticking point in Christian-Muslim dialogue is located. *Tawhid* demands both a rejection of the Trinity—regardless of how you count the persons, three does not equal one in Islam—and also a rejection of the divinity of Jesus. Jesus ~~Jesus~~ is believed to be a great prophet, and the Qur'an speaks very highly of him, but it is also adamant and unequivocal: Jesus is not, and cannot be God; what is created cannot be joined to the Creator. This is also why there are strict prohibitions against depicting God in any form—there are no pictures of a bearded old man in any mosque! To even attempt to image God in any way is deeply sinful and forbidden in all circumstances. Incidentally, this is why there continues to be heated debate about whether or not Christians and Muslims worship the same God. While many Muslims might answer "yes"—with the caveat that Christians have misunderstood Jesus' proper identity as a prophet, and many Christians might answer yes—with the caveat that Muslims, like Jews, do not accept the fullness of God's self-revelation in Jesus Christ; many believers in both faith traditions continue to answer "no," arguing that this difference regarding God's triune nature and the divine nature of Jesus Christ prevents easy agreement.

This belief leads to another important doctrine. In Islam, the worst form of what Christians consider "sin" is to associate something from creation with God, to join the finite to the infinite. John Kaltner describes it this way: "The ~~shirk~~ unity of Allah is the defining feature of the Muslim understanding of God, and anything that disrupts that unity is considered to be the most serious of sins. The term commonly used for this offense is *shirk* (literally, 'association'), which describes the attempt to join or associate something from the created world with the uncreated nature of Allah in a way that violates the divine unity."[33] *Shirk*, then, in essence, is understood as polytheism: worshiping something else alongside God, or worshiping anything less than a strictly monotheistic God. This doctrine seeks to preserve the absolute nature of God, unbounded, unlimited, omniscient, and omnipotent. God is both the perfect judge and deeply merciful, so although God is to be feared and obeyed, lest one be

32. Esposito, *The Oxford Dictionary of Islam*, 317.

33. Kaltner, *Islam: What Non-Muslims Should Know*, 30.

condemned at the final judgment, God is also compassionate and forgiving, inviting people to repent and return to God again and again.

Second is the belief that God revealed Godself to humanity not only in the Qur'an, but also in the sacred texts of Judaism and Christianity. This is the reason why the Qur'an refers to Christians and Jews as "People of the Book," and grants them a special status. However, it is believed that over time, their message was corrupted—most specifically destroyed or lost—and replaced with a false message. Those are the texts we know today as the Hebrew scriptures and the Bible. Let me emphasize this point: while Islam concedes that God did send down God's word—or at least a portion of it—to Jews and Christians, those authentic divine books have been lost to us. All we have now are the corrupt ones written to take the place of the true revelation. As such, neither Jewish nor Christian scripture is considered authoritative. The consequence is that "[o]nly the Qur'an can be trusted."[34]

Along with this comes the belief in multiple prophets and messengers of God, including those well known to Christians from the Bible. In fact, many Christians are surprised when reading the Qur'an for the first time to find stories of Adam, Noah, Abraham, Ishmael and Isaac, Moses, and even Jesus. Islam considers all of these prophets, sent from God. However, important to remember here is that while Muhammad stands in this long line of prophets, he is the last and most perfect.

A third key doctrine in Islam is the belief in angels. While angels also can be found in Christianity, their presence is somewhat ambiguous, doctrinally; and, in the Western church, they exist more robustly in what I would call folk belief and popular culture than they do in orthodox Christian teaching. (However, they do play a significant role in Eastern Orthodox iconography.) By contrast, in Islam, angels are given pride of place, honored for their steadfast, faithful worship of God, and their perfect obedience to God's command. Naturally enough, Gabriel is considered to be at the top of the hierarchy, not least because he is the one who brought the Qur'an to Muhammad, and also accompanied Muhammad on the Night Journey.

Related here is the belief in what are called the *jinn*, creatures created by God out of fire—in contrast both to angels, created out of light, and humans, created out of clay—and typically understood by Muslims to be evil, although they also possess free will, and can therefore be good if they choose. There are several references to them in the Qur'an, including the statement that the devil, known as Iblis in Islam, is one of the *jinn*: "When We said to the angels: 'Bow

---

34. Reynolds, *The Emergence of Islam*, 122.

before Adam in adoration,' they all bowed but Iblis. He was one of the jinns and rebelled against his Lord's command" (Qur'an 18:50). The *jinn* are also common figures in Islamic literature. According to Reynolds, "In Islamic literature, the *jinn* indeed have a special place as magical creatures who are often up to mischief but who can also be compelled to grant favors to humans."[35] A well-known example of this can be seen in the stories in *One Thousand and One Nights*. The Western idea of the "genie" comes directly from the stories involving the *jinn*.[36]

Islam emphasizes the Day of Judgment, also called the Day of Resurrection. The Qur'an speaks about this repeatedly, including various descriptions of heaven and hell. It is believed that on that day, Allah will raise the dead and judge each one individually, based on her actions. As I noted earlier, Islam does not have a doctrine of original sin or the corresponding belief that humans are incapable of doing good. For this reason, there is great emphasis on praxis in Islam, since the right practices are what keep a Muslim on the right path, ensuring reward after death. Of particular importance are the five practices known as "the five pillars of Islam." These are the practices around which one's whole life is structured, which form and shape one's submission to Allah.

THE FIVE PILLARS OF ISLAM

The five foundational practices of Islam traditionally have been called "pillars," which is an apt image for conveying their importance and their role in supporting one's life as a Muslim. The five pillars of Islam, then, are the five practices that Muslims perform to express their religious identity and signal their participation in the larger community. They are important not only in the way they form religious habits and thinking, but also in the way they structure and organize one's whole life. In this way, they are the center around which one's whole life turns, and from which all other activities and beliefs flow.

> Carrying out these obligations provides the framework of a Muslim's life, and weaves their everyday activities and their beliefs into a single cloth of religious devotion. No matter how sincerely a person may believe, Islam regards it as pointless to live life without putting that faith into action and practice. Carrying out the Five Pillars demonstrates that the Muslim is putting their faith first, and not just trying to fit it in around their secular lives.[37]

---

35. Reynolds, *The Emergence of Islam*, 138.

36. Ibid.

37. http://www.bbc.co.uk/religion/religions/islam/practices/fivepillars.shtml.

I will list them first, and then elaborate briefly on each of them. First is the *shahadah*, the Muslim profession of faith. Second is *salat*, the ritual prayers performed five times a day. Third is *zakat*, a form of what Christians would call tithing. Fourth is *sawm/siyam*, the Ramadan fast; and fifth is the *hajj*, the pilgrimage to Mecca.

First, the *shahadah*. The *shahadah*, which means "witness," is the fundamental declaration of what constitutes the heart of the Islamic faith: the belief in the oneness of God, and the status of Muhammad as the definitive messenger of God. The specific text of the declaration is as follows: "There is no God but the God and Muhammad is the messenger of God."[38] It is said at different times, and has a variety of uses. For example, it is used as the declaration of faith for converts: one need only say it twice in the presence of two other Muslims.[39] However, its most common usage is in the context of the call to prayer, which means that in predominantly Muslim countries, it is heard publicly five times a day.

This is an apt transition to the second pillar, *salat*. This is the name for the specific prayers Muslims are required to perform five times a day: at daybreak, noon, mid-afternoon, sunset, and evening. These prayers have a specific set of rituals governing their performance, including a series of ablutions, which, in addition to cleansing the body, also signify the purity necessary to come before God. This ritual washing includes the feet, hands, head, mouth, nose, face, and forearms. Outside many mosques—particularly large ones—there are fountains specifically for this purpose, and sometimes there is even a freestanding structure in the center of a courtyard with multiple taps on all sides.

---

38. *World Religions Today*, ed. John Esposito et al. (Oxford: Oxford University Press, 2009), 239.

39. Actually, one does not need any witnesses at all to convert—it is believed that Allah sees and accepts a genuine conversion. However, for documentation purposes—for the *hajj*, for example—two witnesses are needed.

Figure 4.3. Two different examples of ablution fountains, Istanbul. May 2012.

The prayers can be performed anywhere one finds oneself at the proper time: at home, at work, even in an airport. They can be prayed together or individually, although the Friday noon prayer ideally should be performed communally at a mosque, by men at least. Each prayer has specific wording that is memorized, and all five prayers always are recited in Arabic, whether or not the person actually knows the language. Obviously, this does not preclude or replace individuals praying in their own languages at any other times during the day;

however, for these specific times, the emphasis is on the community: "All Muslims are active in this community of prayer in precisely the same way: with their lips and their whole bodies, praying with exactly the same gestures and words."[40] As I noted earlier, it is believed that Muhammad received the final form of the daily prayers during the Night Journey, although the specifics are not found in the Qur'an itself, but rather in the *hadith*, the various collections of the sayings and deeds of Muhammad.

At this point, let me say a brief word about the mosque. "Mosque" is an English word, which is derived from the Arabic word *masjid*, which means "place for prostration." This is a clear indication of the main prayer posture in the daily prayers: kneeling, with one's forehead touching the ground. When Christians enter a mosque for the first time, they might be surprised: what one first notices in the main hall is its emptiness. There are no pews or chairs, no statues or pictures, only a large open space in which the community is able to gather and pray shoulder to shoulder. (Women and men do not pray side by side; typically there is a partition separating the women from the men. This is both to prevent distraction, and out of modesty and respect—allowing both men and women to avoid close physical contact with someone not in one's family.) The floor is typically carpeted, and the pattern of the carpet indicates the direction one is to face: all five daily prayers are performed facing Mecca. There is also a niche in the wall, called a *mihrab*, which signifies the location of Mecca. The other dominant architectural feature of the great hall is a *minbar*, a narrow series of steps leading to a small platform, typically located next to the *mihrab*. The imam delivers the Friday sermon from here.

40. Küng, *Islam,* 127.

Figure 4.4. A Muslim man at prayer, Istanbul. May 2012.

Each daily prayer time is announced with a ritual call to prayer, the *adhan*, the text of which reads as follows:

> God is the greatest. God is the greatest.
> God is the greatest. God is the greatest.
> I witness that there is no god but God.
> I witness that there is no god but God.
> I witness that Muhammad is the messenger
> of God.
> I witness that Muhammad is the messenger
> of God.
> Come to prayer. Come to prayer.
> Come to prosperity. Come to prosperity.
> God is the greatest. God is the greatest.
> There is no god but God.[41]

41. Esposito, *The Oxford Dictionary of Islam*, 7.

Figure 4.5. The interior of the Blue Mosque, Istanbul, with minbar and mihrab. May 2012.

zakat

The third pillar is *zakat*, typically translated as "almsgiving." As I mentioned above, this concept should be very familiar to Christians, and is motivated by many of the same religious convictions. Muslims, along with Christians and Jews, confess that everything ultimately belongs to God, and all that humans have is a gift entrusted from God. Therefore, humans are only the "trustees" of wealth—God remains the true owner of all. Thus it is believed that one should yearly give back to God a percentage of one's wealth, as a sign of God's ultimate dominion over creation, and of respect and obedience to God. For example, in the Lutheran Book of Worship, one of the offertory prayers used begins with the words: "We offer with joy and thanksgiving what you have first given us: ourselves, our time and our possessions, signs of your gracious love. . . ." It is in this same spirit that *zakat* is given.

It should be stressed that *zakat* is not charity, which should be given throughout the year as the need arises. Instead, *zakat* is more formalized than that, with most Muslims agreeing that 2½ percent of one's entire worth should be given for this purpose.[42] In fact, in some Islamic countries, the government is in charge of both collecting the money from each household (and determining the amount) and also distributing it to specific organizations. In these contexts, *zakat* looks more like a tax. In other places, however, such as the United States, individual Muslim households determine the specific amount on their own, and give it to the recipients of their choosing, following the principles for distribution that have been established by the Qur'an and in Islamic law.

The fourth pillar is *sawm*, fasting from eating, drinking, and sexual activity during the daylight hours of the month of Ramadan, the ninth month of the Islamic calendar. Ramadan is commanded specifically in the Qur'an:

> Ramadan is the month in which the Qur'an was revealed as guidance to man and clear proof of the guidance, and criterion (of falsehood and truth). So when you see the new moon you should fast the whole month; but a person who is ill or travelling (and fails to do so) should fast on other days, as God wishes ease and not hardship for you, so that you complete the (fixed) number (of fasts), and give glory to God for the guidance, and be grateful. (Qur'an 2:185)

This month is the holiest month of the year in Islam, because it commemorates the first revelation of the Qur'an to Muhammad, which occurred sometime toward the end of the month: many Muslims celebrate it on the night before the twenty-seventh day of the month. As I noted earlier, this night is called the "Night of Power," and often Muslim men—and sometimes women—mark this night by staying up all night praying, gathering at the local mosque. All Muslims of a certain age who are healthy are expected to adhere to a strict fast from sunup to sundown; and because Islam follows a purely lunar calendar, Ramadan moves through all twelve months of the calendar over a period of years. This means that Ramadan is particularly challenging during the long,

---

42. Kaltner, *Introducing the Qur'an*, 35.

hot summer days of August; the fasting time is appreciably shorter during December. This is more or less true depending on one's geographical location.

Like the Jewish day, the Muslim day begins at sundown; thus Ramadan begins on the night that the new moon—that is, the first crescent moon—is seen and lasts for either twenty-nine or thirty days, depending on when the next crescent moon is visible. The specific name for this moon is the *hilal*; this is the main symbol of Islam seen on flags, mosques, etc.

Again, this practice has a parallel in Christianity in the Lenten fast formally taught by Roman Catholicism and Eastern Orthodoxy, but also practiced by other denominations and individuals as well. As in Christianity, the fast is not viewed as something negative, as a punishment or a deprivation. Rather, it is understood as a means of rededicating one's life to God, clearing space in one's life to spend more time in prayer and worship, and increasing one's general sense of the awareness of God's presence. For this reason, "*Sawm* is not a negative experience but one to which Muslims look forward throughout the year."[43]

In addition, there is a strong communal emphasis during Ramadan: it is a sign of unity and support that all Muslims fast together, and they often break each day's fast (*iftar*) in community as well. In many Muslim countries, the entire pattern of the day is altered and brought in line with the Ramadan fast, including restaurants being closed during the day, but staying open later into the evening. Ramadan ends with a celebration called *Eid al-Fitr*, the "feast of fast-breaking." It lasts for several days, and includes communal meals, gifts of sweets for children, and prayer. It is preceded by a special almsgiving for the poor.

Finally, the last pillar is the *hajj*, the pilgrimage to Mecca all Muslims should perform at least once in their lifetime, if they have the financial resources and if they are healthy. Every year, roughly two million Muslims from all corners of the globe come to Mecca (located in Saudi Arabia) to share in this powerful experience. Everyone dresses alike in simple clothing, called *ihram*, symbolizing their equal status before God and the state of purity in which the *hajj* is to be performed. In particular, the men wear two unsewn pieces of white cloth, which many save and use as their burial shroud.

The *hajj* consists of a series of rituals that date back to the story of Ibrahim, Isma'il (known as Abraham and Ishmael in the Hebrew scriptures), and Hagar; and the centerpiece of the *hajj*—literally and figuratively—is the Ka'aba, a square structure believed to have been built by Ibrahim and Isma'il as a place to

---

43. Hewer, *Understanding Islam: An Introduction*, 113.

worship the one true God. It is this particular structure that is the physical center of Islam, and it is specifically toward the Ka'aba that daily prayers are directed. As I mentioned previously, over time the Ka'aba had become a polytheistic shrine, but as part of his missionary activity, Muhammad cleansed it of its idols and rededicated it to Allah, and in so doing gave the *hajj* its final form, which is still followed today.

The rituals take roughly a week to perform, and most people use guides to help perform them correctly and in the right order. Some of the key rites of the pilgrimage are as follows. First comes the *tawaf*, the act of circumambulating the Ka'aba in a counterclockwise direction seven times, an act meant to mimic the angels circling God's throne in heaven. During the circumambulations, many attempt to touch, or even kiss, the Black Stone as one passes, although this is somewhat perilous given the sheer masses of people. This stone is believed to have been brought to Ibrahim by Gabriel, and sits in the outer east corner of the Ka'aba. Another important ritual is the *sa'y*, the running back and forth between two small hills seven times, remembering Hagar's frantic search for water for her son. There is a well nearby called Zamzam, believed to have been revealed to Hagar by God, from which pilgrims drink at the conclusion of their run/walk.

Following the *sa'y*, pilgrims walk to the Plain of Arafat, which is where Muhammad gave his final sermon. This is the high point of the *hajj*, as pilgrims stand in prayer and supplication for hours, coming before God in deep humility, seeking forgiveness and God's mercy. The last main rite of the *hajj* is the symbolic stoning of Satan in the valley of Mina, which is performed by throwing small pebbles at three tall pillars of stone. The *hajj* ends on *Eid al-Adha*, the Feast of Sacrifice, with the sacrifice of an animal, recalling the ram that Ibrahim sacrificed in place of Isma'il (in the Hebrew scriptures it is Isaac who was almost sacrificed). Even Muslims who do not make the *hajj* in a certain year celebrate this festival, and many also either commission a sacrifice or make a monetary donation to buy food for the poor at home or abroad.

Currently, the Saudi government oversees the *hajj*, and it is worth noting that technology and modern conveniences have made many aspects of the *hajj* easier and more efficient—no small improvement, given that temperatures soar well above 100 degrees in Saudi Arabia in the summer; and that even in the best circumstances, housing, feeding, and transporting two million people safely is a steep challenge. Here is a description of some advances in the practice of sacrifice:

Given the numbers of pilgrims today and the need to ensure that animals do not suffer, these sacrifices are now mostly performed by trained slaughtermen who act in the name of each pilgrim. During recent years, huge abattoirs have been built to ensure hygiene, and the meat is butchered and loaded into freezer trucks or canned for later distribution among the poor in various countries.[44]

For many, this is the only time they will be able to perform the *hajj*; therefore, once the official rites are finished, many pilgrims make a side trip to Medina, which is where Muhammad is buried, and visit his grave.

THE CONCEPT OF *JIHAD*

Before concluding this chapter, it is necessary to say a word about the concept of *jihad*. No single idea in Islam is more misunderstood or misinterpreted—I would argue both by Christians and by radical Muslim organizations. First, to be clear, Muhammad did indeed talk about the importance of *jihad*, but his explanation in no way resembles the idea the word conveys today, particularly in an American context. The word itself comes from an Arabic root that means "to strive" or "to exert." In both the Qur'an and Islamic tradition, it is used in two different ways, to describe two different "struggles": the struggle within oneself to be faithful and obedient to God, and the military struggle against enemies of God. Certainly Muhammad did refer to this latter type of *jihad*, and the Qur'an does provide encouragement to those who "fight in the way of God" (Qur'an 2:218; 9:20), and "struggled in the cause of God" (8:74). However, the vast majority of Muslims today see these verses as relating to a specific time in the development and spread of Islam; and while there is still a legitimate tradition of "holy war" in Islam, the conditions under which one might be fought are strictly regulated, carefully formulated, and only warranted in rare situations. It should go without saying that the type of terrorist activities carried out under the false banner of *jihad* have been resoundingly and unequivocally rejected by the overwhelming majority of the world's Muslims, precisely because those above-mentioned conditions were blatantly violated.

Instead, most Muslims interpret *jihad* to refer to the first type of struggle, the struggle within oneself, often using the well-known tradition that tells of the time when Muhammad returned from a battle and told his followers: "We

---

44. Hewer, *Understanding Islam: An Introduction*, 24.

return from the lesser jihad to the greater jihad."[45] Here, we see Muhammad downplaying the idea of *jihad* as a military struggle in favor of what is much harder and actually more important: one's own internal struggle to resist temptation, obey God, and follow God's will. The Qur'an also speaks of this type of struggle, exhorting believers to "strive in the way of God with a service worthy of Him" (Qur'an 22:78), and promising "We shall guide those who strive in our cause to the paths leading straight to Us" (Qur'an 29:69). This idea is found in another *hadith* that recounts the following exchange: "The Prophet was asked about the best kind of jihad. He replied, 'It is a just word in the presence of an unjust ruler.'"[46] At the very least, the word should be very carefully used, and viewed with suspicion when tossed out casually without proper nuance or explanation.

CONCLUSION

Especially since 9/11, American Muslims have labored under ignorance, deep distrust, and outright hostility from their neighbors, as far too many Christians and others in this country have allowed Al-Qaeda and other terrorist organizations to represent Islam in the media and in the culture more broadly. Still today, communities reject the construction of new mosques in their neighborhoods, women wearing *hijab* are stared at and derided, and men with the wrong "look" or surname are barred from certain educational opportunities, jobs, and travel. This is an unjust and indefensible situation.

Christians have an obligation to combat such ill-informed stereotypes and discrimination by learning more about Islam and getting involved in interreligious dialogue. Most Muslim communities welcome the opportunity to talk with Christians and are eager to build bridges of friendship and peace. This is one situation in particular in which new knowledge actually can be transformative, both for us as individuals and for society as a whole.

45. One finds this quote in almost every book discussing the concept of *jihad*. See, for example, Esposito et al., *World Religions Today*, 243.

46. As quoted in Reynolds, *The Emergence of Islam*, 37.

PART II

A Comparative Approach to Christian Theology

5

God-Talk

The chapter has five main sections, organized under five different fundamental assertions Christian theology makes about God. As a part of each section, relevant doctrines from different religious traditions are introduced, inviting the reader to raise questions and make connections. At the conclusion of the chapter, there is a series of interreligious questions for further discussion and reflection.

1. GOD MAKES GOD-TALK POSSIBLE

The most basic claim that grounds a Christian understanding of God is that it is God first and foremost who makes knowledge of God possible. Certainly, human questioning of God's nature and action is possible, and human reason is capable of reflecting upon and describing God's being and work. In fact, once God has revealed Godself to humanity, it is incumbent upon humans to respond to that revelation with faithful consideration. Saint Anselm, Archbishop of Canterbury from 1093 to 1109, is famous for categorizing the Christian theological enterprise as *fides quaerens intellectum*—"faith seeking understanding." This phrase was the original title of a text that he ultimately named *Proslogion*, in which he seeks to prove the existence of God through what has come to be known as the "ontological argument."[1] The point Anselm wants to make is based on Isa. 7:9, which he quotes in *On the Incarnation of the Word*: "Unless you have believed, you will not understand."[2] Anselm argues that all the knowledge in the world will not lead to faith; instead, it is for

[margin annotation: possibility of knowledge of God]

---

1. The gist of the argument is that God is "something-than-which-nothing-greater-can-be-thought"—and, obviously, one of the attributes of this superlative greatness is existence: something "real" is greater than something that exists only in the mind. The developed argument can be found in *Proslogion*; see, for example, *Anselm of Canterbury: The Major Works*, ed. Brian Davies and G. R. Evans (Oxford: Oxford University Press, 2008), 82–104.

2. *On the Incarnation of the Word*, found in *Anselm of Canterbury*, ed. Davies and Evans, 235.

those who believe in God's self-revelation to seek after greater knowledge and understanding of God.

The main point here, then, is that human activity is a second act, a response to God's prior self-communication to us. The simple reason for this is that because of human finitude and sin, knowledge of God is impossible without God's prior self-revelation. As Karl Barth forcefully insisted, when left to our own devices, human beings construct idols that serve our own needs, and religions that tell us what we want to hear. Thus he writes, "From the standpoint of revelation religion is clearly seen to be a human attempt to anticipate what God in [God's] revelation wills to do and does do. It is the attempted replacement of the divine work by a human manufacture. The divine reality offered and manifested to us in revelation is replaced by a concept of God arbitrarily and willfully evolved by [people]."[3] Thus Barth offers a stark conclusion: "Religion is never true in itself and as such. . . . No religion is true."[4] In Barth's view, therefore, the only thing that saves Christianity from this falsehood is the presence of Jesus Christ, the definitive self-revelation of God that allows humanity to speak an authentic word about God, and sets Christianity apart as the one true religion.

While I appreciate Barth's clarity here, and also his reminder that all Christian God-talk must be grounded in God's antecedent action toward us—God's coming to and dwelling with humanity in grace and truth, I would challenge the notion that God cannot also be present in other religions, even where the name "Jesus Christ" is unknown and unacknowledged. This seems not only to presume too much knowledge about the working of God in the world, but also to set limits upon God that Christians have no right to establish. Barth's exclusivism is particularly difficult to defend when looking at the other two monotheistic world religions, Judaism and Islam. Like Christianity, both of these Abrahamic faiths also believe that God willingly and freely reveals God's will and God's nature to humanity, establishing a relationship with humanity—and, through them, the whole creation. What, exactly, God reveals, and to what extent God reveals, varies from tradition to tradition; but all three cousins share the same core conviction that it is the God of Adam, Abraham, Isaac, and Ishmael who makes possible any God-talk.

3. Karl Barth, *Church Dogmatics* I/2, ed. G. W. Bromiley and T. F. Torrance (New York: Scribner's, 1956), 302.

4. Ibid., 325.

GOD'S SELF-REVELATION IS UNIVERSAL

Perhaps there is warrant for extending this assertion even further. When discussing God's self-revelation it is important to remember that within the Christian tradition itself there has been strong affirmation from the very beginning that God's self-disclosure is universal: that is, God does not reveal Godself only to Christians, but rather to all. We see this even in scripture, in Acts 17 for example, where Paul proclaims to the Athenians the identity of the "unknown God" they were worshiping (Acts 17:26-28). This conviction is evident in much (though, sadly, not all) of Christian missionary activity as well, particularly in the act of translating the Bible, which, by the mere fact of using indigenous words to define and describe God, presumes God is already known—present and at work in all places, with all peoples.

The universality of God's self-revelation was affirmed strongly during the Second Vatican Council, held in the 1960s. In many ways, the documents that came out of this council laid the foundation for much of the fruitful interreligious dialogue that has followed it. Two documents in particular deserve mention. First is *Nostra Aetate*, the Declaration on the Relation of the Church to Non-Christian Religions. This document marks a stunning shift in Catholic doctrine, proclaiming a new openness to recognizing and acknowledging God's revelatory work in non-Christian religions. The document reads, in part: "The Catholic Church rejects nothing of what is true and holy in these [non-Christian] religions. She has a high regard for the manner of life and conduct, the precepts and doctrines which, although differing in many ways from her own teaching, nevertheless often reflect a ray of that truth which enlightens all [people]."[5]

A second document echoes these ideas. *Lumen Gentium*, the Dogmatic Constitution on the Church, states that God is not remote from "those who in shadows and images seek the unknown God, since he gives to all [people] life and breath and all things."[6] Therefore, the document continues, "Those, who, through no fault of their own do not know the Gospel of Christ or his Church, but who nevertheless seek God with a sincere heart, and, moved by grace, try in their actions to do his will as they know it through the dictates of their conscience—those too may achieve eternal salvation."[7]

5. "Declaration on the Relation of the Church to Non-Christian Religions," in *Vatican Council II* (Collegeville, MN: Liturgical Press, 1987), 739.

6. "Dogmatic Constitution on the Church," in *Vatican Council II* (Collegeville, MN: Liturgical Press, 1987), 367.

7. Ibid.

Perhaps the best contemporary articulation of this idea comes from Paul Tillich, who, in the last years of his life, teaching at the University of Chicago, came to a more explicitly universalist understanding of God's self-disclosure. In his final public lecture, he stated that "revelatory experiences are universally human."[8] Simply put, this means that Christians do not have exclusive rights on God's self-disclosure: God reveals Godself wherever, whenever, and to whomever God wills, and we cannot be so presumptuous as to assume that God chooses only to come to us. Or, as Tillich says, "There are revealing and saving powers in all religions. God has not left himself unwitnessed."[9] There is, then, no reason to assume that Christians have nothing to learn about God from non-Christian religions; instead, we can assume that new discoveries and insights await, and that another facet of God might be revealed in another's witness to the Divine, which may look very different from our own.

Let me conclude this section with one caveat. Even though God discloses Godself fully in revelation—that is, there is not some important "piece" or aspect of God that God intentionally withholds—God never can be fully known or understood by finite, sinful human beings: neither individually, nor collectively. As Catherine LaCugna says, "Although the ineffable mystery of God truly is revealed, we cannot do away with the fact that our understanding of God's self-revelation remains ever imperfect and partial. . . . The essence of God remains permanently unknowable, even though it is fully bestowed."[10] Elizabeth Johnson makes the argument this way: "Human beings simply cannot understand God. No human concept, word, or image, all of which originate in experience of created reality, can circumscribe divine reality, nor can any human construct express with any measure of adequacy the mystery of God who is ineffable."[11] To emphasize her point, she quotes St. Augustine: "*Si comprehendis, non est Deus*"—"If you have understood, then what you have understood is not God."[12] This is a reminder to Christians that any talk of God must be infused with humility, and the recognition that we always must be willing to reconsider, reexamine, and revise what we have said, in light of a fresh revelation and new knowledge. In short, Christian God-talk is an ongoing activity that will not end until God has the final word in the eschaton.

8. Paul Tillich, *Christianity and the Encounter of World Religions* (Minneapolis: Fortress Press, 1994), 64.

9. Ibid.

10. Catherine Mowry LaCugna, *God for Us: The Trinity & Christian Life* (New York: HarperCollins, 1991), 324–25.

11. Elizabeth Johnson, *She Who Is: The Mystery of God in Feminist Theological Discourse* (New York: Crossroad, 1992), 105.

12. Ibid.

2. God's Self-Revelation in Jesus Christ

While many aspects of God's self-revelation are debated among Christians, one point that is not is the defining assertion of the Christian faith that the definitive expression of God's self-revelation is found in the person of Jesus Christ: his life, death, and resurrection. For Christians, this is the starting point and the standard for all knowledge of God. Indeed, the belief that Jesus is the fully divine, fully human son of God and the savior of the world is "the linchpin of Christians' distinctive worldviews and beliefs. Jesus' mediation of God's revelation stands as the foundation of Christian faith."[13]

What this means, then, is that the task of Christian God-talk in particular is about not only responding to God's initiative, but even more describing this God from the specific vantage point of the unique relationship that God has established with humanity in the incarnation. Let me be clear about the ramifications of that: this means that the Christian starting point is not "God in general," as if Christian God-talk consists of little more than some broad ideas, concepts, or philosophical reflection on "the Divine." Instead, Christian God-talk begins with the God who has revealed Godself most deeply, most intimately, and most openly in the incarnation.

It is obvious, but worth stating nonetheless: an overstatement of the importance of Jesus' unique person and work in the Christian faith is hardly possible, and issues of Christology cannot be avoided in an interreligious conversation that professes to take Christian faith claims seriously.

THE "TWO BOOKS" OF GOD'S SELF-REVELATION

Alongside this unique Christian teaching about the incarnation, however, it also must be noted that this revelation of God in Jesus Christ—sometimes called "special revelation"—does not negate what is sometimes called "general revelation," that is, the revelation of the creator in God's creation; instead, they are complementary. Together, these two ways of receiving God's self-disclosure traditionally have been called the "two books" of divine revelation.

In his book *Sun of Righteousness, Arise!,* Jürgen Moltmann writes that "[t]he idea of 'the two books' derives from Christian tradition, and was widespread in the era before the scientific revolution."[14] The point of the image of the "book" is to allow a positive correlation between scripture and scientific knowledge

13. *Constructive Theology: A Contemporary Approach to Classical Themes*, ed. Serene Jones and Paul Lakeland (Minneapolis: Fortress Press, 2005), 163.

14. Jürgen Moltmann, *Sun of Righteousness, Arise! God's Future for Humanity and the Earth*, trans. Margaret Kohl (Minneapolis: Fortress Press, 2010), 194.

of nature: "More precisely, this metaphor lets us understand nature as a 'book' whose characters we can learn to read. Nature is just as intelligible as the human mind is rational. The metaphor assumes that nature has a language, and it calls the signatures of nature a 'script' which human beings can read."[15]

He goes on to note the importance of this metaphor in the writings of the early church fathers:

> The Syrian Church Fathers and the Cappadocians used the idea of the two books. A certain third-century abbot Antonius said: "My book is the created nature, one always at my disposal whenever I want to read God's words." Basil the Great believed that our reason was so perfectly created by God that "through the beauties of created things we can read God's wisdom and providence as if these beauties were letters and words." For Augustine, although only the person who has learnt to read can read Holy Scripture, even the illiterate can understand the book of the universe. For Maximus the Confessor, nature and Scripture are the two robes of Christ which shone bright as his transfiguration, his humanity and his divinity: in Christ the "two books" have the same content. The Celtic theologian Scotus Eriugena thought that the two books were the two theophanies, the one through the medium of letters, the other through forms.[16]

Of importance here is the affirmation that even apart from the incarnation, there is something to learn of God in creation: God's fingerprints are on God's handiwork, and the signs of God's loving nature are written into the very fabric of the web of life itself.

Islam: Another "Word" of God
God's Self-Revelation in the Qur'an

As described previously, Muslims believe that the Qur'an is the literal, uncreated word of God. Therefore, in Islam, the starting point of God's self-revelation is also a "word incarnate," as it were: a flawless, incomparable, inerrant revelation of God's will that cannot ever be surpassed or superseded. Simply put, it is believed that ". . . God gives a perfect revelation in the Koran."[17] This is the reason why the Qur'an has such unshakable

---

15. Ibid., 194–95.

16. Ibid., 195–96.

17. Keith Ward, *Religion and Revelation* (Oxford: Clarendon, 1994), 175.

authority in Islam, and is followed so literally. Allow me to repeat the quote from Gabriel Said Reynolds from Chapter 4: ". . . the prevailing Islamic tradition is that the Qur'an has always existed in heaven, along with God. . . . In this understanding, God did not 'inspire' Muhammad. He sent down a preexisting book to him. Thus the Islamic view of the revelation of the Qur'an is closer to the Christian view of the incarnation of the World of God in Jesus than it is to the Christian view of the Bible."[18] To emphasize this point, Hans Küng describes the Qur'an's place in Islam using language Christians typically reserve for Jesus:

Indeed for all Muslims the Qur'an is:

- the truth: the original source of the experience of God and piety and the mandatory criterion of right faith;
- the way: the true possibility of coping with the world and the eternally valid standard for correct action (ethic);
- the light; the abiding foundation of Islamic law and the soul of Islamic prayer, already the material for the instruction of Muslim children, the inspiration of Islamic art and the all-permeating spirit of Islamic culture.[19]

Again, this is also why translation is so problematic: How does one translate the literal speech of God without losing something in the process? One cannot possibly grant equal authority to a text rendered in a secondary language when "The Qur'an, as the Revealed Word of God, actually exists only in the Arabic language. It is this Arabic Qur'an that is used in all formal prayers, teaching, and scholarship. . . . Translations of the Qur'an into other languages, and many exist in English alone, are considered only interpretations. . . ."[20] In spite of the theological difficulties with translation, however, the missionary impulse in Islam won out, resulting in a compromise position that translations of the Qur'an into vernacular languages would be allowed, even encouraged, but it would remain clear that those translations do not have the authority of the original Arabic.

Incidentally, related to this issue of translation are the challenges and opportunities created by new technologies, particularly media technologies. Even though there were initial concerns around the mass-production of the

18. Gabriel Said Reynolds, *The Emergence of Islam: Classical Traditions in Contemporary Perspective* (Minneapolis: Fortress Press, 2012), 96.

19. Hans Küng, *Islam: Past, Present and Future,* trans. John Bowden, (Oxford: Oneworld, 2009), 66.

20. C. T. R. Hewer, *Understanding Islam: An Introduction* (Minneapolis: Fortress Press, 2006), 53.

Qur'an, "particularly in the early stages, when copies were often of inferior quality and marred by errors,"[21] the clear advantages of being able to reach a global audience were undeniable. What that means is that in the twenty-first century, the "'democratization' of the Qur'an has enabled it to play a larger role in the everyday lives of Muslims everywhere."[22] Free hardcopies are available from a variety of sources, in a variety of languages; and a plenitude of different translations are available free online. The result is that comparisons between Jesus and the Qur'an are challenging, interesting, and fruitful, as they push Christians to rethink the whole concept of "divine word" in fresh and stimulating ways.

EXPANSIVE VIEWS OF SALVATION

Given that one of the key claims of Christianity is that Jesus Christ is the savior of the world, when it comes to believers in other religious traditions, the Christian is left with several options: some Christians limit salvation to within the Christian church, while others suggest that there is a way to think about salvation more broadly. If one chooses the first option, then the conversation is over: all that is left is to try to convince others in the most loving and persuasive way possible of the ultimate necessity of belief in Jesus Christ. However, if one favors the second option, then one is faced with (at least) two different possibilities: the first is the possibility of universal salvation; and the second is the possibility of *salvations*, plural—the possibility that there exists more than one ultimate end. I will discuss each of these briefly.

The doctrine of universal salvation, often called by its traditional Greek name *apokatastasis*, refers to the belief that in the end, all "free moral creatures"—this includes not only humans but also angels and devils—will be saved.[23] While the Bible certainly has much to say about the idea in general, the word itself only appears once, in Acts 3:21. And, even though many Christians often assume that this is a modern idea, brought about by engagement with a more liberal, secular society, this doctrine actually has a long history in the Christian tradition, beginning with Clement of Alexandria. Clement, who lived and wrote in the second century CE, was the first Christian author to

21. John Kaltner, *Introducing the Qur'an for Today's Reader* (Minneapolis: Fortress Press, 2011), 40.

22. Ibid.

23. *The Oxford Dictionary of the Christian Church*, 2nd edition, ed. F. L. Cross and E. A. Livingstone (Oxford: Oxford University Press, 1990).

hypothesize the idea of universal salvation, in book seven of the *Stromateis*.[24] He believed that there would be punishment after death—so he did not discount the idea of hell entirely—but he believed that the punishment would have a purifying effect and thus be limited: it would, for all people, come to an end at some point.

While Clement used a variety of texts from scripture to ground this idea, most influential for him were 1 John 2:2 and Phil. 2:10, both of which emphasize the universality of Jesus' saving work: ultimately, Christ has atoned for the sins of the whole world, and thus in the end, "every knee should bend" at the name of Jesus. Clement interpreted both of these passages literally, which meant that he sought to explain how they could be harmonized with other passages that seemed to assert the existence of a place of punishment after death. In the end, what Clement ended up with was a kind of both/and: yes, hell exists, but it will not exist forever.

The second early church father who discussed this idea was Gregory of Nyssa, who elaborated his understanding of universal salvation primarily in *On the Soul and the Resurrection*.[25] Gregory, like Clement, also believed in the limited, purifying power of the punishments of hell, but he also had an additional rationale for arguing against eternal damnation. Gregory believed that evil does not have positive ontological existence; instead, it exists solely as a parasite, living off the existence of the good. For this reason, evil, unlike the good that God has created, has only finite existence. Ultimately, once all free moral beings are purged from evil and are able to choose the good, evil—and hell—will cease to exist.

In twentieth-century theology, the doctrine of *apokatastasis* has been revisited and revised for a contemporary audience by the Swiss Catholic theologian Hans Urs von Balthasar. In the aptly named *Dare We Hope That All Men Be Saved?*, he does not attempt to definitively prove universal salvation: he believes that decisive knowledge of ultimate ends lies outside the scope of human reason, as salvation is under the sole purview of God. Instead, he argues that it is a Christian's duty to *hope* that all will be saved, based not only on the scriptural witness to a universally loving God, but also based on our Christian

---

24. Particularly book seven, chapter two. The context of Clement's thought here is his attempt to rehabilitate the Alexandrian Gnostics. *The Ante-Nicene Fathers: Translations of the Writings of the Fathers Down to A.D. 325*, ed. Alexander Roberts and James Donaldson, vol. 2 (Edinburgh: T. & T. Clark/Grand Rapids: Eerdmans, 1989), 523ff.

25. St. Gregory of Nyssa, *On the Soul and the Resurrection*, trans. Catharine P. Roth (Crestwood, NY: St. Vladimir's Seminary Press, 1993).

responsibility to love our neighbor. His position is that "[c]ertainty cannot be attained, but hope can be justified."[26]

It must be stated, of course, that this doctrine always has been controversial, and it continues to generate heated speculation and argumentation—the most recent participant in the arena is Rob Bell and his book *Love Wins*. Even almost 2,000 years later, the same issues continue to be opposed: the will of a loving God to save the whole world, and the freedom of the human being to reject that love, even everlastingly. Jean Daniélou says it well in his book on Origen—another early Christian father who elaborated a doctrine of universal salvation—when he writes that the "great theological symphony" of a doctrine of *apokatastasis* must somehow reconcile two things: "God's love and [humans'] freedom."[27]

The second possibility I mentioned is that of plural religious ends: the idea that there is more than one positive ending to a life of faith, whether that is the paradise described in the Qur'an, or the enlightenment described in the Heart Sutra. Mark Heim elaborates on this possibility at length in two different books. In the first, titled *Salvations*, Heim argues against those pluralists, such as John Hick, who insist on an ultimate oneness, a transcendent unity of some sort that ultimately will reconcile the differences we experience between religions here and now. Heim finds this position wanting, as it does not, in the end, uphold the deep divergences between the visions different religious traditions offer regarding the end of human life.

He argues instead that more integrity must be given to the faith commitments and practices of the believers in any religious tradition, and the hopes attached to those practices. In other words, if at the end of his life a Hindu travels to Varanasi in the hopes of dying on the banks of the Ganges and achieving *moksha*, Christians have to take that practice, and the belief associated with it, seriously: otherwise, as Heim notes, "The specific details of the faiths seem to become irrelevant."[28] What he advocates, then, is what he calls "an eschatological plenitude"—the affirmation of a variety of religious ends, not all of which might be deemed of equal value, but all of which can be seen to glorify God.[29]

He refines this idea further in *The Depth of the Riches*, where he uses Dante's *Divine Comedy* as a model for imagining what this eschatological plenitude

26. Hans Urs von Balthasar, *Dare We Hope That All Men Be Saved?*, trans. David Kipp (San Francisco: Ignatius, 1988), 187.

27. Jean Daniélou, *Origen*, trans. Walter Mitchell (London: Sheed & Ward, 1955), 288–89.

28. S. Mark Heim, *Salvations* (Maryknoll, NY: Orbis, 1997), 7.

29. Ibid., 165.

might look like. He grounds his argument on the fact that, in the *Comedy*, Dante has drawn an elaborate picture of an afterlife in which there are divergent ends for different human beings. Heim adapts this model to a religiously plural context, suggesting that in a similar way, people's different choices and desires land them in different places after death; and similar to the way that not all of Dante's destinations are equally fulfilling or rewarding, Christians need not affirm the parity of the different ends. Thus Heim recognizes that, for Christians, "To realize something other than communion with the triune God and with other creatures through Christ, in the continuing relationship of created being, is to achieve a lesser good. It is not the abundant life that Christians know and hope for in Christ. There is no reason to avoid this judgment, as long as we realize that other traditions make similar reciprocal judgments about the supremacy of their religious end."[30]

At the same time, however, he does go further, arguing that even if Christians do not see equal value in the different religious ends, they can still affirm that the triune God is at work for the good somehow in all of them.

> We could say instead that the prospect of persons realizing religious ends alternative to salvation should enhance our sense of God's majesty and love all the more. God's willingness to honor and incorporate this kind of freedom within creation's consummation redounds greatly to God's glory. God is glorified in opening up to creatures participation in the triune life of communion, but also in honoring the free alternative choices of creatures, meeting them not with punishment but with the best possible gifts their choices will allow.[31]

Ultimately, Heim suggests that "God allows each of us to become what we wish to become. Or, more exactly, God allows each of us to freely form our most profound desires, and then to fulfill them. Short of the total resistance to God that leads to annihilation, each person's aim for fulfillment includes relation with God in some dimension."[32] This is not the doctrine of *apokatastasis*, but something even more mysterious, and perhaps, even greater.

---

30. S. Mark Heim, *The Depth of the Riches: A Trinitarian Theology of Religious Ends* (Grand Rapids: Eerdmans, 2001), 44.
31. Ibid., 263.
32. Ibid.

3. THE TRIUNE NATURE OF GOD: ONE GOD, THREE PERSONS

The Christian claim about the nature of God is both quite specific, and quite unique. While Christians are monotheists by virtue of their confession of belief in the "one God," that monotheism has a distinct character, in that its "oneness" finds expression in "threeness." Obviously, it is not the math here that is important, but rather the fact that God exists as communion, as relationality; and because of the dynamism and openness of that communion, God's self-disclosure and relationship to creation take on a special character. Therefore, even though Christians tend to emphasize the oneness of God, in actuality, given the claims Christians make about how God has revealed Godself (most definitively in Jesus Christ), it makes more sense to start a Christian conversation about God with the three persons. William Placher argues the point this way: "If, however, as I believe, we can know God only as revealed in Christ through the Holy Spirit, then we *start* with three."[33] Indeed, this starting point is of particular importance given that every work of God always is a work of all three persons together: God's self-revelation is always triune. To emphasize that point, Placher quotes Gregory of Nyssa: "Every operation which extends from God to the creation . . . has its origin from the Father, and proceeds through the Son, and is perfected in the Holy Spirit."[34]

THE LEXICOGRAPHY OF THE EARLY CHURCH COUNCILS

The particular language that has become standard for describing the distinctively Christian form of monotheism came out of the early church councils, specifically the Council of Nicaea (325) and the Council of Constantinople (381). These councils continue to serve as the gold standard of Christian belief, and the doctrines established there still serve as the measure by which one determines heresy and orthodoxy.

At the time, no one set out to define a "doctrine of the Trinity" per se. Instead, the pressing theological issue was the nature of Jesus Christ. Jaroslav Pelikan states the central question this way: "Is the divine that has appeared on earth and reunited [hu]man with God identical with the supreme divine, which rules heaven and earth, or is it a demigod?"[35] This question points to the fact that salvation was actually the key issue at stake in the debate: "if the pre-existent Son

---

33. William C. Placher, *The Triune God: An Essay in Postliberal Theology* (Louisville: Westminster John Knox, 2007), 1.

34. Ibid., 146–47.

35. Jaroslav Pelikan, *The Christian Tradition: A History of the Development of Doctrine*, vol. 1 (Chicago: University of Chicago Press, 1971), 172.

were not one with the Father, how could he bring salvation to humanity even if he became incarnate in Jesus? And how could salvation depend upon someone who was not eternal and not fully divine?"[36] In a nutshell, the problem is this: only God can save, therefore, Jesus Christ must be equal to God; however, unless the existence of two different gods is admitted, it must be the same God who redeems who also creates.

It is hard to imagine now, centuries and centuries removed from the debates of that time, but there were several live options to the doctrine of the Trinity we know today that drew many followers. For example, Arians believed that Jesus was not divine from eternity, but rather created by God the Father as the first being of creation. Modalists (or Monarchians) such as Sabellius argued that there was only one divine person who took the form of the Son, the Father, and the Spirit at different times, as though God were one actor, wearing different masks to play different roles. The Arian position was particularly strong, and it took many centuries before it finally was suppressed. At Nicaea, the language used to refute Arius was the Greek word *homoousios*, which means "of the same substance." In English, it has been translated in the second article of the Nicene Creed as ". . . of one being with the Father . . ."

The second ecumenical council, the Council of Constantinople, continued to hammer out the theological details of Nicaea, including the trinitarian question of how the person of the Holy Spirit related to the Father and the Son. Some Christians at this time, the so-called *Pneumatomachoi*, argued that the Spirit was a creature and therefore should not be seen as equal to the Father or the Son. Especially helpful in countering this idea were the Cappadocian fathers: Basil of Caesarea, his brother Gregory of Nyssa, and their friend, Gregory of Nazianzus. In his text *On the Holy Spirit*, Basil emphasized the full divinity of the Holy Spirit, arguing that the Holy Spirit is both "pre-existent and co-eternal, part of the Father's instrument in creation."[37] Together, the three church fathers stressed not only the individuality (and equality) of the three persons of the Trinity, rather than their unity, but also their "co-inherence"—that is, the way in which the three were in relationship.

This emphasis on a God who is not only in external relationship with God's creation, but who is also internally fundamentally relational has continued up to the present day. It serves as a core component of the argument that the economic Trinity (the triune God revealed through God's work in the world, specifically through God's plan of redemption in Jesus Christ) and the

36. Stephen W. Need, *Truly Divine & Truly Human: The Story of Christ and the Seven Ecumenical Councils* (Peabody, MA: Hendrickson, 2008), 41–42.

37. Ibid., 69.

immanent Trinity (the eternal being of God, inaccessible to human eyes) are the same. That is, God in God's essence is the same as the God revealed in God's work. One of the best twentieth-century books on the Trinity is Catherine Mowry LaCugna's *God for Us*, in which she elaborates on and reinterprets the doctrine of the Trinity for a contemporary context. One particularly compelling aspect of her argument uses the concept of *perichoresis*, an idea first elaborated upon by John of Damascus in the eighth century. The term itself means "being-in-one-another, permeation without confusion,"[38] and it points to a dynamic understanding of the divine that is fundamentally relational. LaCugna argues that *perichoresis* "expresses the idea that the three divine persons mutually inhere in one another, draw life from one another, 'are' what they are by relation to one another."[39]

Through the centuries a variety of images have been used to illustrate this idea, perhaps none as compelling as that of the "divine dance." Here is how LaCugna describes it:

> Choreography suggests the partnership of movement, symmetrical but not redundant, as each dancer expresses and at the same time fulfills him/herself towards the other. In inter-action and inter-course, the dancers (and the observers) experience one fluid motion of encircling, encompassing, permeating, enveloping, outstretching. There are neither leaders nor followers in the divine dance, only an eternal movement of reciprocal giving and receiving, giving again and receiving again.[40]

For Christians, the great strength of this image is that it moves away from language that suggests a static, unchangeable, untouchable God in favor of a dynamic, engaged, relational God: a God who acts *and* reacts, a God who gives *and* receives, a God who is flexible, responsive, and innovative. However, this is exactly the point at which other religious traditions would disagree.

Islam's Pure Monotheism

At the start of any discussion of monotheism in Islam, particularly for a Christian audience, it must be noted that in Islam, Jesus is revered; indeed, he is deeply respected and esteemed by Muslims. When reading the Qur'an

---

38. LaCugna, *God for Us*, 271.

39. Ibid., 270–71.

40. Ibid., 272.

for the first time, Christians are often surprised to find that the Qur'an testifies to the virgin birth (Qur'an 3:42-48; 19:16-21), and repeatedly extols Jesus as a great prophet (Qur'an 3:45-51; 5:109-20). However, this reverence for Jesus extends only to his humanity; at the same time that the Qur'an lifts up Jesus' human prophethood, his divinity is sharply and strongly rejected, for one very particular and critical reason: "The doctrine of the incarnation is rejected by Islam because it seems to compromise the utter transcendence and sovereignty of God."[41]

Thus it is fair to say that the main source of theological disagreement between Muslims and Christians is the divinity of Jesus Christ, which, for Muslims, directly relates to the affirmation of Allah as the one God. Keith Ward writes: "A deep difference exists between Islam and Christianity as to whether it is proper to worship Jesus Christ. The Muslim view stresses the utter transcendence of God, and denies that there can be any form of union between Creator and creature. Christians, however, claim that Jesus imaged and expressed the Divine Being and Will. He was united to God in such an intimate manner as to be the complete expression in human terms of what God is."[42] Regardless of how much agreement one can find between the two faith traditions—and there is much to be found—at this particular point, the difference is critically important. No matter how much Jesus is honored, he is not—in fact cannot—be viewed as divine. Such a teaching fundamentally compromises the core assertion of God's oneness, and Islamic doctrine is unambiguous on this point: ". . . the gulf between the world and God remains absolute and no finite thing can be associated with God in any way—the grievous sin of *shirk* is that of associating any other thing with God."[43]

This uncompromising emphasis on the oneness of God—and the corresponding rejection of any sort of "partner" or "son" for God—can be seen throughout the Qur'an. For example, "God does not forgive that compeers be ascribed to Him, though He may forgive aught else if He please. And he who ascribes compeers to God is guilty of the gravest sin" (Qur'an 4:48).[44] Further, "Creator of the heavens and the earth from nothingness, how could He have a son when He has no mate?" (Qur'an

---

41. Ward, *Religion and Revelation*, 181.

42. Ibid.

43. Ibid., 176.

44. All citations of the Qur'an are taken from *Al-Qur'an: A Contemporary Translation by Ahmed Ali* (Princeton: Princeton University Press, 2001).

6:101). For Muslims, the issue is not only God's uniqueness as creator and lord, but also God's sole power and authority over all creation: "God is so self-sufficient that he stands in no need of a son; and, since God possesses all things, he cannot stand in a special relation of possession to just one person, Jesus."[45]

Ward argues that at least some of the emphasis one finds on God's uncompromised unity, sovereignty, and omnipotence relates to the Arabian context in which Islam was born. He writes, "In reaction to tribal polytheism in the Arabian peninsula, all talk of sons and daughters of god, who might divide Divine power between them and be worshiped as competitors with the Divine Father, is forbidden. This largely accounts for Muslim antipathy to the doctrine of God as Trinity."[46] We see evidence of this in the story of Muhammad himself and the spread of the teachings of Islam, particularly as it relates to the Ka'aba. One of the centerpieces of Muhammad's religious activity was to purge the Ka'aba of its many idols, and rededicate it to Allah alone. This was considered the crowning event of the Muslims' victory over the warring tribes of Arabia, and the definitive event establishing the importance of Mecca and the *Hajj* in Islam. Therefore, the Qur'an teaches:

> O people of the Book, do not be fanatical in your faith, and say nothing but the truth about God. The Messiah who is Jesus, son of Mary, was only an apostle of God, and a command of His which He sent to Mary as a mercy from Him. So believe in God and His apostles, and do not call Him "Trinity." Abstain from this for your own good; for God is only one God; and far from His glory it is to beget a son. All that is in the heavens and the earth belong to Him; and sufficient is God for all help (Qur'an 4:171).

Hinduism's One and Many

Swinging the pendulum far to the other side now, it is also worth mentioning in this context the way in which the "oneness" of the Divine is described and understood in Hinduism. As a way of introducing this idea here, let me repeat what I said in an earlier chapter. Hinduism encompasses

---

45. Ward, *Religion and Revelation*, 179.
46. Ibid., 188.

a lush, expansive understanding of the divine—richer by far than the relatively narrow range of conceptions, images, and language typically used for God in the Christian tradition. There is a simple, yet profound reason for that: "To Hindu ways of thinking, the ultimate reality is so far beyond our imagining, so complex, so utterly rich in potential, that a single image or even a mere handful of images will not do. If the absolute must be portrayed, then many, many images and symbols will be more successful than just one or a few."[47] Simply put, in Hinduism god is not either one or many, but both; god is not male or female, but both; god is not formless or embodied, but both. For this reason, "... in the Hindu religions, monotheism is basically considered disdainful of the divine since it presumes that one knows how the divine is manifested."[48]

As one concrete example of how this one and many are experienced in Hinduism, one need look only to the role of Krishna in the *Bhagavad-Gita*. The *Bhagavad-Gita* is a later insertion into the *Mahabharata*, the longest of the two most important pan-Indian epics. At its heart, the *Mahabharata* is the story of two groups of cousins, the Pandavas and the Kauravas, and the rivalry between them—particularly the disputed kingship, which provides the impetus for the warfare that ultimate breaks out between them. The *Bhagavad-Gita* begins as the two sides stand on the cusp of war, as the two vast armies stand facing each other in the field of battle. It is at this point that Arjuna, the hero of the Pandavas, loses heart. Standing next to Krishna, his charioteer, he sees all too clearly the death and destruction that await him and his family members—cousins, uncles, etc., and in the face of such monumental loss, he slumps down in his chariot and refuses to fight.

It is into this crisis of moral despair that Krishna enters to explain the truth of reality to Arjuna and inspire him to fight. In the course of this conversation, Arjuna asks Krishna for a vision of his "supremely powerful form" (*Bhagavad-Gita* 11:3); and out of affection for Arjuna, and a desire for him to know the truth, Krishna agrees to Arjuna's request, bestowing upon him the "divine eyes" he will need to behold such a vision, which mortal eyes are not able to grasp. The vision, which the text goes on to describe, is impossible to conceive: "What Arjuna witnesses is beyond the scope of the human mind to comprehend. The *Gita* can only give us a hint,

47. Mark W. Muesse, *The Hindu Traditions* (Minneapolis: Fortress Press, 2011), 132–33.

48. Axel Michaels, *Hinduism Past and Present*, trans. Barbara Harshav (Princeton, NJ: Princeton University Press, 2004), 208.

an inkling. If we can imagine the entire span of the cosmos, every event that has ever taken place, is taking place, and will ever take place, every form, every being, every thing, manifested endlessly in the infinite body of the divine Person, we can begin to understand."[49] Thus Krishna shows himself to have multiple mouths full of crushing teeth in which the worlds are destroyed; he has multiple eyes and unlimited arms; he has no end and no beginning; "multitudes of celestial beings" sing praises to him; and the very cosmos trembles at his revelation. Indeed, we are told that the brilliance emanating from his being shines like the light of a thousand suns, rising in the sky at once, burning the universe with his splendor.

This vision solidifies Krishna's existence as the highest and ultimate reality in the universe. From the perspective of the *Gita*, there is only the appearance of many gods—in reality, Krishna dwells within them all, sustaining them with his being, possessing the power to create and destroy them all. Thus, "The dialogue between Krishna and Arjuna opens up a whole new dimension of religion in Hinduism. Krishna presents himself as the Supreme Lord, the Highest Personal God. All other gods are merely manifestations of him in accordance with their time, place, and spiritual aptitude."[50] What this means is that ". . . within the new ontology [described in the *Gita*], the entire world is a part of God, including the bodies and psyches of all people, and the ultimate, unchanging, eternal part of all people, the ultimate self in each, is also God."[51] God is one, but God is also many; and the "many-ness" of the divine self-revelation only enhances and deepens the understanding of God's oneness.

THE TRINITY AND THE RELIGIONS

It is possible to argue that because the Christian doctrine of the Trinity is so precise and distinctive it excludes any way of understanding God that deviates from its specific definition. However, one also might argue that the doctrine of one God in three persons does create room for thinking creatively with non-Christian religions. This openness is reflected in three streams of interreligious engagement, each of which has its source in a specific understanding of one person of the Trinity. First is the stream that flows from the first person

49. Barbara Powell, *Windows into the Infinite* (Fremont, CA: Asian Humanities Press, 1996), 63.

50. James Robinson, *Hinduism*, Religions of the World (New York: Chelsea House, 2004), 33.

51. James L. Fitzgerald, "The Great Epic of India as Religious Rhetoric: A Fresh Look at the *Mahabharata*," *Journal of the American Academy of Religion* 51, no. 4 D (1983): 618.

of the Trinity, God the Father, and more precisely, God's creative activity. Specifically, this stream explores "the implications of trust in God as the sole source of a unitary creation."[52] What this means is that if one takes seriously the belief that God created all that is, one is led to see "a fundamental universal fit between humanity and its Maker, an imprinting of the divine nature in all that is an endowment of persons with the capacity to perceive that imprint."[53] The influential Catholic theologian Karl Rahner described this very well in his doctrine of the "supernatural existential," which states that ontologically present in human nature is God's self-revelation, and it is God's invitation of love and grace that calls humanity into being. Rahner writes, "In this sense, really and radically *every* person must be understood as the event of a supernatural self-communication of God,"[54] and this is true even when that communication of God is rejected. In this view, it is not first and foremost baptism that conveys God's grace to Christians, but rather "all people were created from the very beginning for grace; it belongs to the very essence of concrete human nature to be called to grace, to be able to find God in the particularities of all history."[55] If one takes this idea literally, one can conclude that God reaches out to all people, and is in a relationship with everyone—believers of all faith traditions, and even nonbelievers—whether or not that relationship is acknowledged.

The second stream flows from an understanding of the second person of the Trinity, God the Son, and explores "what we might call preincarnate, incarnate, and postresurrection modalities."[56] This language refers to the many different ways of thinking about the incarnate Word: for example, using John 1, and emphasizing the universality of the Word as existing eternally "in the beginning with God" and participating in the creation of all that exists; or looking at a text like Colossians 1, and emphasizing the universality of Christ's reconciling work in the resurrection. Another possibility is to reinterpret the uniqueness of the incarnation by seeing the "one and only" language of the New Testament as "love language," testifying to the special nature of the disciples' relationship with Christ, rather than making an exclusive ontological claim about his person. Paul Knitter describes the shift this way: "If Christians

---

52. S. Mark Heim, "Accounts of Our Hope," in *Grounds for Understanding*, ed. S. Mark Heim (Grand Rapids: Eerdmans, 1998), 10.

53. Ibid.

54. Karl Rahner, *Foundations of Christian Faith: An Introduction to the Idea of Christianity*, trans. William V. Dych (New York: Crossroad, 1997), 127–28.

55. "Theology in a New Key," by William V. Dych, in *A World of Grace*, ed. Leo J. O'Donovan (Washington, DC: Georgetown University Press, 1995), 11.

56. Heim, "Accounts of Our Hope," 10–11.

could reclarify and repossess the original and enduring intent of christological language—that is, if 'one and only' could mean 'I'm fully committed to you' rather than 'no one else is worthy of commitment'—then many Christians would feel more honest about their faith and doors would be opened more widely to dialogue with other believers equally committed to their saviors."[57]

Finally, the third stream flows from an understanding of the third person of the Trinity, God the Holy Spirit, and emphasizes "the continued freedom and providence of God's action. The Spirit blows where it will, and the religions can be viewed through the lens of possibility of this direct, spontaneous action and presence of God."[58] This is in many ways the most fertile ground for growing interreligious insights, given the freedom and mystery of the movement of the Holy Spirit, and the consistent witness throughout Christian scripture and tradition that human beings cannot track or predict the movement of the Holy Spirit, nor are they able to definitively state where or when She will be found: "The Spirit blows where it chooses, and you hear the sound of it, but you do not know where it comes from or where it goes" (John 3:8). It is at this point where Christians can most easily recognize and affirm the absolute sovereignty of God to move where and when God chooses, and respond with openness to discovering the previously unexplored places where God might be found.

HOW SHALL WE CALL YOU?

Few issues evoke more passion and argument than language for God. For many questions, the issue is straightforward and clear cut: they endorse the conclusion of Lutheran theologian Robert Jenson, who argues that in the doctrine of the Trinity we have a "proper name" for God—that is, Father, Son, and Holy Spirit; and that this proper name is of critical importance for the Christian faith.[59] For this reason, in Jenson's view, no other language for God can be used without falling into either blasphemy or absurdity. Unfortunately, this doctrinal rigidity has promulgated a too-literal mandating of God's "fatherhood," excluding any female metaphors for God, as if being a "father" means that God is also a man, for example.

However, in spite of Jenson's conviction, there is another way of thinking about the language we use for God that offers many more faithful, fruitful possibilities for envisioning who God is and how God is in relationship to us.

---

57. Paul Knitter, *No Other Name? A Critical Survey of Christian Attitudes Toward the World Religions* (Maryknoll, NY: Orbis, 1996), 186.

58. Heim, "Accounts of Our Hope," 11.

59. "The Triune God," by Robert Jenson, in *Christian Dogmatics*, vol. 1, ed. Carl E. Braaten and Robert W. Jenson (Philadelphia: Fortress Press, 1984), 89ff.

Another Lutheran theologian, Ted Peters, takes this route, challenging Jenson's claim and arguing instead that "to say that the trinitarian formula is God's proper name is to say too much."[60] The primary reason Peters makes this statement is that these "names" for God—Father, Son, and Holy Spirit—are not proper names, but rather metaphors: important metaphors, certainly—and not just ones among others—but metaphors all the same. Thus Peters challenges the exclusivity of Jenson's claim with the assertion that "[t]he trinitarian set of terms constitutes a family of symbols within a larger clan of biblical symbols we use to identify the God of Christian faith."[61] This metaphorical understanding of how religious naming for God can function warrants further explanation.

Peters notes that when Christians use the word "God," it typically has one of three referents. He writes, "First, we use the word 'God' to refer to the general notion of divine reality as it can be found in most of the world's religions and, more specifically, to refer to Yahweh, the Holy Lord of Israel. Second, 'God' may on occasion refer to the first person of the Trinity, to God, the Father of Jesus. Third, we may speak of the entire Trinity—inclusive of the Father, Son, and Holy Spirit—as the 'Godhead' or simply 'God.'"[62] Particularly when it comes to the last two usages—most common in Christian theology—one of the most important, and often contentious, issues around a Christian doctrine of God is that of language and imagery: specifically, what is permissible and what is not.

Frustrating to many contemporary theologians is the fact that while there are a wide variety of images in both Scripture and the tradition, only a tiny fraction of that language has made it into standard ecclesiastical nomenclature. For example, when was the last time you heard a sermon in which the image for God used in Hos. 13:8 (a mother bear robbed of her cubs) was used? Moreover, equally as problematic as the paucity of images is the standard that has been used to determine whether a particular word or phrase, or visual image, can serve as a legitimate descriptor for God: plainly put, that standard is an older white king. Thus, language that calls to mind royal attributes such as powerful lord, mighty sovereign, ruler of the heavens, creator of the world, etc., is favored—in both Christian art and liturgical practices; and language that seems to suggest an alternate image—particularly anything that suggests female imagery—continues to be suspect.

---

60. Ted Peters, *God as Trinity: Relationality and Temporality in Divine Life* (Louisville: Westminster John Knox, 1993), 53.

61. Ibid., 54.

62. Ibid., 13.

Far from being a side-issue in theology, the way we talk about God is of the utmost importance: not only for understanding who God is and how God is in relationship to us, but also for understanding who we are and how we bear the image of God. Susan Brooks Thistlethwaite experienced the power of language firsthand. She writes of being on the National Council of Churches' *Inclusive Language Lectionary* committee, which spent nine years translating not only the three-year lectionary texts but also the Psalms into more inclusive English. Of that experience she writes, "These efforts to translate the scripture more inclusively have been met with resistance, derision and outright hostility and threatened violence. Initially, I had not understood the full depth of the liberation potential of language. It was in this enormous backlash that I learned the power of this form of resistance. *The hysterical rejections that 'Language doesn't matter' prove the reverse. Language matters immensely.*"[63]

Although we don't often think of this as an issue of idolatry, Rosemary Radford Ruether reminds us that, in fact, this is the case: "Christian theology has always recognized, theoretically, that all language for God is analogical or metaphorical, not literal. . . . To take one image drawn from one gender and in one sociological context as normative for God is to legitimate this gender and social group as the normative possessors of the image of God and the representative of God on earth. This is idolatry."[64] Elizabeth Johnson explains the problem this way. Inherently, there is nothing wrong with using male imagery for God; the problem comes in *how* those images are used. More specifically, the issue is that they are used *exclusively*, *literally*, and *patriarchally*. By this, she is pointing to the fact that first, when only male metaphors are used for God, "speech about God in female metaphors or in images taken from the natural world lies fallow, and can even appear deviant."[65] Second, when our inflexibility leads us to think of God uncritically as literally male, we have—consciously or not—signified that "maleness is an essential character of divine being."[66] Finally, when language for God is narrowed even further by drawing only from one specific male image—that is, a male ruler—"divine mystery is cast in the role of a monarch."[67] And, even when this monarch is depicted as kind and merciful, the problem does not go away: as she wryly

---

63. Susan Brooks Thistlethwaite, "On the Trinity," in *Lift Every Voice: Constructing Christian Theologies from the Underside*, ed. Susan Brooks Thistlethwaite and Mary Potter Engel (Maryknoll, NY: Orbis, 1998), 115, my emphasis.

64. As quoted in Anne M. Clifford, *Introducing Feminist Theology* (Maryknoll, NY: Orbis, 2002), 92.

65. Johnson, *She Who Is*, 33.

66. Ibid.

67. Ibid., 34.

observes, "Benevolent patriarchy is still patriarchy."[68] She thus comes to the same conclusion as Ruether:

> [Such speech] for God fails both human beings and divine mystery. In stereotyping and then banning female reality as suitable metaphor for God, such speech justifies the dominance of men while denigrating the human dignity of women. Simultaneously this discourse so reduces divine mystery to the single, reified metaphor of the ruling man that the symbol itself loses its religious significance and ability to point to ultimate truth. It becomes, in a word, an idol.[69]

In this situation in which we find ourselves, then, a reminder of the metaphorical function of "God-talk" can be immensely helpful, freeing Christian theology today to be no less bold and creative than that of our mothers and fathers in the faith, echoing the breadth and depth of God-talk that we find in both scripture and the tradition.

Sallie McFague continues to be an excellent resource in this regard. In her book *Models of God*, she begins by describing what she calls "metaphorical theology"—that is, a theology that takes seriously the need for new metaphors and models of God in the new contexts in which we find ourselves. In the course of this endeavor, she makes one point that has particular relevance in the context of this chapter. She emphasizes that "metaphor always has the character of 'is' and 'is not': an assertion is made but as a likely account rather than a definition."[70] What she means by this is that when Christians say, for example, that "God is mother," the implication is not that God is a literal mother—with literal breasts and a literal uterus, for example. Instead, we are using a category that is familiar to us and suggests certain characteristics (not always in evidence in every mother, obviously) that are generally true: mothers are loving, life-giving, nurturing, protective, etc. Then, by analogy, we ascribe those characteristics to God as well—asserting at the same time that God is both like mothers we know and unlike any human mother, in that God surpasses all human experience of motherhood.

---

68. Ibid.

69. Ibid., 36. Johnson emphasizes this point even more succinctly in her later book, *Quest for the Living God: Mapping Frontiers in the Theology of God* (New York: Continuum, 2011), in which she writes, "dead metaphors make good idols" (p. 20).

70. Sallie McFague, *Models of God: Theology for an Ecological, Nuclear Age* (Philadelphia: Fortress Press, 1987), 33.

This simple example evidences how all language for God is incomplete, and why we must continually press for more and varied images for God, both to enhance and expand our understanding of who God is, and better to envision the many ways God comes to us and is in relationship to us. In this way, we come to see that our language for God is never perfect, never complete, and always in process. *And*, far from being a loss, this is actually a gift, in that it not only allows, but actually encourages Christians to continue to imagine and reimagine God in every new context, in every situation, responding to God's continued self-revelation that is also never-ending.

Elizabeth Johnson makes this process clear in her book, *Quest for the Living God: Mapping Frontiers in the Theology of God*, in what she calls three "ground rules for the journey." She argues that when seeking to describe and define God, Christians first must always keep in mind that "the reality of the living God is an ineffable mystery beyond all telling."[71] That is, God is always more than we can know, always more than we can describe, and always lies outside our grasp. As soon as we forget that and think that we have captured the essence of God in one particular word or image, we have ceased talking about the living God and are instead worshiping an idol. Second, Christians must remember that "no expression for God can be taken literally."[72] She uses the Catholic tradition of analogy to describe how this works: first, language for God affirms something positive, in the way that "God is mother" affirms God's loving care for humanity; second, language for God negates the limitations of that image, asserting that God does not exhibit the weaknesses and sinfulness human mothers exhibit. Then, finally, language for God "negates the negation," affirming the image in a "supereminent" way, saying that God is the source and font of all perfect motherhood, existing as "mother" in a way we can only imagine.[73] She concludes by citing Aquinas, arguing that "we see the necessity of giving to God many names."[74] That is, "since no one term alone is absolute or adequate, a positive revelry of symbols pours forth to express divine being."[75]

Now, practically, why is all this significant? One of the most important real-world explanations of why a proper understanding and use of metaphorical language for God is of such critical importance is that "God-language is more about *relationship* than definition."[76] What that means is that every image we

---

71. Johnson, *Quest for the Living God*, 17.

72. Ibid., 18.

73. Ibid., 18.

74. Ibid., 21.

75. Ibid.

76. Clifford, *Introducing Feminist Theology*, 95, my emphasis.

use to describe God also suggests a mode of relationship for God and creation, a specific way in which God acts towards us, and a specific way we are called to respond to God. And, frankly, some of these ways are not only more authentic to the God revealed to us in scripture, but also healthier and more life-giving—both for humanity and the whole cosmos. Therefore, when we unnecessarily restrict language for God to one narrow set of images, we risk not only distorting and misrepresenting God, but also alienating and excluding those for whom specific images do not facilitate a positive transformative relationship. This is why Thistlethwaite endorses Caroline Walker Bynum's contention that any time we use an image for God, we must ask the question: "For whom does it mean?"[77] By this, she is pointing to the fact that "what" an image means cannot be divorced from those who have determined that meaning and sanctioned it. Certain images invest power and authority in certain groups of people—and divest power and authority from others. Language for God is not—and has never been—neutral.

Islam: The Ninety-Nine Names of God

In several places in the Qur'an, the idea of the "many beautiful names of God" is mentioned: for example, "All the names of God are beautiful . . ." (7:180); ". . . all His names are beautiful" (17:110); and "God: There is no god but He. To Him belong the attributes most beautiful" (20:8). These passages inspired a practice in which ninety-nine attributes of God's perfection were chosen, each of which is found in the Qur'an, and codified into a list that is often memorized and used in personal prayer—typically with a set of thirty-three beads called *subha*. The most famous explication of the names is found in a treatise by Abu Hamid al-Ghazali (1058–1111), who was asked by a "brother in God" to "elucidate the meanings of the most beautiful names of God."[78] These names are as follows:[79]

1. Allah
2. Al-Ākhir—The Last
3. Al-Awwah—The First
4. Al-'Adl—The Just
5. Al-'Afū—The Effacer of Sins
6. Al-'Alī—The Most High

---

77. As quoted in Thistlethwaite, "On the Trinity," 117.

78. Al-Ghazali, *The Ninety-Nine Beautiful Names of God*, trans. David B. Burrell and Nazih Daher (Cambridge: Islamic Texts Society, 1992), 1.

79. Ibid., 197–200.

7. Al-'Alīm—The Omniscient
8. Al-'Aẓīm—The Tremendous
9. Al-'Azīz—The Eminent
10. Al-Badī'—The Absolute Cause
11. Al-Bā'ith—The Raiser of the Dead
12. Al-Bāqī—The Everlasting
13. Al- Bāri'—The Producer
14. Al-Barr—The Doer of Good
15. Al-Baṣīr—The All-Seeing
16. Al-Bāsiṭ—He Who Expands
17. Al-Bāṭin—The Hidden
18. Al-Ḍārr—The Punisher
19. Dhu'l-Jalāl wa'l-Ikrām—The Lord of Majesty and Generosity
20. Al-Fattāḥ—The Opener
21. Al-Ghaffār—He Who Is Full of Forgiveness
22. Al-Ghafūr—The All-Forgiving
23. Al-Ghanī—The Rich
24. Al-Hādī—The Guide
25. Al-Ḥafīẓ—The All-Preserver
26. Al-Ḥakam—The Arbitrator
27. Al-Ḥakīm—The Wise
28. Al-Ḥalīm—The Indulgent
29. Al-Ḥamīd—The Praised
30. Al-Ḥaqq—The Truth
31. Al-Ḥasīb—The Reckoner
32. Al-Ḥayy—The Living
33. Al-Jabbār—The Compeller
34. Al-Jalīl—The Majestic
35. Al-Jāmi'—The Uniter
36. Al-Kabīr—The Great
37. Al-Karīm—The Generous
38. Al-Khabīr—The Totally Aware
39. Al-Khāfiḍ—The Abaser
40. Al-Khāliq—The Creator
41. Al-Laṭif—The Benevolent
42. Al-Mājid—The Magnificent
43. Al-Majīd—The All-Glorious
44. Al-Malik—The King
45. Mālik al-Mulk—The King of Absolute Sovereignty
46. Al-Māni'—The Protector
47. Al-Matīn—The Firm

48. Al-Mu'akhkhir—The Postponer
49. Al-Mubdi'—The Beginner
50. Al-Mudhill—He Who Humbles
51. Al-Mughnī—The Enricher
52. Al-Muhaymin—The Guardian
53. Al-Muhṣī—The Knower of Each Separate Thing
54. Al-Muhyī—The Life-Giver
55. Al-Muʿīd—The Restorer
56. Al-Muʿizz—The Honourer
57. Al-Mujīb—The Answerer of Prayers
58. Al-Mu'mim—The Faithful
59. Al-Mumīt—The Slayer
60. Al-Muntaqim—The Avenger
61. Al-Muqaddim—The Promoter
62. Al-Muqīt—The Nourisher
63. Al-Muqsiṭ—The Equitable
64. Al-Muqtadir—The All-Determiner
65. Al-Muṣawwir—The Fashioner
66. Al-Mutakabbir—The Proud
67. Al-Mutaʿālī—The Exalted
68. Al-Nāfiʿ—He Who Benefits
69. Al-Nūr—Light
70. Al-Qābiḍ—He Who Contracts
71. Al-Qādir—The All-Powerful
72. Al-Qahhār—The Dominator
73. Al-Qawī—The Strong
74. Al-Qayyūm—The Self-Existing
75. Al-Quddūs—The Holy
76. Al-Rāfiʿ—The Exalter
77. Al-Rahīm—The Merciful
78. Al-Rahmān—The Infinitely Good
79. Al-Raqīb—The All-Observant
80. Al-Rashīd—The Right in Guidance
81. Al-Ra'ūf—The All-Pitying
82. Al-razzāq—The Provider
83. Al-Ṣabūr—The Patient
84. Al-Salām—The Flawless
85. Al-Ṣamad—The Eternal
86. As-Samīʿ—The All-Hearing
87. Al-Shahīd—The Universal Witness
88. Al-Shakūr—The Grateful

89. Al-Tawwāb—The Ever-Relenting
90. Al-Wadūd—The Loving-Kind
91. Al-Wahhāb—The Bestower
92. Al-Wāḥid—The Unique
93. Al-Wājid—The Resourceful
94. Al-Wakīl—The Trustee
95. Al-Wālī—The Ruler
96. Al-Walī—The Patron
97. Al-Wārith—The Inheritor
98. Al-Wāsiʿ—The Vast
99. Al-Ẓāhir—The Manifest

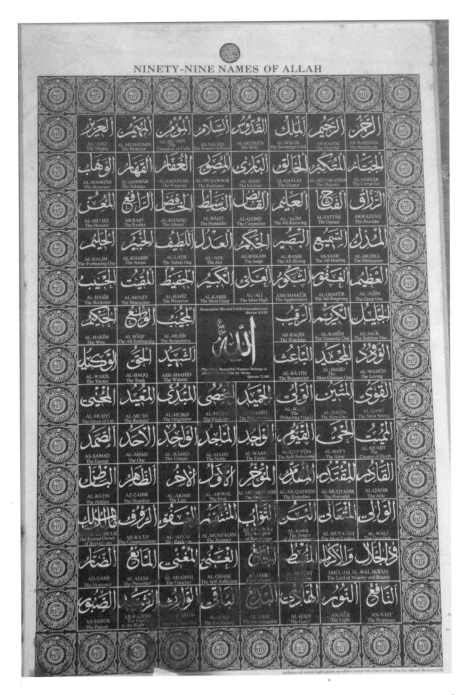

Figure 5.1. The ninety-nine names of Allah are shown here in the original Arabic. Courtesy of Wikimedia Commons.

What one notices about these names is that very few of them suggest a specifically male image. Instead, the names are primarily verbal descriptions: they image a God doing something, but that God could be viewed in a variety of embodiments—young, old, black or white, male or female (although, to be fair, the Qur'an uses only male imagery and language for Allah). Further, they suggest a complex deity that does not easily fit into one particular type or portrait: Allah is both the Life-Giver and the Slayer, both the Patient and the Avenger, both the Manifest and the Hidden. This complexity also suggests an abundance of images that resist reduction into one particular form or category.

Hinduism: The Role of the Goddess

One of the well-known aspects of Hinduism is the role of the goddess. "Shaktism" (*Shakti* is the female personification of divine creative power) or goddess worship is, for many Hindus, a central aspect of religious practice; and in the same way that the Divine is seen as both one and many, it is accurate to talk about both the Goddess, singular—that is, Devi, or Mahadevi—and "goddesses," plural. There are myriad goddesses in India, from local goddesses, unknown outside a limited geographical area but still worshiped in "small, inconspicuous places,"[80] to pan-Indian goddesses, whose worship is ubiquitous in both India and in the Indian diaspora.

There are two broad categories of goddesses. "First are those goddesses who generally manifest as benevolent, gentle, and life-giving; they are regarded as cool goddesses. Second are those who often become malevolent, terrifying, and lustful; these are the hot goddesses."[81] They have starkly different appearances and activities, and they solicit different types of relationships with their devotees. For example, Axel Michaels, using the language of "wild and mild" aspects of the goddesses, notes that the mild goddesses typically receive fruit and sweets, while the "wild" goddesses typically receive eggs, blood, and even animal sacrifice.[82]

The most important "cool" goddesses are those whose primary representation is as the consort, or wife, of a god: Sarasvati with Brahma; Parvati with Shiva; and Lakshmi with Vishnu. Each of these goddesses is depicted as placid, beautiful, benign, and gracious. In addition to their role as consorts, however, they also each have their own festivals and are frequently worshiped independently as well. This reflects the fact that "the

---

80. Michaels, *Hinduism Past and Present*, 223.

81. Muesse, *The Hindu Traditions*, 157–58.

82. Michaels, *Hinduism Past and Present*, 225.

goddesses are powerful in their own right and govern domains of particular concern to human beings"[83]—wealth, learning, and music, for example.

Of the "hot" goddesses, certainly Kali is the most well known, and her imagery is unmistakable. She often is worshiped as a consort of Shiva, although she also is worshiped alone; and in some cases she is even seen as superior to him. She always is depicted with dark skin, a lolling tongue, fangs instead of teeth, a ferocious stare, and a mouth streaming blood. She wears a necklace of human skulls and sometimes cobras on her arms. Even today, animal sacrifices are offered at her temples, and she revels in death and destruction. Why, then, is she worshiped? For the truth about reality she reveals:

> To be Kali's child is to suffer, but to know the source of that suffering. The Shakta tradition holds that Kali does not always give what one wants or expects. What devotees experience as cruelty forces them to reflect on the true nature of the phenomenal world, as well as of their own selves, and ultimately to transcend them.[84]

Durga is the second "wild" goddess that is widely worshiped. Durga typically is represented as a powerful warrior, sitting on a tiger, with different celestial weapons in each arm. This particular image comes from a well-known story in which she slays the mighty buffalo demon Mahisha, whom even the great gods Shiva and Vishnu were unable to kill. Their solution was to infuse Durga with their power and weapons; so armed, she was able to successfully vanquish Mahisha and his demon army.

Finally, it is worth mentioning that the goddess also can be personified in aniconic aspects as well. For example, as mentioned previously, the Ganges River is typically referred to as a goddess, *Ganga Mata*, the Mother Ganges. In addition, the earth itself can be worshiped as a goddess; in particular, the country of India is called *Bharat Mata*, Mother India. In fact, in Varanasi, there is a temple dedicated to *Bharat Mata*, which, instead of an anthropomorphic image of the divine, houses as its central image a map of India.

---

83. Muesse, *The Hindu Traditions*, 158–59.
84. Ibid., 161–63.

KATAPHATIC AND APOPHATIC LANGUAGE FOR GOD

One helpful way that Christians traditionally have categorized language for God is using the following two types: *kataphatic* attributes of God, and *apophatic* attributes of God. Both of these words come from the Greek: *kataphatic* comes from *kataphatikos*, which means "positive"; and, according to Alister McGrath, in this particular context "it denotes an approach to theology which holds that positive statements may indeed be made about God."[85] By contrast, apophatic comes from *apophatikos*, which means "negative"; and "it denotes an approach to theology which stresses that we cannot use human language to refer to God, who ultimately lies beyond such language."[86] Another set of terms that point to the same idea are *"via positiva"*—the positive way of thinking about God; and *"via negativa"*—the negative way. McGrath notes that while both ways of describing God have been used broadly in the Christian tradition, the generalization is also true that "the apophatic approach tends to be found in Eastern Orthodoxy, whereas the Western theological tradition has tended to be much more kataphatical."[87] Both ways of thinking about God are important, and both need to be held together so that they can work complementarily in the human quest for God.

Kataphatic language works by analogy, applying positive qualities to God that we know from our experience in creation. Thomas Aquinas describes how this functions in his *Summa Theologiae*, writing that from the point of view of our use of a word (though not of its meaning), we start with our human experience, and apply that word to God analogically.[88] So, for example, since we know from human experience what love is like, we can ascribe the quality of love to God, stating affirmatively that God is loving (recognizing, however, as noted previously, that God's love is perfected and supereminent in a way we can barely fathom). In the same way, Christians describe God as good, life-giving, merciful, motherly, holy, etc. These are all kataphatic attributes of God, and all seek to say something positive about God, thereby deepening our understanding of who God is.

The value of kataphatic attributes of God is that they enable us to function with some image, some concept of God—even though it is limited and imperfect—with whom we can be in relationship: to whom we can pray, for

---

85. Alister McGrath, *Christian Theology: An Introduction*, 5th ed. (Malden, MA: Wiley/Blackwell, 2011), 188.

86. Ibid.

87. Ibid.

88. Thomas Aquinas, *Summa Theologiae*, vol. 3, *Knowing and Naming God*, 1a, 12–13, trans. Herbert McCabe, O.P. (London: Blackfriars, 1964), question 13, article 6, p. 71.

example, and whom we can share with others in witness and proclamation. If all we can say about God is that God is nothing like anything we can know, nothing like anything we can imagine, nothing like anything we can understand, we are left with an empty cipher that can hardly have any significance or meaning in daily life. Instead, kataphatic language invites creative thinking that is always evolving, responding to contemporary human experiences and relating those experiences to an understanding of God. Kataphatic language encourages Christians to say more, not less, about God.

Yet there is a danger on the other side as well—the danger of too much familiarity and theological arrogance; and it is this danger from which apophatic language seeks to protect us. Apophatic language accentuates God's mystery and transcendence by emphasizing God's difference from creation—the radical otherness of God, and the ultimate unknowability of God. Ted Peters writes that "the preeminent apophatic attribute of God is ineffability," which points to the ultimately indescribable nature of God.[89] McGrath makes the point this way: ". . . while we can indeed say that God exists, human language is totally unable to comprehend God's nature. It does not have the capacity to enfold God. It is impossible for human reason to grasp the nature of God. . . ."[90] The theological value of these statements is that they caution humans to avoid the temptation to presume too much about what we can know and what we can say about God. The ever-present danger is that humans continually attempt to create God in our image; fashioning a God who looks like us, pleases our sensibilities, and blesses our vision of how we think the world should work. Apophatic language for God keeps us humble, and always mindful of our own finitude and limitations. Apophatic language encourages us to say less about God, rather than more.

5. A LOVING GOD: THE HEART OF GOD'S IDENTITY

To conclude this chapter and prepare for the next, which will treat human beings, it seems appropriate to end on an attribute of God, which, by wide consensus in the Christian tradition, is thought to indicate the very essence of the Divine being, and the core of who God is in relationship to God's creation. That attribute, of course, is love. That God not only loves, but *is* love itself, comes out of Scripture, particularly 1 John 4:16: "God is love, and those who abide in love abide in God, and God abides in them."

89. Ted Peters, *God—The World's Future*, 2nd ed. (Minneapolis: Fortress Press, 2000), 93.
90. McGrath, *Christian Theology*, 188.

Love, of course, needs relationship: one can say that one loves oneself, but if oneself is all there is, it becomes a rather meaningless designation. One can really only love oneself in the larger context of relationships with others. Thus the fact that God not only has relationships but *is*, fundamentally, relationality itself, is of central importance here, and is rooted in the triune nature of God: in confessing a triune God, the Christian faith asserts that God in God's very being exists in communion, in relationship. And, what's more, this communion is not neutral, but it is a communion of love.

Augustine, writing on the Trinity, emphasizes two things inherent in this doctrine. First, we can best understand the triune God as an expression of love: "the lover, what is being loved, and love."[91] Second, in loving our neighbor, we also love God; love of our brothers and sisters is inextricable from love of God: ". . . if a [hu]man loves his neighbor, it follows that above all he loves love itself. . . . So it follows that above all he loves God."[92] Love of God and love of each other are inherently connected; and human love is both inspired by and an expression of God's love.

The nature of this love is also important. In *On the Mystery*, Catherine Keller expands and elaborates on this idea of God as love, using categories found in process theology that describe two different aspects of God's creative, loving activity in the world. Eros, or desire, is what she calls "the creative love of God," which can be described as "a cosmic appetite for becoming, for beauty and intensity of experience."[93] This is the love of God that creates out of the sheer joy of seeing something new develop, out of the thrill of watching the movement and growth of God's creatures, out of the passion for God's children. Keller writes that this creative eros "is a lure to our own becoming, a call to actualize the possibilities for greater beauty and intensity in our own lives."[94] This is God's love rousing us and leading us into deeper experiences of God's grace and mercy, and new paths of opportunity in our life with God. This is God's love at its most insistent, its most urgent, its most creative and artistic.

Agape—spiritual or selfless love—is what she calls the "responsive love of God": "The Eros attracts, it calls: it is the invitation. The Agape responds to whatever we have become; in com/passion it feels our feelings: it is the reception."[95] This is God's love abiding with us, bearing us up and inspiring our response to God's initiative in our lives. This is God's love mending our

91. Augustine, *The Trinity*, trans. Edmund Hill, O.P. (Hyde Park, NY: New City Press, 1991), 255.

92. Ibid., 252.

93. Catherine Keller, *On the Mystery: Discerning God in Process* (Minneapolis: Fortress Press, 2008), 99.

94. Ibid.

95. Ibid.

brokenness, forgiving our rejection of God's love and the love of others, and guiding us with gentle wisdom and patience, tuning us to a more faithful hearing of God's call in every moment. Together, these twin movements of God's love, pouring out into creation, reaching into the heart of every creature, leading Keller to suggest that "[p]erhaps every creature in a creature's own way is *called*. Persons personally, animals bestially, plants vegetably. . . ."[96] And in this way, each creature is able to experience and respond to God's love in a way appropriate to each creature. This puts the love of God not only at the center of God's being, but at the nexus of the universe as well, radiating out, connecting each of us with another, connecting all of us together. What this means for human existence will be taken up in more detail in the following chapter.

Buddhism: The Concept of Upaya

The concept of *upaya*—or "skillful/expedient means"—mentioned in Chapter 3, has particular relevance in this context of describing God as love. It relates to the bodhisattva path, developed specifically in Mahayana Buddhism, and, as noted earlier, it points to the willingness—indeed, eagerness—of the Buddha to do anything, to appear anywhere at any time, in order to teach human beings the truth about reality, thereby leading them to enlightenment. Paul Williams defines it this way: ". . . the doctrine of skillful means maintains that the Buddha himself adapted his teaching to the level of his hearers."[97] Yet it is not the adaptation itself that is important here; rather, it is the reason for the adaption that makes it worthy of note. Again Williams: "The Buddha teaches out of his infinite compassion for sentient beings. All teachings are exactly appropriate to the level of those for whom they were intended."[98] The point here is that compassion overrides every other concern: nothing is more important than rescuing those caught in ignorance and suffering, and even if the Buddha—or a bodhisattva—has to violate the Buddhist code of ethics, he or she will do so, if it means bringing a sentient being to enlightenment. Some texts even describe bodhisattvas appearing to animals, to teach them as well.

Two well-known examples where we see compassion placed above ethics are found in the *Upayakausalya Sutra*. First is the story in which a celibate monk commits the great sin of sexual intercourse with a poor girl who has threatened to kill herself (a terrible act that would cause her

---

96. Ibid., 100.

97. Paul Williams, *Mahayana Buddhism: The Doctrinal Foundations* (London: Routledge, 1989), 143.

98. Ibid., 144.

great suffering upon rebirth) if her love is not returned. The second is the story of a man (really the Buddha in a previous life) who commits the even greater sin of killing another man, who, if he had been allowed to live, would have killed five hundred men, and thus fallen into the lowest realm of hell. Since this act was motivated purely out of compassion, "not only did the Bodhisattva progress spiritually and avoid hell, but the potential murderer was also reborn in a heavenly realm."[99] In Mahayana Buddhism, compassion, combined with wisdom, is both one's overriding concern and the defining motivation for all action.

Perhaps the finest example of *upaya* in action can be found in the Lotus Sutra, one of the most popular and well-known texts in East Asian Buddhism. While its earliest origins are unknown, the earliest translation we have of the Lotus Sutra is a Chinese translation made in 255 ce. The definitive translation, however, is that of Kumarajiva, made in 406.[100] The sutra begins with Ananda, a close disciple of the Buddha, present at all the Buddha's sermons and therefore the most trusted witness to his teachings, saying, "This is what I heard . . ." Thus it purports to be an account from the Buddha's own life and to carry the authority of the Buddha himself.

In the various chapters of the sutra, the point is made that everyone possesses Buddha-nature, and all can hope for enlightenment—if only one is taught correctly, and one's innate potential is developed. Thus the bodhisattva practice contains an inherent ethical mandate to use whatever "skillful means" (*upaya*) are at one's disposal to help others attain their potential and live with wisdom and compassion. The text narrates a variety of stories to illustrate this principle, most notably the famous "story of the carts." In this story a rich man lives in an enormous, but rotting mansion, with only one gate. A fire breaks out in the house, and he is unable to get his children—who are blissfully playing, unaware of the danger—to come out of the house. The text reads, "At that time the rich man had this thought: The house is already in flames from this huge fire. If I and my sons do not get out at once, we are certain to be burned. I must now invent some expedient means that will make it possible for the children to escape harm."[101] So, he bribes them with wonderful descriptions of a goat-cart, an

99. Ibid., 145.

100. *The Lotus Sutra*, trans. Burton Watson (New York: Columbia University Press, 1993), ix.

101. Ibid., 57.

ox-cart, and a deer-cart; and, so tempted, they rush out of the house and are saved. The moral of the story?

> . . . the Thus Come One [a name for the Buddha] is like this. That is, he a father to all the world. . . . He is endowed with expedient means and the paramita of wisdom, his great pity and great compassion are constant and unflagging; at all times he seeks what is good and will bring benefit to all. . . . [The Buddha] . . . thinks to himself, I am the father of living beings and I should rescue them from their sufferings and give them the joy of the measureless and boundless Buddha wisdom so that they may find their enjoyment in that.[102]

It is not only the Buddha who acts this way; bodhisattvas also are avid practitioners of *upaya*. And, what's more, the sutra teaches that all Buddhists are to act this way in the world, nurturing and deepening their own practice for the sake and salvation of others—*all* others in need.

Judaism: God and the Covenant

Standing at the heart of the relationship between the Jewish people and God is the covenant, a rich and complex metaphor that gets to the core of who God is, and also speaks to the origins of the Israelites as well. The Hebrew scriptures testify to this reality: "It has been said that Israelites are not 'the hero' in the *Tanakh*; rather, it is the ongoing story of a *relationship*, between God and a people God has cultivated. In most religious systems, gods appear as more powerful than humans, while in Judaism the relationship takes on the form of a covenant, or *berit*. God and Israel agree to commit to each other, even though it is not an agreement between equals. . . ."[103] One of the most important aspects of God in Judaism, then, is that God freely and willingly binds Himself (the *Tanakh* uses male pronouns exclusively for God) to a specific people, a reality most clearly signified in the covenantal formula "they shall be My people and I shall be their God," found in Exod. 6:7 and Ezek. 14:11, among other places.

102. Ibid., 59.

103. Harvey E. Goldberg, "Judaism as a Religious System," in *The Cambridge Guide to Jewish History, Religion, and Culture*, ed. Judith R. Baskin and Kenneth Seeskin (Cambridge: Cambridge University Press, 2010), 289.

This covenant begins with the call of Abram in Genesis 12, but it is formalized in what is called "The Book of the Covenant," which comprises the verses found in Exod. 20:19–23:33, immediately following the theophany and giving of the Law to Moses on Sinai. *The Jewish Study Bible* notes that the name "Book of the Covenant" comes from a phrase found in Exod. 24:7: "Then [Moses] took the record of the covenant and read it aloud to the people. And they said, 'All that the LORD has spoken we will faithfully do!'" The commentators go on to note that "[t]he most literal translation would be 'we will do and listen,' and the midrash inferred from this that the people trusted Yahweh so thoroughly that they committed themselves to obeying His commands before they even heard their contents."[104]

Central to this covenant—and the book of Exodus as a whole—are the motifs of deliverance and presence,[105] and it is clear when the Hebrew scriptures are read as a whole that these themes are central to God's relationship with God's people. Even though God punishes the people when they turn from God, God's patience is never exhausted, and there is always another chance, another opportunity for the people to respond in kind to God's steadfast faithfulness and love. Additionally, God never ceases to listen to the cries of God's people, and respond to them when they are in need: the paradigmatic example is, of course, the deliverance of the people out of Pharaoh's hand in Egypt. Further, the covenant also includes God's promise to dwell with God's people; and the instructions for building the Tabernacle, given in Exod. 25:1–31.17, are designed to enable God to reside in a tangible, concrete way with God's people, "that they may experience God's guiding presence."[106]

This scriptural witness, then, leads Walter Brueggemann to argue that "the distinctiveness of 'God' in Old Testament tradition concerns YHWH's deep resolve to be a God *in relation*—in relation to Israel, in relation to creation, in relation to members of Israelite society and of the human community more generally."[107] And, because God willingly and freely

104. *The Jewish Study Bible*, ed. Adele Berlin and Marc Zvi Brettler (Oxford: Oxford University Press, 2004), 162.

105. See Walter Brueggemann, *An Introduction to the Old Testament* (Louisville: Westminster John Knox, 2003), 65ff.

106. Ibid., 163–64.

107. Walter Brueggemann, *An Unsettling God: The Heart of the Hebrew Bible* (Minneapolis: Fortress Press, 2009), 4.

enters into this relationship, God also then reveals Godself as a God fully dynamic and interactive, "always emerging in new ways in response to the requirements of the relationship at hand."[108] Brueggemann notes how this means that God also willingly suffers and makes Godself vulnerable in relationship—not only acting, but also being acted upon. This makes clear that the covenantal relationship God has chosen with Israel entails both love and suffering on God's part, and that God willingly accepts both for the sake of Israel.

Brueggemann goes on to explain how there are three verbs that are typically used by Israel to explain its understanding of who God is in the relationship: 'ahab (love), bahar (choose), and ḥashaq (set one's heart).[109] In Israel's view, then, God is one who, first and foremost, loves Israel superlatively, with an everlasting love (Jer. 31:3); has made Israel special in choosing Israel for this unique relationship with God; and finally, demonstrates a "personal commitment that has a dimension of affection and in which YHWH is emotionally extended for the sake of Israel."[110] Even though this final verb is used only twice, in Deut. 7:7 and 10:15, it is significant because "the verb ḥashaq has strong, passionate emotional overtones. The term bespeaks a lover who is powerfully in pursuit of the partner, perhaps in lustful ways."[111] God deeply and passionately loves God's people, and in responding through the upholding of their side of the covenant, the Jewish people deeply and passionately love God in return.

GOD'S POWER, JUDGMENT, AND OMNISCIENCE

Many of the traditional attributes of God rely on an image of God as an unassailable monarch, who exists in a self-chosen bubble of immutability and supremacy. This God controls every aspect of creation, knows from the beginning of time everything that is going to happen, and is unmoved by any of it. This God is an impartial judge, a changeless ruler, and an all-knowing, all-seeing king of the universe. The problem is that such a God is not actually capable of love or relationship; and it is hard to square that image of God with the God of the incarnation: a God who was born in poverty, ate with prostitutes

108. Ibid.
109. Ibid., 20.
110. Ibid., 22–23.
111. Ibid., 22.

and outcasts, and suffered a humiliating, torturous death on a cross in order to rescue from death and destruction those who could not ever save themselves.

Thus in many ways, a stronger, richer understanding of God as love provides a much more helpful lens for viewing all the other attributes of God, and can serve well as the standard by which the others are measured. For example, it enables Christians to appreciate how God's omniscience might be better described as seeing and knowing all possibilities at every moment, for every creature, every relationship—but not actually determining which of those possibilities will be chosen. (Relevant here is Elizabeth Johnson's endorsement of John Haught's suggestion that "we should no longer think of God as having a *plan* for the evolving universe, but rather a *vision*."[112]) In a similar way, it enables Christians to accept God's judgment as falling on all humans equally—for our failure to love God and love our neighbor—but at the same time being inextricably linked with God's mercy and forgiveness. And, finally, it makes possible a celebration of how God responds and even changes in relationship, and is profoundly affected by the joys and sorrows experienced in creation. Love is not simply one more in a long line of attributes of God: it is the definitive word of who God is, and how God has revealed Godself to us; and it is therefore the definitive word for humanity's existence as well.

INTERRELIGIOUS QUESTIONS FOR FURTHER DISCUSSION

1. What kind of insights and challenges are raised by the Islamic teaching of the Qur'an as the literal word of God, particularly for Christian thinking on scripture and Jesus?
2. How is Christian monotheism different from and similar to that found in Islam? How is it different from and similar to the Hindu understanding of the Divine as both One and Many?
3. Looking at the list of the ninety-nine names of God in Islam, which ones resonate with your understanding of the God revealed in the Hebrew scriptures and the New Testament? What "names" of God would you choose for such a list?
4. How does the concept of the Goddess in Hinduism both challenge and inform a Christian understanding of God?
5. Is there a parallel to the Buddhist doctrine of *upaya* in Christianity? Is this a helpful concept for thinking about how God reveals Godself to humanity?

112. Johnson, *Quest for the Living God*, 197.

6. How is the concept of "covenant" unique to Judaism? Is it helpful in a Christian context for thinking about how God relates to humanity?

6

Human Being, Being Human

INTRODUCTION

Of the many things the Christian church says about the human being, there are three affirmations that stand at the core of any Christian anthropology. Sequentially, they are as follows: first, human beings are created good, in the image of God. This pronouncement of goodness is the first word God says to humanity, and this ontological goodness of human nature endures, in spite of the indelible stain of sin that distorts it. Second, human beings are fundamentally, profoundly, and inescapably sinners. The Christian doctrine of sin points to the fact that human sinfulness is not merely a series of mistakes—even bad mistakes—which, with proper training and knowledge, can be fixed. Instead, sin warps the core of who we are, and we are powerless to "right" ourselves on our own. Third, human beings are justified and forgiven in the life, death, and resurrection of Jesus Christ; in Jesus Christ, humans are both empowered and freed to live a life of love, in service to one's neighbor for the glory of God. Together, these statements form the core of what Christians affirm to be true about human nature.[1] In what follows, I expand upon each one of these, elaborating on what these assertions mean for human life in the twenty-first century, and asking what Christians might learn from engagement with non-Christian doctrine and practice in each of these areas.

THE QUESTION OF THE HUMAN BEING IN THE TWENTY-FIRST CENTURY

As was described in the previous chapter, Christianity asserts that human beings find their core meaning and purpose in relationship to God. Yet, the way in which this meaning is sought and found varies greatly from time and

---

1. Daniel Migliore argues something similar in chapter seven of *Faith Seeking Understanding: An Introduction to Christian Theology*, 2nd ed. (Grand Rapids: Eerdmans, 2004), 139ff.

place. Therefore, while humanity's quest for meaning and self-understanding is perpetual and timeless, the shape of the quest itself is dependent to a large degree on the context: the where and the when of the questioner. This means that while there certainly are similarities across continents and centuries, each society and generation has the responsibility to frame the question of human existence in its own way.

Many argue that in the late twentieth- and now early twenty-first-century Western context, the quest for meaning has taken on a deeply existential character. Paul Tillich described this well in the second volume of his *Systematic Theology*. He writes, "The state of existence is the state of estrangement. [The human being] is estranged from the ground of his being [by which Tillich means God], from other beings, and from himself."[2] The result is that, as Robert Kolb argues, "[t]he critical question at the end of the twentieth century, at least in the West, is not the sixteenth-century question, 'How can I find a gracious God?' It expresses itself in different forms: 'Who am I?' 'What am I doing here?'"[3] This is still true today, where the realization of one's estrangement results in a deep longing for connection and transformation, relationship and community, and meaning and relevance. What does contemporary Christianity have to say in the face of such longing?

The goal of this chapter is to provide a long answer to that question, but for those who are looking for a brief synopsis of a mainline Christian response a good place to look is Martin Luther's Small Catechism, which moves in a sweeping arc from problem to solution—that is, from law to gospel. Luther described it this way: "The Ten Commandments are like the diagnosis; they disclose the sickness of sin because believers are forced to realize they can never perfectly obey them. The Apostles' Creed identifies the remedy. . . . The Lord's Prayer and the sacraments provide the treatment; prayer, absolution, baptism, and the Lord's Supper are means through which the Holy Spirit applies the remedy of redemption to us."[4]

Briefly, then, the order of the main parts of the Catechism is designed to first acknowledge and emphasize that there is a rupture in human existence: a void, an ache, an alienation. It does this by beginning with the Ten Commandments, the law. Kolb describes it this way: "The decalog does no more than to pose the question, 'Why do I feel uncomfortable in my own skin?'

---

2. Paul Tillich, *Systematic Theology*, vol. 2 (Chicago: University of Chicago Press, 1957), 44.

3. Robert Kolb, "'That I May Be His Own': The Anthropology of Luther's Explanation of the Creed," *Concordia Journal* (January 1995): 28.

4. Günther Gassmann and Scott Hendrix, *Fortress Introduction to the Lutheran Confessions* (Minneapolis: Fortress Press, 1999), 166.

'What is this pressure which makes me dissatisfied with life as I experience it? Where does it come from? Who or what has put the squeeze on me?' These are all extensions of the question, 'Who am I, really?'"[5] Once this reality has been confirmed, it moves to the gospel—first and foremost the Apostles' Creed, where God's love and grace are revealed in triune form: in the first article, we read the good news of God's creative love that establishes humanity in a vast network of graced existence; in the second article, we read of God's liberating love in the life, death, and resurrection of Jesus Christ that redeems and preserves human existence even beyond death; and finally, in the third article, we read of God's sustaining love that makes us holy and enables us to live lives of joyful service in community. The Small Catechism then concludes with the means through which the Holy Spirit preserves and sustains Christians in their life with Christ.

This is the "short" answer Christianity provides to the meaning of human existence and life; there is, however, much, much more to be said, as the three major components of Christian anthropology—human goodness, sinfulness, and justification and forgiveness—warrant further exploration and elaboration.

HUMAN GOODNESS: "INSCAPE," "INSTRESS," AND GERARD MANLEY HOPKINS

Even though human beings are profoundly and ineluctably marked by sin (more about that shortly), humans also are inherently and indelibly good. The former is humanity's own fault—individually and collectively, but the latter is the result of being created by God. God is not the author of evil—God is pure goodness, and thus all that God creates is good: this is the point of the repeated phrase ". . . and God saw that it was good" that caps each episode of God's creative work in the first creation story in Genesis. Therefore, regardless of how sin, brokenness, and malice mar God's creation in ways large and small, its goodness remains, a defiant witness to both God's continuing love and care for all God has made, and also God's promise to redeem and transform creation at the end of time.

[margin note: goodness of creation]

However, while this profession of human goodness might sound nice in theory, one might well ask for more specifics: in what way, specifically, is human goodness visible, demonstrable; and here we need something more than merely a murky reckoning of individual and/or corporate acts of kindness and mercy, which may or may not balance out individual and/or corporate acts of wickedness and deceit. To what evidence can we point that demonstrates

5. Kolb, "'That I May Be His Own,'" 31.

ontologically, rather than merely epistemologically, human goodness? As one possible answer, I suggest that one of the primary ways in which Christians are able to observe and affirm the inherent goodness of humanity is in human uniqueness and diversity; and I look to the poetic theology of Gerard Manley Hopkins to make the case.

I am aware that Hopkins might, at first glance, seem to be an odd voice to bring to the conversation. In textbooks on nineteenth-century theology, Hopkins hardly has pride of place—in fact, he is rarely mentioned at all. The big names, of course, are Friedrich Schleiermacher, G. W. F. Hegel, John Henry Newman (who was himself quite influential on Hopkins), and Albrecht Ritschl; even the poet Samuel Taylor Coleridge could be included in this list, but not Hopkins. To those of us in the twenty-first century who know and love his poetry and have a great appreciation for his theological passion and insight, this omission seems a remarkable oversight. However, when we step out of our own context and examine the situation as it was then, there is a ready explanation. In brief, Hopkins was not part of the "great conversation" of the day. He could not read German, and had little desire to engage with either Hegel or Schleiermacher. The main passion in his life was his Ignatian spirituality, and there continues to be debate today as to whether he ever fully reconciled his vocations as poet and priest. None of his poems were published until after his death, and it is only comparatively recently that his poetic genius has been justly acknowledged.

Hopkins was born in 1844, ten years after Coleridge's death. To the dismay of his parents, he was received into the Catholic Church by Newman in 1866, and entered the Jesuit Novitiate in 1868: in the same year, he burned all his earlier poems. He began writing poetry again with *The Wreck of the Deutschland*, in 1875, and wrote for the rest of his life. He was ordained as a Jesuit priest in 1877, and died in 1889 of typhoid fever. It was not until 1918 that the then-Poet Laureate of Britain, Robert Bridges, first published Hopkins's poems.

In the context of this chapter, what is most significant about Hopkins's theology is his preoccupation and fascination with the individual self, specifically the way he viewed each individual person—and indeed, each individual created animal, and all creation itself—showing forth in its very being God's grandeur (to use the title of one of his most famous poems). In many ways, this preoccupation was an important characteristic of nineteenth-century thought as a whole. Walter Ong writes, "Thanks in part to studies of Hopkins and his milieu, we have become increasingly aware of how widely fascination with particularity and the self marks 19th Century thought. It shows not only in the British Isles, but also on the Continent, where, even more than Hume, Fichte and Hegel had made the self a major focus of philosophical speculation."[6]

For Hopkins, this interest manifested in a belief that each individual "self" reflects inherently the presence, beauty, and goodness of God, especially when that "self" was doing that which it was created to do. He coined a neologism to describe what he meant by that idea—"inscape," which basically refers to the distinctive set of characteristics and abilities that both makes the being what it is and also connects it distinctively with everything else: it is the created essence of a being. It is "that which makes this oak tree this oak tree only, or this rose this rose only, or this person this person only, and not another—something unique and separate, God's infinite and incredible freshness of Creation every nanosecond of every day, world without end."[7] As a result, when one observes a "self" engaged in an activity that expresses its essence, God is both revealed and glorified; and, furthermore, when we see such a thing—*really* see it—that self also becomes a window into the Divine, giving us a glimpse of God as well.

In this moment of observation, the perceiver is joined to the perceived, and both are simultaneously linked to God; this experience he named "instress." In this way, the twin concepts of "inscape" and "instress" serve to describe the inherent goodness of each individual created being, the connection between them, and the revelatory experience of God's glory and goodness: "Perceiver and perceived landscape (inscape) are joined in such an act of sacramental participation . . . 'an instress of inscape [is] received through [the viewer's] own inscape—which transcends separateness into unity'."[8]

It is at this point that the influence of John Duns Scotus can be most clearly seen, particularly in Scotus's concept of *haecceitas*—Latin for "thisness." Basically, it refers to that which makes an individual who s/he is: it is his or her particular "essence." By emphasizing the particularity of each individual created being, Hopkins champions and celebrates the inherent goodness in each individual being that God has created, noting that each individual reveals the presence of Christ not by conforming to some universal "type" or manifesting some universal quality, but rather through the manifestation of his or her individual uniqueness.

Let me offer as an example one of his most beautiful and theologically powerful poems, "As kingfishers catch fire, dragonflies dráw fláme."

6. Walter Ong, S.J., *Hopkins, the Self, and God* (Toronto: University of Toronto Press, 1986), 3.

7. Paul Mariani, *Gerard Manley Hopkins: A Life* (New York: Viking, 2008), 110.

8. Katharine Bubel, "Nature and Wise Vision in the Poetry of Gerard Manley Hopkins, *Renascence* 62, no. 2 (Winter 2010): 123.

As kingfishers catch fire, dragonflies dráw fláme;
As tumbled over rim in roundy wells
Stones ring; like each tucked string tells, each hung bell's
Bow swung finds tongue to fling out broad its name;
Each mortal thing does one thing and the same:
Deals out that being indoors each one dwells;
Selves—goes itself; *myself* it speaks and spells,
Crying *Whát I do is me: for that I came.*
Í say more: the just man justices;
Kéeps gráce: thát keeps all his goings graces;
Acts in God's eye what in God's eye he is—
Chríst—for Christ plays in ten thousand places,
Lovely in limbs, and lovely in eyes not his
To the Father through the features of men's faces.[9]

In describing this poem, Paul Mariani writes, "The kingfishers sonnet is about the Scotist individuation of things, where once again the opening lines flame out, and where things reveal themselves. . . . But more: it is about Christ playing—acting in all seriousness, at the same time delighting in the never-again-to be-repeated distinctiveness of human beings in ten thousand separate places and revealed in the faces of those who keep God's graces."[10] Human sin may be strong, human alienation from God may be profound, and human brokenness may be, at times, shocking in its breadth. Yet—and this "yet" is of critical theological import—that sin does not, cannot obliterate the face of Christ that is manifest in human beings in all their diversity and individuality. In Hopkins's theological poetry, then, we see a beautiful, compelling affirmation of the goodness of humanity—indeed, the goodness of all creation—in "God's variegated abundance," the "splendor and grandeur and goodness"[11] of all God has made. No amount of sin, regardless of its power and devastation, can destroy this grandeur, this goodness.

IRENAEUS AND THE GOODNESS OF BODIES

In today's context, as we affirm human goodness, what must be remembered and highlighted is the goodness of human *bodies*, specifically, which sometimes

---

9. Gerard Manley Hopkins, *Poems* (London: Humphrey Milford, 1918); Bartleby.com, 1999, www.bartleby.com/122/.

10. Mariani, *Gerard Manley Hopkins: A Life*, 173.

11. Ibid., 181.

seems to get lost in the discussion. The great early church father Irenaeus emphasized this very point, which is encapsulated in his well-known affirmation *"gloria enim Dei vivens homo, vita autem hominis visio Dei"*—that is, "the glory of God is the living human being, and the human person has true life only in the vision of God."[12] In his magnum opus, *Adversus haereses*, in which he defends the Christian faith against the Gnostics (the Valentinians in particular) and their denigrated view of both the body of the world and human bodies, he describes a view of salvation that has come to be known as the doctrine of recapitulation. Irenaeus's understanding of salvation emphasizes in particular the salvation of the *flesh*—the flesh that is shared between humanity and the incarnate Christ. He does this by accentuating the connection between the incarnation and the resurrection, arguing that all human bodies have been forever sanctified and transformed in the Word becoming flesh. In Irenaeus's view, we have been made by God, molded by divine hands from the soil of the earth, and it is our very flesh and blood that God has chosen to redeem in Jesus Christ. In this way, Irenaeus categorically refuses to allow any spiritualizing of human nature that would deny either the created goodness of human bodies, or the redemption of bodies.

The goodness of human bodies warrants special mention here because it is a point about which there has been much confusion in the Christian tradition, and even more damaging and unhelpful language. In the world in which we live in today, which includes organ transplants, artificial knees, pigs' hearts, gender reassignment surgery, and cloning, bodies matter more and more—and Christian theology must have something relevant and revelatory to say in such a world. Here, contemporary theology can and should draw on the fact that the body always has mattered in Christian theology, which is, at its core, a theology of creation, incarnation, physical resurrection, and physical sacramentality. In fact, the Christian tradition asserts the goodness of human bodies not only in creation, but also in redemption, in its confession of the resurrection of the body.

The Christian insistence on the resurrection of the body is grounded in Jesus' own bodily resurrection, which is attested to in various places in scripture: his appearance to the women, who grasped his feet and worshiped him (Matthew 28); his incognito conversation with two of his disciples on the Emmaus Road (Luke 24); his command to Mary not to hold onto him as he ascended (John 20); his invitation to Thomas to touch his side (John 20); and his

---

12. Mary Ann Donovan, S.C., *One Right Reading? A Guide to Irenaeus* (Collegeville, MN: Liturgical Press, 1997), 119–20.

request for a piece of fish at the first Easter breakfast (John 21). Paul emphasized this point repeatedly in his theology, pinning human hopes for their own resurrection on the fact of Jesus' resurrection: "For if we have been united with him in a death like his, we will certainly be united with him in a resurrection like his" (Rom. 6:5). Indeed, in 1 Corinthians 15, Paul makes an extended argument for the resurrection of the body—even while acknowledging that the physical bodies we know now will be transformed and changed; the language he uses is that of a "spiritual" body.

However, at this same time, it must be acknowledged that Paul also has been part of the problem. In various places—particularly in Romans—he castigates "the flesh," suggesting a dichotomy wherein the "spirit" is considered superior to the "body," and the body is viewed as the place of sin and corruption. So, for example: "flesh and blood cannot inherit the kingdom of God" (Rom. 15:50); "While we were living in the flesh, our sinful passions, aroused by the law, were at work in our members to bear fruit for death" (Rom. 7:5); "So then, with my mind I am a slave to the law of God, but with my flesh I am a slave to the law of sin" (Rom. 7:25); and "For God has done what the law, weakened by the flesh, could not do: by sending [God's] own Son in the likeness of sinful flesh, and to deal with sin, [God] condemned sin in the flesh, so that the just requirement of the law might be fulfilled in us, who walk not according to the flesh but according to the Spirit. . . . To set the mind on the flesh is death, but to set the mind on the Spirit is life and peace" (Rom. 8:5-6). Even Jesus seems to endorse this line of thinking, when he scolds the disciples for sleeping in the Garden of Gethsemane: ". . . the spirit is willing but the flesh is weak" (Matt. 26:41).

Thus even though a strong case can be made that Paul did not intend to perpetuate such a dichotomy, this idea worked its way into the mainstream of Christian theology—undergirded at various times and places by Manicheism, Platonic philosophy, and Gnostic theology—and physical bodies, particularly women's bodies, were marginalized. The result has been a centuries-long complex and uneasy relationship with the body, evidenced in both scripture and the tradition. Lisa Isherwood and Elizabeth Stuart, in their book *Introducing Body Theology*, write that "The perception of the body as friend *and* enemy was to echo down the Christian ages";[13] and they cite John Climacus, sixth/seventh-century Eastern monastic as evidence of this struggle.

Early Christian monastics had a particularly complex relationship with the body, and in their writings we see the tension they felt between the body

13. Lisa Isherwood and Elizabeth Stuart, *Introducing Body Theology* (Sheffield: Sheffield Academic Press, 1998), 67.

and the soul—"two irreconcilable antagonists yoked together for a lifetime. The body was the foe—gross, corrupt, and greedy, reaching out for its own crass satisfactions or else generating subtle, even civilized, needs against which the soul had always to struggle."[14] This "deadly antagonism" became a center point of monastic reflection. Climacus exemplifies this tradition well, and in his masterwork, *Ladder of Divine Ascent*, he writes repeatedly about this tension, most pointedly in the following passage:

> By what rule or manner can I bind this body of mine? By why precedent can I judge him? Before I can bind him he is let loose, before I can condemn him I am reconciled to him, before I can punish him I bow down to him and feel sorry for him. How can I hate him when my nature disposes me to love him? How can I break away from him when I am bound to him forever? How can I escape from him when he is going to rise with me? How can I make him incorrupt when he has received a corruptible nature? . . . He is my helper and my enemy, my assistant and my opponent, a protector and a traitor.[15]

However, even in spite of this tension, the affirmation of the goodness of the body persisted in Christian theology; it was never fully effaced. Thus Isherwood and Stuart conclude: "Much more characteristic of the Christian tradition [as opposed to a thoroughgoing mind/body dualism] is an uneasy acceptance of embodiment: uneasy because the body is liable to decay, excess, instability and distraction, whereas perfection is associated with changeless stability. Nevertheless there is generally a clear sense that the body and soul are in the process of redemption together."[16] Caroline Walker Bynum, in her masterful study of the resurrection, endorses this conclusion. She writes: "The idea of a person, bequeathed by the Middle Ages to the modern world, was not a concept of soul escaping body or soul using body; it was a concept of self in which physicality was integrally bound to sensation, emotion, reasoning, identity—and therefore finally to whatever one means by salvation. Despite its suspicion of flesh and lust, Western Christianity did not hate or discount the body. Indeed, person was not person without body. . . ."[17] Certainly, this is still true today.

14. John Climacus, *The Ladder of Divine Ascent*, trans. Colm Luibheid and Norman Russell (New York: Paulist, 1982), xviii.

15. Ibid., 185–86.

16. Ibid., 73.

One other aspect of this conversation also needs to be mentioned here, and that is the role race places in contemporary conversations about bodies. Still today, in countries all over the world, different bodies are given different values, depending on their ethnicity, caste, and/or color; and still today, in an American society that continues to evince a pervasive racist character, African American bodies are particularly devalued and oppressed. Christians have a special responsibility to speak up and step out against this kind of exploitation and violence, given that we worship a God who willingly bore marginalization, persecution, and a criminal's death, in order to redeem and transform the bodies of others who are marginalized, persecuted, and criminalized. James Cone, one of the strongest, most compelling voices in Black theology, makes this association persuasively in his book *The Cross and the Lynching Tree*. There, he teases out the links between the crucifixion and the lynching of black bodies that occurred in the United States in the nineteenth and twentieth centuries, during the "lynching era" of 1880–1940—not nearly as far in the past as American society would like to think. He argues that "God saw what whites did to innocent and helpless blacks and claimed their suffering as God's own. God transformed lynched black bodies into the recrucified body of Christ. *Every time a white mob lynched a black person, they lynched Jesus.* The lynching tree is the cross in America."[18]

In a similar vein, one of the best books on the topic of anthropology, bodies, and race is Shawn Copeland's *Enfleshing Freedom: Body, Race, and Being*. Her vantage point is that of black women's bodies; and as she resists the dominant narratives that have constructed those bodies—beginning with, but not limited to, slavery—she tells a different story, one that recognizes "that the black body is a site of divine revelation and, thus, is a 'basic human sacrament.'"[19] She goes on to note that, not only for black women but for all of us, it is only in, with, and through the body that a person "achieves and realizes selfhood through communion with other embodied selves."[20]

In light of this complicated and equivocal history, it is of critical importance today that Christian theologians emphasize the goodness of physical bodies—all colors, shapes, and sizes—and the positive role they play in our salvation. We are embodied now, and we will be in the eschaton. As Wolfhart

17. Caroline Walker Bynum, *The Resurrection of the Body in Western Christianity, 200–1336* (New York: Columbia University Press, 1995), 11.

18. James Cone, *The Cross and the Lynching Tree* (Maryknoll, NY: Orbis, 2011), 158, author's italics.

19. M. Shawn Copeland, *Enfleshing Freedom: Body, Race, and Being* (Minneapolis: Fortress Press, 2010), 24.

20. Ibid.

Pannenberg writes, "The soul is not on its own the true person as though the body were simply a burdensome appendage or a prison to which the soul is tied so long as it has its being on earth. Instead, the person is a unity of body and soul, so that we can think of a future after death only as bodily renewal as well."[21]

"Good Is the Flesh": Disabilities and Sexuality

One of the main reasons why this affirmation of physical goodness is so important is that it impacts how Christians view disability and sexuality—two aspects of human bodily existence that traditionally have been either ignored or excluded from theological discussions about human goodness.[22] This is particularly problematic in the twenty-first-century context, where those bodies society has labeled as "dis-abled" have been devalued and disadvantaged, without realizing the extent to which the very categories of "abled" and "disabled" are social constructs. Ultimately, all bodies are both "abled" and "disabled" in a variety of ways; and over time, all of us will be "disabled" at some point in our lives, whether because of accident, illness, or old age. In his book *Far from the Tree*, Andrew Solomon quotes disability-rights scholar Tobin Siebers, who says "[t]he cycle of life runs in actuality from disability to temporary ability back to disability, and that only if you are among the most fortunate."[23] Thus when Christianity affirms the goodness of human bodies, it must necessarily wrestle with issues of ability and disability, struggling with a myriad of complex questions that have profound theological ramifications.

So, for example, how might the Christian theologian respond to the question: Are "disabilities" part of God's good creation, or distortions of it? Should scientists work to identify and eradicate genetic disorders such as cystic fibrosis? What about deafness? Should all deaf children be given cochlear implants? What about dwarfism? Should all children born with dwarfism have limb-lengthening surgery? What about when we look to the future: Will "disabilities" remain in the kingdom of God? Will someone who is blind in this life have her sight restored in the resurrection? Is that what it means to be "perfected"? And, even more pointedly, might we imagine a "disabled God," as Nancy Eisland does in her classic text *The Disabled God: Toward a Liberatory*

21. Wolfhart Pannenberg, *Systematic Theology*, trans. Geoffrey Bromiley, 3 vols. (Grand Rapids: Eerdmans, 1991–1998), 3:572.

22. "Good Is the Flesh" is the title of a hymn by Brian Wren. The full text of the hymn can be found at http://www.hopepublishing.com/media/pdf/hset/hs_2381.pdf.

23. Andrew Solomon, *Far from the Tree: Parents, Children, and the Search for Identity* (New York: Scribner, 2012), 22.

Theology of Disability; and, if so, what does that say about both who God is and how God creates? These are critical questions for society today, with which Christian theology must wrestle, keeping the inherent goodness of the human body always in mind.

Related to questions around bodies are issues of sexuality, another topic fraught in today's culture. In the West, sexuality has managed to be both an unhealthy obsession and a target of stringent religious morality—simultaneously overindulged and rigorously shunned. This is true of heterosexuality in particular; when it comes to the LGBTQ community, the situation is much worse, as gay men and lesbians, transsexual men and women, and those who self-identify as bisexual or queer face not only societal persecution, but legal and economic discrimination, and the very real threat of violence. These desperate circumstances leave the most vulnerable—particularly children and young adults—contemplating, and in some tragic cases completing, suicide. In such an uncertain cultural milieu, Christian theology can offer a positive message that first and foremost affirms the inherent goodness of sexuality: humans have been created as sexual beings, and the healthy exercise of that sexuality is to be celebrated and encouraged. Not only that, but as Jesus Christ was fully human, Christianity affirms that Jesus also was a sexual being, with all the thoughts and behaviors that accompany a healthy expression of sexuality. Perhaps he desired Mary Magdalene, as so many authors have speculated over the centuries. Perhaps he experienced nocturnal emissions as a young man. None of this should be seen as shameful or sinful—neither for Jesus, nor for us.

However, at the same time, unlike Jesus Christ, whose sexuality was untainted by the stain of sin, Christian theology recognizes that human sin and brokenness affect all of who we are, and therefore our sexuality is also broken. As such, the exercise of our sexuality requires great care—both for oneself and for the neighbor, recognizing the high degree of vulnerability and risk it always involves. Perhaps as Christians, then, we should be less concerned about *who* one loves, and more concerned about *how* one loves. In this, we could be governed by the principle of "do no harm"; and take for our guidelines in sexual relationships those suggested by Marie Fortune: choosing a "peer" (someone with equal power) as a partner; establishing authentic consent for both partners ("Both of us must have . . . the option to say 'no' without being punished as well as the option to say 'yes.'"[24]); taking responsibility for protecting both oneself and one's partner against both sexuality transmitted diseases and unplanned

---

24. Marie Fortune, *Love Does No Harm: Sexual Ethics for the Rest of Us* (New York: Continuum, 1995), 38.

pregnancies; being committed to facilitating one's own pleasure and intimacy as well as that of one's partner; and finally, being faithful to one's promises and commitments.[25] This seems to me at the very least to be a good starting point for Christian conversation around sexuality, one that is consistent both with the command to love one's neighbor, and also the recognition of our inherent relationality and the good place sexuality can hold within those relationships.

Buddhism: Inherent Buddha-Nature in All Sentient Beings

As noted in the previous chapter on Buddhism, it is taught in several of the Mahayana schools of Buddhism that one attains *nirvana* in the here-and-now, right in the midst of one's daily life. What's more, one does not need any special prowess or experience to attain enlightenment—rather, one already possesses the seed of enlightenment within oneself, only this seed is obscured in the mire of ignorance and suffering. Once one is freed from those despoliations, one's true enlightened nature is revealed. This teaching is grounded in the doctrine that every sentient being possesses within herself the potential for buddhahood; that is, every sentient being possesses innately what is called "Buddha-nature." The technical term for this is *tathagatagarbha*, which means something like "Buddha-womb" or "Buddha-storehouse." (One author translates it as "Buddha within."[26])

Donald Lopez Jr. notes the many similes used in different sutras to describe it, all of which point to something of great value that is obscured by something worthless or undesirable, until its true nature is revealed by the eye of wisdom. Thus the *tathagatagarbha* is "like pure honey in a cave, entirely covered by bees, which prevent one from seeing it"; or "like a kernel of wheat that is covered by a husk so coarse that an unknowing person might discard it"; or "like a piece of gold that has lain at the bottom of a cesspool for many years"; or "like a treasure hidden beneath the house of a poor family." "In the same way, the Buddha nature abides silently within the bodies of all beings, untainted by their afflictions, as they take rebirth in samsara again and again."[27]

Certainly, there was and continues to be controversy about this teaching within the various schools of Buddhism,[28] particularly around

---

25. Ibid., 38–39.

26. John S. Strong, *The Experience of Buddhism: Sources and Interpretation* (Belmont, CA: Wadsworth, 1995), 155.

27. Donald S. Lopez Jr., *The Story of Buddhism: A Concise Guide to Its History and Teachings* (San Francisco: HarperSanFrancisco, 2001), 99–100.

the problem of the self: some argued that in teaching a doctrine of some enduring "inherent nature," the result is an affirmation of an abiding "self," which is antithetical to Buddhist teaching. Nevertheless, this idea proved to be a popular teaching, particularly in East Asia, where it was used as a way to encourage the realization of one's true nature, and the true nature of all sentient beings right now, right in the midst of *samsara*. As should be obvious, the doctrine of the *tathagatagarbha* is a deeply optimistic, positive teaching about not only human beings, but indeed, all sentient beings; and it connects the entire cosmos of living beings to each other, and to the Buddha, through the promise of a latent enlightened state that already inheres in us all.

IMAGO DEI—RELATIONALITY AND LUTHER'S FOUR *CORAMS*

As mentioned in the previous chapter, a strong theological consensus has emerged in the twenty-first century affirming that the most constructive and compelling way to understand the meaning of humanity's creation as *imago Dei* is through the concept of relationality. Humanity bears the image of God in our fundamentally relational existence. Echoing the triune communion of persons, human beings do not simply *have* relationships; instead, it is accurate to say that human beings *are* relationships: that is, human identity—both individually and communally—comes into being only in and through the myriad network of relationships that create us. There are many different ways to articulate this reality in Christian theology, but one of the most helpful can be found in Martin Luther's theology, in particular his use of the preposition *coram*, a Latin word that means "before" or "in the presence of."

Gerard Ebeling discusses the importance of this concept for Luther in the context of his larger "Two Kingdoms" explication. The overall point for Ebeling is that, in Luther's theology, a Christian is "one and the same person in both kingdoms";[29] and, fundamentally, it is one's relationship to God, the primary relationship out of which all others flow, that provides the foundation for the whole of one's life, in both sacred and secular spheres, both private and

28. See, for example, *Pruning the Bodhi Tree: The Storm over Critical Buddhism*, ed. Jamie Hubbard and Paul L. Swanson (Honolulu: University of Hawai'i Press, 1997).

29. Gerhard Ebeling, *Luther: An Introduction to His Thought*, trans. R. A. Wilson (Philadelphia: Fortress Press, 1970), 192.

public, both home and work. What is most interesting here is the way Luther describes this relationship to God as being so deeply connected to the other relationships that make up human existence. The way he does this is through the use of the word *coram*. Ebeling writes:

> It is not very difficult to find an expression which will characterize the very basis of Luther's mode of thought. It can be found in a preposition which might be described as the key word to Luther's understanding of being: the preposition *coram*, which can be translated into German by the word "*vor*" and into English by "before."[30]

By "before," of course, Ebeling is not pointing to a chronological state of being, but rather a "spatial" state of being; in this context, "before" means "before the face of," or "in the sight of"—which itself means "in the presence of."[31] In short, Luther's use of the word *coram* points to a life in relationship; as Ebeling describes it: "the fundamental situation is that something is defined here not in itself, but in its outward relations with something else, or more properly in terms of the relationship of something else with it."[32] That "something" being defined is the human being; and the point here is that the very definition of what it means to be human requires consideration of the different relationships that delineate human life: "This *coram*-relationship, in which [hu]man always finds himself, is in fact the characteristic human situation, without which he would not be [hu]man at all. In it the way in which he encounters others, others encounter him, and he encounters himself are interwoven."[33]

The most important *coram* relationship is, of course, human life as *coram Deo*: "existence in the sight of God, in the presence of God, under the eyes of God, in the judgement [*sic*] of God, and in the word of God."[34] Yet, this relationship never stands alone. Instead, it is interwoven through and through with the other three *coram* relationships that Luther defines: "existence in my own sight (*coram meipso*), existence in the sight of [people] (*coram hominibus*), and existence in the sight of the world (*coram mundo*)."[35] All four of these relationships interpenetrate, and none is separable from the others. This means

30. Ibid., 193.
31. Ibid.
32. Ibid., 194.
33. Ibid., 196.
34. Ibid., 199.
35. Ibid.

that the human being's relationship with God includes and finds expression in the myriad web of relationships one experiences in the concrete context of daily life.

Caryn Riswold emphasizes this point, arguing that "[o]ne cannot be in relationship to God without a life in the world, a personal sense of self, and relationships with fellow human beings."[36] In this way, viewing human existence through the lens of Luther's four *corams* provides a fruitful means of articulating what being created in the image of God really looks like in the here and now: it means acknowledging God's presence in every aspect and every moment of our lives; it means engaging in the particular geography of the places in which we find ourselves—including local landscapes, animals, and plants—but also being aware of the interconnections that exist between the near and the far; it means loving and serving the neighbor, stretching and strengthening networks of brothers and sisters as far as possible; and finally, it means being self-aware, and attending to one's own vocation and place in the complex web of existence. Riswold sums it up this way: "Women and men find their lives *coram mundo* grounded in their existence *coram deo*, lived out *coram hominibus*, and defined *coram meipso*."[37]

Hinduism: Darshan and Puja

The concept of *darshan* is an important way of understanding the relationship between the human being and the divine in Hinduism. In her book *Darśan: Seeing the Divine Image in India*, Diana Eck notes that while the simplest meaning of *darshan* is "seeing," more specifically, in a religious context, it points to the viewing of the deity—visually apprehending God. She writes, "The central act of Hindu worship, from the point of view of the lay person, is to stand in the presence of the deity and to behold the image with one's own eyes, to see and be seen by the deity."[38] This is not the passive activity it might appear to be: in fact, in Hinduism, this religious seeing is a form of touching, a form of knowing[39]—it is not only a profound form of worship, but also a primary means of blessing. By receiving the gaze of the divine, one also receives a blessing from the god or goddess

---

36. Caryn D. Riswold, "*Coram Mundo*: A Lutheran Feminist Theological Anthropology of Hope," *Dialog: A Lutheran Journal of Theology* 48, no. 2 (Summer 2009): 126.

37. Ibid., 132.

38. Diana L. Eck, *Darśan: Seeing the Divine Image in India*, 3rd ed. (New York: Columbia University Press, 1998), 3.

39. Ibid., 9.

present in the image itself. In fact, one also can receive *darshan* from holy men and women, such as Gandhi, for example; and one can even receive *darshan* from aniconic images of the divine, such as the Ganges River.

The importance of this mode of worship, and this tangible connection between the human and the divine, makes clear how central images of God are in Hinduism, a tradition Eck calls "an imaginative, an 'image-making,' religious tradition in which the sacred is seen as present in the visible world."[40] These tangible images mediate one's relationship with God in the daily life of Hindus. Again, Eck writes, "The day to day life and ritual of Hindus is based not upon abstract interior truths, but upon the charged, concrete, and particular appearances of the divine in the substance of the material world."[41] Hindus experience their own physical existence in the world as met and undergirded by the physical embodiment of the divine, present in a vast multiplicity of locations and images.

Therefore, the experience of *darshan* typically is accompanied by and grounded in a variety of other practices, which together can be called *puja*. This word has several different meanings, but it is most often translated as "worship" or "homage." In practice, however, what it refers to is the act of offering and/or devotion to a deity; and it is thoroughly, deeply corporeal, engaging all the senses of the divine with a variety of pleasing sensory offerings including flowers, incense, chanting, foods, clothes, and baths of milk and oil. In return, the deity gives back what is called *prasad*—grace, goodwill, or blessing. This gift takes the form of the return of the offered substances, now transformed by the blessing of the god: flowers are returned to the devotees by the priest and placed in one's hair, for example; the food is eaten; incense is wafted around one's head, etc. Certainly, *puja* occurs in large temples, which house larger-than-life images of specific gods—this is particularly true on festival days; but it also takes place daily in the home, at small altars and/or *puja* rooms—also called *mandirs*—present in almost every Hindu household, certainly in the homes of those Hindus who are considered "higher" caste.

The different rituals that make up a *puja* can be elaborate or abbreviated, depending on the context; however, even the shortest home *puja* emphasizes welcoming the divine, reverencing him or her and receiving in return a blessing. Nancy Auer Falk describes a typical *puja*

puja ε
prasad

40. Ibid., 10.
41. Ibid., 11.

ritual as follows, familiar to anyone who has ever attended a Hindu temple—either in this country or abroad:

> The "divine guest" is invited in and offered a seat. Its feet are washed, and it is offered water for washing its face, rinsing its mouth, and taking a cooling drink after its "journey." Then, it may be bathed and wrapped with a cloth signifying clean new "clothing." It is anointed with cooling sandalwood ointment and/or decorated with red kumkum powder applied to the center of its forehead. Next, it is decked with flowers, while sweet-smelling incense burns before it. Finally, a burning lamp is waved before it, and food is offered, including the family's intended breakfast or supper. The food is returned to the family as *Prasad*, a manifestation of divine grace. All worshipers present do *namas* or *pranam*. The first is a gesture of pressing both palms together and raising them before the face. In the second, the worshiper drops to the knees and touches his or her forehead to the floor or stretches out full length with palms pressed together and extended in front of her or his head. . . . After pranams, the god is bade good-bye, and the family can turn to other pursuits.[42]

In this way, the relationship between the human and the divine is daily reconstituted and reaffirmed, grounding human existence in the divine presence.

Judaism: The Chosen People

The understanding of the human person in Judaism is fundamentally communal: the individual is who she is in the larger context of her participation in the Jewish community. Jonathan Sacks writes: "The governing assumption throughout the Hebrew Bible is that when Israel is rewarded, it is rewarded collectively. When it is punished, it is punished collectively. It experiences fate as a people, which is to say, together . . .

42. Nancy Auer Falk, *Living Hinduisms: An Explorer's Guide* (Belmont, CA: Thomson Wadsworth, 2006), 122.

Judaism is a collective faith. Despite its principled attachment to the dignity of the individual its central experiences are not private but communal."[43]

What's more, this community itself is constituted through its relationship to God, specifically through God's act of "choosing" Israel. The concept of the "chosen people" comes out of the Hebrew scriptures, and, over the centuries, it has been elaborated upon across the breadth of Jewish literature—including both rabbinic texts and even texts outside the Jewish tradition. The scriptures witness to the fact that out of all the peoples on earth, God chose Israel for the covenant: they would be God's people, and God would be their God. The people Israel were not chosen for their strength, size, or any other characteristic they possessed inherently; rather, they were chosen on the basis of God's will alone: "It is not because you are the most numerous of people that the LORD set His heart on you and chose you—indeed, you are the smallest of people; but it was because the LORD favoured you . . ." (Deut. 7:7-8).

This concept of chosenness found expression through various creation myths that are told in multiple Jewish texts. Here is one such story:

> The world and everything in it was created only for the sake of Israel. Indeed, all worlds, above and below, were only created for the sake of Israel. Everything that was brought forth, created, formed, and made, everything the God did, was for the sake of His holy people Israel. Israel was the first thing that arose in God's thought. That is why the sages commented about the verse *In the beginning God created the heaven and the earth* (Gen. 1:1), that "beginning" means Israel, since God's first thought was of Israel. . . . When God created the world, it did not have the power to endure. God created Israel so that the world would be able to endure, for Israel is the sustenance of all universes. If not for Israel, everything would revert to its original state of nothingness.[44]

While some Jews are uneasy with the concept of chosenness—particularly insofar as it seems to suggest an exclusive notion of privilege—the dominant

43. Rabbi Jonathan Sacks, *To Heal a Fractured World: The Ethics of Responsibility* (New York: Schocken, 2005), 86.

44. As quoted in Howard Schwartz, *Tree of Souls: The Mythology of Judaism* (Oxford: Oxford University Press, 2004), 327.

contemporary interpretation of chosenness is that it points to a responsibility for the sake of the whole world. That is, Israel is not chosen for itself, but to be a "light of nations" (Isa. 42:6 and 49:6), and a sign of God's universal redeeming will. In this way, the concept of chosenness, specifically as it was created in the context of the covenant with God, is used by contemporary Jews to emphasize their collective responsibility not just for each other, but for the entire cosmic community that God has created. This is a gift Judaism offers to the world, particular contemporary society: "The message of the Bible for the politics of the contemporary West is that it is not enough to have a state. You also need a society—meaning, that *common belonging* that comes from a sense that we are neighbours as well as strangers; that we have duties to one another, to the heritage of the past and to the hopes of generations not yet born. . . ."[45]

It is with this in mind, then, that Jewish worship, prayers, study, and rituals are carried out: to structure human life according to the way of God, in fulfillment of the covenant made with God: the covenant that was first written in the flesh of Abraham (the rite of circumcision) and subsequently given to the people at Sinai (the Torah)—a covenant made for the sake of the whole world.

45. Sacks, *To Heal a Fractured World*, 125.

Figure 6.1. An exhibit from the Mevlevi Museum at the Mevlevi Lodge, an eighteenth-century Sufi monastery, Istanbul. May 2012. It includes the traditional Sufi garb, as well as a drawing of the whirling dance.

Islam: Sufism

Sufis generally are described as Islamic mystics—although some more conservative strains of Islam do not recognize them as legitimate practitioners. They are not a separate "sect" of Islam—Sufis can be Sunni or Shi'a—instead, Sufis represent a dimension of Islam that pervades the whole of it: some Islamic scholars call it the "inner" or "esoteric" aspect of Islam. It is important to state up front that Sufis follow the Qur'an and the teachings of Muhammad; indeed, in general, Sufis consider themselves to be in direct line with Muhammad. However, their view of both is unique: Sufis consider that the Qur'an is "the first and foremost mystical text of Islam and that the Prophet is the first and the greatest of the Sufi sages and saints."[46]

---

46. Victor Danner, "The Early Development of Sufism," in *Islamic Spirituality: Foundations*, ed. Seyyed Hossein Nasr (New York: Crossroad, 1987), 242.

What this means is that Sufis are not concerned with obedience to specific rules and regulations. Instead, they seek what is considered to be the highest stage of faith, unity with the Divine, which consists of a direct experience of the Divine that is achieved through repeating the name of God, meditating on God's ubiquitous presence, and breaking one's attachments to the world. The Sufi path thus has been described as "the progressive unveiling of the inner eye, which then begins to see what it had not perceived before."[47] This relates to the Sufi understanding of the highest stage of religious practice, which, "according to the words of the Prophet to the archangel Gabriel" consists of "adoring Allah as though thou didst see Him, and if thou dost not see him He nonetheless seeth thee."[48] In this state of devotion and union with God, the human being "rediscovers 'the most beautiful form' in which he was created (according to the Qur'an XCV, 4), because his heart is like a pure, well-polished mirror in which the Divine can be reflected."[49]

The word *Sufi* is said to come from *suf*, which means "white wool." (This is also the source of the Arabic name for Sufis—*tasawwuf*, which indicates both Sufis themselves, and also the mystical Sufi path.) The reason for this is that the white wool clothing said to have been favored by Muhammad and his early followers soon became a mark of an ascetic lifestyle: "a symbol of ascetic renunciation and orientation toward the contemplative life."[50]

Sufis train in a community, with a master, and the master/disciple relationship is of critical importance—"a condition *sine qua non* for spiritual success":[51] "Masters of the Way say that every [person] has inherent within him the possibility for release from self and union with God, but this is latent and dormant and cannot be released, except with certain illuminates gifted by God, without guidance from a leader."[52] This is because the way in which Sufis approach God—and open themselves up to the Divine—is through "intuitive and emotional spiritual faculties," which must be properly cultivated with careful guidance.[53] This explains both the Sufis' traditional distain for dogmatic theorizing, and also the suspicion with

---

47. Danner, "The Early Development of Sufism," 240

48. Jean-Louis Michon, "The Spiritual Practices of Sufism," in *Islamic Spirituality: Foundations*, 266.

49. Ibid.

50. Ibid., 267.

51. Ibid., 271.

52. J. Spencer Trimingham, *The Sufi Orders in Islam* (Oxford: Clarendon, 1971), 3.

53. Ibid., 1.

which they are often viewed by Islamic scholars and traditional practitioners: their emphasis is on ecstatic experience and inner transformation, not Qur'anic study or obedience to Islamic law.

However, let me say again that this should not imply that Sufis ignore, or even less, disparage, the Qur'an. Instead, they consider their practice in line with Qur'anic teaching, particularly such verses as ". . . We are closer to [the human] than his jugular vein" (50:16), and "Remember that God intervenes between man and his heart" (8:24), which Sufis take as evidence of the fact that God dwells within the heart of the human being, and that there is, in fact, a union between them. To facilitate this union, prayer and worship are intense, including in particular repeated recitation of the Divine Name, which is considered an example of *dhikr*, which means "remembrance"—remembering God. This is a key aspect of Sufi practice, and it includes a variety of set prayers for both individual and group devotions.

There are many different orders of Sufis, each of which traces its lineage back to Muhammad in one form or another, but the one that is the most well-known in the West is the Mevlevi order, the order of the "whirling dervishes," whose founder is the famous Sufi mystic and poet Jalal al-Din Rumi, who lived in the thirteenth century. In this order, the particular means by which the disciples ("dervishes") seek union with God is not only through more traditional means of study, fasting, and prayer, but particularly through a complex litany of twirling dance, called the "sema." The sema is a 700-year-old ritual that comprises a highly ritualized series of movements, each of which carries deep religious meaning. The ceremony as a whole represents a mystical journey of humanity to God; there are four specific periods of "whirling," called "selams" or "salutes." They represent the stages of humanity's ascension to God and the purification of the soul. During the sema the disciples shed their black cloaks, which represent their worldly attachments—their tomb—and twirl in all white garments, which represent their burial garments. In addition, the special hat they wear (called a tarboosh) represents the tombstone. It actually takes over a year for a dervish to learn how to whirl properly: not only the physical technique, but also the mental focus: during the dance they repeat the name of God constantly, which keeps them from getting dizzy or losing their balance.

The Sufis, then, follow a mystical path that seeks two goals simultaneously: knowledge of self, and knowledge of God. And, in fact, once that knowledge is attained, the disciple realizes that it was really one goal all along—the knowledge of one is embedded in the knowledge of the other—as the veil that separates the Creator from the creation becomes transparent. Once this happens, the individual "is said to have 'disappeared' (*ghā'ib*), to be absorbed by the One invoked and 'made one' with Him."[54]

WE ARE SINNERS: *SIMUL JUSTUS ET PECCATOR*

Having established humanity's essential, created goodness, we now shift to the second and third fundamental assertions Christianity makes about the human being: she is inherently, inescapably sinful; and, in Christ, she is justified and made right with God. These two aspects of humanity are always taken together, because even after baptism, sin remains, and one must struggle against the "old Adam" for as long as one lives. The Latin phrase for this is *simul justus et peccator*—at the same time justified and sinful. It is a way of articulating this central Christian paradox: even though humanity continues to resist and reject God, God continually seeks humanity out in love, rescuing and forgiving them in Christ. Without Christ, the individual can do nothing but sin against God, but with Christ, through the work of the Holy Spirit, she is able to love God and the neighbor. As one needs a clear, thorough understanding of sin before one can appreciate justification, I begin here with the latter word, *peccator*—sinner.

WHAT IS SIN?

When seeking a definition for sin, it is hard to resist applying the familiar phrase, famously used by Supreme Court Justice Potter Stewart, "I know it when I see it." This is because while all of us quickly can identify multiple concrete examples of sin—both from personal experience and global, historical knowledge—a single definition is difficult to articulate, not least because sin is at once so complex, underhanded, and shape-shifting. It is simultaneously deeply personal and particular, and broadly sweeping and universal; it is both flagrant in the flush of evil, and subtle, almost imperceptibly interwoven with the good; and it manifests itself in both discrete acts of individuals and entire social structures. It appears in a multitude of guises: as pride—rebellion against God, indifference—apathy toward one's neighbor, and selfishness—self-absorption that refuses to live in loving relationships with others.

Here are a variety of definitions from several prominent twentieth-century theologians, each of which emphasizes a different, but equally compelling, facet

---

54. Michon, "The Spiritual Practices of Sufism," 289.

of sin. Peter Hodgson describes sin as *disruption*: "Sin entails a disruption of the personal and interpersonal structures of human being. These disruptions—to be identified as idolatry, flight, and alienation—correspond to specific features of the tragic vulnerability that attends finite freedom."[55] Gustavo Gutiérrez says that sin is ". . . the *breach of friendship* with God and others. . . ."[56] Daniel Migliore argues that sin is *opposition to grace*: "Sin can be described as the denial of our relatedness to God and our need for God's grace . . . sin is fundamentally *opposition to grace*, saying No to the invitation to be human in grateful service to God and in friendship with our fellow creatures."[57] James Cone emphasizes the *communal nature* of sin: "Sin is a community concept . . . to be in sin is to deny the community . . . sin warps a person's existence in the world."[58] And, in one of the most well-known definitions of sin from the twentieth century, Reinhold Niebuhr names sin as *pride*: "The religious dimension of sin is [humanity's] rebellion against God."[59] His point is that in sin, the human pretends to be more than she is, seeking to transcend the limits God has set for her: "[The human's] inclination to abuse his freedom, to overestimate his power and significance and to become everything is understood as the primal sin."[60]

In light of the contemporary explanation of the *imago Dei* as human relationality, many theologians emphasize the unwillingness to be in relationship as a primary manifestation of sin. Carter Heyward writes that sin is *radical self-absorption*: "our sin is in living as if we and others are, or can be, self-contained, well-boundaried, selves set apart from others . . . our sin is in failing to know ourselves together, connected at the root of our humanness/creatureliness."[61] Dietrich Bonhoeffer makes a similar point, recognizing that sin is *isolation*: "The reality of sin places the individual in the utmost loneliness, in a state of radical separation from God and [humanity]."[62]

---

55. Peter C. Hodgson, *Christian Faith: A Brief Introduction* (Louisville: Westminster John Knox, 2001), 91.

56. Gustavo Gutiérrez, *A Theology of Liberation* (Maryknoll, NY: Orbis, 1988), 100–101, my italics.

57. Migliore, *Faith Seeking Understanding*, 130, my italics.

58. James Cone, *A Black Theology of Liberation* (Maryknoll, NY: Orbis, 1998), 104–8.

59. Reinhold Niebuhr, *The Nature and Destiny of Man*, vol. 1 (New York: Scribner's, 1964), 179.

60. Ibid., 92.

61. Carter Heyward, *Saving Jesus from Those Who Are Right: Rethinking What It Means to Be Christian* (Minneapolis: Fortress Press, 1999), 84–85.

62. *Dietrich Bonhoeffer: Witness to Jesus Christ*, ed. John de Gruchy (London: Collins Liturgical Publications, 1988), 68.

At the same time, sin does not just affect the human community, either—it also finds expression in humanity's relationship with creation, as Sallie McFague emphasizes, in her definition of sin as "a refusal to accept our place." She writes:

> . . . both sin and salvation are earthly matters—fleshly, concrete, particular matters having to do with disproportion and well-being *in relation to* the forms of God's presence we encounter in our daily, ordinary lives: other bodies. Sin against the many different bodies—the bodies of other people, other animals, and nature—*is* sin against God in the model of the world as God's body. . . . Sin is not just breaking divine laws or blaspheming God; rather it is living falsely, living contrary to reality, to the way things are.[63]

This is a sentiment echoed by Marjorie Hewitt Suchocki, who states, "Sin is a rebellion against creation in the unnecessary violation of the well-being of any aspect of existence. Because it is a violation of creation, it is also sin against God."[64]

CHARACTERISTICS OF CHRISTIAN SIN-TALK

When thinking about sin, there are several key doctrinal affirmations that are important for Christians to keep in mind. First, one should always begin from the stance that "I am the first among sinners"—with one important caveat. Christian theology as a whole is indebted to many feminist theologians and others for pointing out that the tradition's instance on convicting people of their sinfulness before presenting the good news of grace and forgiveness sometimes has the deleterious effect of pushing the already cracked and fragile to the breaking point. For people who already are drowning in despair, convicted by feelings of worthlessness, helplessness, and hopelessness, a further word of condemnation is more than unnecessary—it can be deadly. Sensitivity, then, is always required when talking about the reality of sin with real people in concrete situations: when it's clear that someone is already mired down in her sinfulness, instead of pushing her in further with the law, reach in and pull her out with the gospel.

That being said, however, the larger point remains that, when it comes to sin, an almost irresistible temptation remains to focus on the speck in the neighbor's eye while ignoring the log in one's own eye. That is, people have

---

63. Sallie McFague, *The Body of God: An Ecological Theology* (Minneapolis: Fortress Press, 1993), 114.

64. Marjorie Hewitt Suchocki, *The Fall to Violence: Original Sin in Relational Theology* (New York: Continuum, 1995), 66.

a tendency to want to emphasize the sins of other people as worse than their own (her adultery is much worse than my greed, for example), in order to make themselves feel better, and to try and justify their own actions. Thus when we commit to starting every conversation about sin with the recognition of our own sinfulness, we are better able to approach our neighbor with compassion and care, rather than judgment and condemnation. Karl Barth acknowledged this in his statement, "Precisely when we recognize that we are sinners do we perceive that we are brothers [and sisters]."[65] This is why Alcoholics Anonymous uses only members as leaders: they know the truth that one is best able to stand in solidarity with the lost and suffering if she knows that suffering firsthand.

Along with this, it is important to keep several other aspects of sin in mind as well. First, a Christian doctrine of sin is about much more than simply moral, ethical, and legal violations: to put it even more bluntly—Christian sin-talk is more than just "sex-talk," even though it can seem as if sex gets a disproportionate amount of attention in contemporary Christian theology. In reality, sin is not merely about action—in word or deed—but also about the way we view others: our prejudices, convictions, blind spots, and assumptions. The fact is, a Christian doctrine of sin points to an entire worldview; a way of being in the world. Barbara Brown Taylor writes: "Sin is not simply a set of behavior to be avoided. Much more fundamentally, it is a way of life to be exposed and changed, and no one is innocent."[66]

Second, sin is always contextual: that is, sin always is experienced and defined in specific situations, by specific societies; and while some understandings of sin translate well from context to context, others do not. This fact reminds Christians to use a hermeneutic of suspicion when examining a doctrine of sin, attending to those who have positions of power, and those who do not—those who are responsible for naming sin, and those whose voices are marginalized or overlooked.[67]

Third, sin is both an individual and a social phenomenon. As humans, in our actions, we always maintain some degree of agency and free will—though some clearly have more than others—which means that we all sin individually

[margin note: not about behavior but world view]

65. Karl Barth, *The Epistle to the Romans*, 6th ed., trans. Edwyn C. Hoskyns (Oxford: Oxford University Press, 1933), 101 (iii., 23, 24).

66. Barbara Brown Taylor, *Speaking of Sin: The Lost Language of Salvation* (Cambridge, MA: Cowley, 2001), 58.

67. As an example from the twenty-first-century American context, one would do well to ask whose interests are served in the insistent emphasis on homosexuality as a sin, while economic greed and environmental devastation are all too often ignored or exegeted away.

through the choices we make. However, at the same time, we also are born into sinful systems, making us sinners by simply living in a particular time and place. This aspect of sin—typically called "structural" or "social" sin—points to complex, deeply engrained patterns of behavior that are interiorized and normalized within entire societies from generation to generation, such that they become part of the "background noise" of a culture, existing unseen and unnoticed—particularly by the advantaged majority—most of the time. This dimension of sin reminds us that sin is more than just the sum total of the individual acts of human beings; it exists in the very fabric of human society, and it includes the "silent" sins of indifference and neglect as well as the boisterous patterns of sinning that manifest themselves in sexism, bigotry, xenophobia, and classism.

One oft-mentioned example of this expression of sin is the racism embedded in the United States. A recognition of this structural sin present in our own society demands that whites in the United States admit and confront their own racism, including the privilege accorded to them in a racist society, even when they are sure that they "don't see color," and do not discriminate. As we might sometimes wish it were so (although that would be deceiving ourselves!), sin is never simply a matter of controlling one's own behavior: it is far more complex than that.

Finally, we can never lose sight of the perspective of the "sinned-against"—that is, the victims of sin.[68] If sin is about broken relationships, then the perspective of the sinned-against points to the experience of being rejected in relationship, being exploited, being violated, being betrayed. This language also provides one way to talk about the difference between the related terms "sin" and "evil," categories that serve as different "vantage points from which to talk about suffering and destruction."[69] In this view, sin points to the vantage point of the sinner: the one who is culpable for malevolence in a specific situation; and evil points to the vantage point of the sinned-against: the one who is trapped in wickedness one had no part in creating, and over which one has no control. To fully grasp sin and its consequences, both terms are necessary: "If sin is the term with which we designate culpable ways of being in the world, then evil points to the reality that every sin carries with it a surplus of malevolence. This surplus of malevolence can, and frequently does, coalesce

68. See the essays in *The Other Side of Sin: Woundedness from the Perspective of the Sinned-Against*, ed. Andrew Sung Park and Susan L. Nelson (Albany: State University of New York Press, 2001).

69. *Constructive Theology: A Contemporary Approach to Classical Themes*, ed. Serene Jones and Paul Lakeland (Minneapolis: Fortress Press, 2005), 118.

with other contingencies in such a way that a reality is created that can only be termed a *world of evil*."[70]

SIN AS ACT: THE BONDAGE OF THE WILL

Keeping all this in mind, then, we now turn to the two primary aspects of any Christian doctrine of sin: sin as *act*, and sin as *fact*. We resist both, and both make us squirm with denial. This first aspect points to the actual activity of sin in which all humans engage, and in which we are deeply enmeshed in every aspect of our lives. Martin Luther wrote his treatise "The Bondage of the Will" in response to Erasmus, who had written "The Freedom of the Will," in order to emphasize that without God's own intervention—the grace of Christ and the work of the Holy Spirit—humans are completely captive to sin, and cannot take even a first step at freeing themselves. He used the phrase "the bondage of the will" to describe the comprehensiveness of this enmeshment, indicating that in the sight of God, humans are utterly incapable of being anything other than sinners. It is not a matter of not trying hard enough, or not knowing enough, or not praying enough; instead, before God, humans simply cannot, on their own, do anything other than sin.

Note the prepositional phrase "before God"—it is not unimportant. No one argues—least of all Luther—that Christians do not have freedom when it comes to what are called "matters of reason": we are capable of obeying the speed limit; we are capable of refraining from murder or adultery; and we are even capable of going to church, tithing, etc. That is, humans are capable of making reasonable choices and obeying laws—if not, it would make no sense to punish someone for breaking them. However, obeying the law can coincide very well with sin: hating my boss and fantasize daily about killing her, refraining from doing so only because I am sure I would get caught hardly qualifies as sinless behavior. And even though my boss certainly would appreciate not being killed, in God's eyes I am as much of a sinner as the one who actually pulls the trigger or wields the knife.

Again, note the phrase "in God's eyes." No one is saying that here on earth it is irrelevant whether someone only thinks about murder or actually carries it out—the works of the law are much needed among the human community, and our neighbor greatly appreciates when we act rightly: defending the victimized, sharing our wealth, visiting the sick, etc. Therefore, of course Christians would agree that it is important in the human community for people to respect others,

70. Ibid., 120.

refrain from harming them, and care for the needs of the vulnerable in their daily encounters with other people: they *can* do this, and they *should*.

However, and this the key point, none of those activities get us closer to God, win us reward from God, or somehow mitigate our sinfulness before God. All of us, every human being, no matter how "good" we are or how well we live our lives, is *equally* sinful before God, and *equally* in need of forgiveness and redemption. In fact, in the sight of God, none of those external works can even rightly be called "good"—because they are not inspired by the love and grace of God. Thus Luther writes, ". . . no [hu]man is brought any nearer to righteousness by his works; and what is more, that no works and no aspirations or endeavors of free choice count for anything in the sight of God, but are all adjudged to be ungodly, unrighteous, and evil. For if the [hu]man himself is not righteous, neither are his works or endeavors righteous; and if they are not righteous, they are damnable and deserving of wrath."[71]

This is hard for Christians to hear, I know. We desperately want to believe that our works on earth somehow "count" before God, even if just in the smallest amount. We want to think that if we are "good enough" God will reward us, and if we just work hard enough, we can somehow become "less" of a sinner. All of these things are untrue—delusions we tell ourselves to avoid facing the hard reality that we are just as sinful before God as our neighbor next door—the jerk who doesn't even go to church; and therefore we are as much in need of Christ's forgiveness as the murderer, the embezzler, the liar, etc. We cannot justify ourselves before God; our sinfulness is comprehensive and complete.

SIN AS FACT: THE IMPORTANCE OF "ORIGINAL" SIN

The second aspect of sin is sin as *fact*, and it points to the bare truth that before we think a thought, complete an action, or say a word, we are sinners: we are born sinners and we die sinners—sin comes with being human, and there is nothing we can do about it. In the Christian tradition—particularly in the West—the doctrine that has been used to describe this reality is the doctrine of original sin. At its core, this doctrine points to the fact that sin is not simply an *act*—or even a complex system of combined and interrelated acts. Instead, sin is also terribly and simply a *fact* of human existence. That is, original sin is the Christian teaching that sin is an inescapable dis-order that warps every human

---

71. Martin Luther, *Luther's Works: Career of the Reformer III*, ed. Jaroslav Pelikan, Hilton C. Oswald, Helmut T. Lehmann (Philadelphia: Fortress Press, 1999), 33:270

being from the moment of her birth: we cannot escape it, we cannot avoid it—sin is as much a part of the human condition as breathing.

The doctrine of original sin finds its inception in the biblical story of Adam and Eve, and the "fall" from paradise—the expulsion from the Garden of Eden. The ramifications of the fall have been cosmic and cataclysmic: as Paul emphasizes both in Romans and in 1 Corinthians, sin and death came into the world through Adam, and all humanity suffers condemnation as a result of Adam's trespass. I would argue that even today, in a twenty-first-century context when many Christians appreciate that the story of Adam and Eve cannot and should not be read as biological history or scientific explanation—the Bible is neither a history nor a science text book, it is the story of God's salvation history with God's people—an understanding of original sin continues to keep that story relevant for human existence. This is because the truth of the story of Adam and Eve is the very real fact of human alienation from God: our willful turning from God, putting ourselves at the center of existence, where, in fact, only God belongs. One of the most powerful metaphors that conveys the devastation and grotesqueness of this "turning" is the image of the human curved in upon herself: *homo incurvatus in se*.[72] She is misshapen, misanthropic, and mistrustful—incapable of knowing God and loving God, let alone knowing and loving another. This willful incapacity stands at the core of a Christian doctrine of original sin.

Paul Ricoeur explains what he calls the "Adamic myth" in this way. First, it is a story that enables us to think of humanity as one: "Adam signifies [humanity]."[73] This points to the fact that when we understand the story of Adam and Eve as a myth, we are better able to understand how their story is our story, and how these two specific figures continue to represent humankind in general. ("Myth," incidentally, does not mean a false story, but rather a story not limited to historical veracity that reveals a deep truth about human nature and God.) Second, this story offers critical insight into a core fissure at the heart of human existence: "namely, the discordance between the fundamental reality—state of innocence, status of a creature, essential being—and the actual modality of [humanity], as defiled, sinful, guilty."[74] In other words, it explains how humanity got from "created good" to "sinful and unclean."

In the West, Christian theology owes much of its thinking about original sin to Augustine, who was an unblinking realist on the subject—and who,

---

72. See Matt Jenson, *The Gravity of Sin: Augustine, Luther and Barth on* Homo Incurvatus in Se (New York: T. & T. Clark, 2006).

73. Paul Ricoeur, *The Symbolism of Evil*, trans. Emerson Buchanan (Boston: Beacon, 1967), 162.

74. Ibid., 163.

incidentally, interpreted the story of Adam and Eve as literal history, a hermeneutical given until the nineteenth century. For Augustine, Adam and Eve's transgression had catastrophic ramifications for humanity as a whole, and we who are descended from this first couple have inherited the crippling disease of sin in the same way a child inherits her eye color from her parents. He writes, "How fortunate, then, were the first human beings! They were not distressed by any agitations of the mind, nor pained by any disorders of the body. And equally fortunate would be the whole united fellowship of [hu]mankind if our first parents had not committed an evil deed whose effect was to be passed on to their posterity. . . ."[75]

Later theologians, such as Luther and Calvin, perpetuated this interpretation, emphasizing both humanity's pride and disobedience. Calvin, in his *Institutes of the Christian Religion*, wrote that after Adam's fall, "After the heavenly image in [hu]man was effaced, he not only was himself punished by a withdrawal of the ornaments in which he had been arrayed—viz. wisdom, virtue, justice, truth, and holiness, and by the substitution in their place of those dire pests, blindness, impotence, vanity, impurity, and unrighteousness, but he involved his posterity also, and plunged them in the same wretchedness. This is the hereditary corruption to which early Christian writers gave the name of Original Sin, meaning by the term the deprivation of a nature formerly good and pure. . . ."[76] He goes on to reiterate the biological metaphor: "All of us, therefore, descending from an impure seed, come into the world tainted with the contagion of sin."[77] Sin is a disease, an infection, a genetic corruption from which it is impossible to be cured, or escape.

In a similar vein, Luther, in characteristically vivid language, discusses the concept of original sin liberally throughout his biblical commentaries and sermons. For example, in his *Lectures on Genesis*, he writes, "Thus original sin, which was contracted in Paradise, clings to us. It is the devil's yeast. Our nature is infected with it."[78] And, even more intensely in his *Lectures on Romans*:

> Therefore, as the ancient holy fathers so correctly said, this original sin is the very tinder of sin, the law of the flesh, the law of the members, the weakness of our nature, the tyrant, the original

75. St. Augustine, *City of God*, trans. Henry Bettenson (London: Penguin, 1972), 567 (Book XIV, 10).

76. John Calvin, *Institutes of Christian Religion*, vol. 1, trans. Henry Beveridge (Grand Rapids: Eerdmans, 1975), 214.

77. Ibid.

78. Martin Luther, *Luther's Works, vol. 7: Lectures on Genesis: Chapters 38–44*, ed. Jaroslav Pelikan, Hilton C. Oswald, Helmut T. Lehmann (Saint Louis: Concordia, 1999), c1965 (Luther's Works 7), S. 7:233.

sickness, etc. For it is like a sick man whose mortal illness is not only the loss of health of one of his members, but it is, in addition to the lack of health in all his members, the weakness of all of his senses and powers, culminating even in his disdain for those things which are healthful and in his desire for those things which make him sick. Thus this is Hydra, a many-headed and most tenacious monster, with which we struggle in the Lernean Swamp of this life till the very day of our death. It is Cerberus, that irrepressible barker, and Antaeus, who cannot be overcome while loose here on the earth.[79]

This understanding of original sin influenced other Reformers as well, including Philipp Melanchthon, who described original sin as an "innate disease,"[80] and Jacob Andreae and Martin Chemnitz, who called it "spiritual poison and leprosy."[81] Original sin is inevitable and inexorable, and it affects every aspect of our being.

To conclude this section on original sin, it is important to give serious consideration to the arguments of some Christian theologians who argue that the doctrine of original sin either should be radically reinterpreted or expunged entirely from the Christian tradition. The argument is that the concept of original sin does more harm than good, preventing proper appreciation and celebration of our created goodness, debilitating the already downcast and despairing, and destroying confidence, paralyzing any potential good we might seek or work for in the world. This critique certainly is not without merit, specifically in the case of those who already are in danger of being unable to hear the gospel, certain that they are unworthy of God's love and entirely incapable of receiving God's forgiveness.

Yet, there is one very good reason why the doctrine of original sin continues to have an important role in Christian doctrine, and that is the way in which it highlights the critical necessity of Jesus Christ as savior. One of the core claims of the Reformers, which they saw as being challenged by the Catholic theology of the day, was that humanity cannot fully understand and appreciate the radical nature of Christ's grace until we know the depth and breadth of original sin. Simply put, until we are thoroughly convinced of our own absolute inability to contribute in any way to our salvation—that is, until

79. Martin Luther, *Luther's Works, vol. 25: Lectures on Romans*, ed. Jaroslav Pelikan, Hilton C. Oswald, Helmut T. Lehmann (Saint Louis: Concordia, 1999), c1972 (Luther's Works 25), S. 25:300.

80. CA II, *The Book of Concord: The Confessions of the Evangelical Lutheran Church*, ed. Robert Kolb and Timothy J. Wengert (Minneapolis: Fortress Press, 2000), 38.

81. Formula of Concord, Solid Declaration, Article 1, ibid., 537.

we accept that we cannot do anything at all to make ourselves right or good before God—we cannot rely fully on the mercy and grace of Jesus Christ. Instead, we always will be tempted into seeing ourselves as contributing, even in the smallest of ways, to our salvation—cooperating with Christ in his saving work. Augustine fought a similar battle against Pelagius, who taught that if humans just "did what was in them"[82]—that is, rely on their God-given abilities and gifts, they would be able to actively participate in Christ's saving activity.

The problem this creates is twofold: first, it leads to a doctrine of Christ as a 90 percent savior. If humanity can contribute, say, 10 percent to their own salvation, we just need 90 percent of Christ's life, death, and resurrection to save us. Obviously, this is untenable to Christian theology: even if the numbers were 1 and 99 percent, the idea that humanity does not need to rely on Christ 100 percent for its salvation disparages Christ and diminishes the significance of his person and work. Second, it leads to a frantic scorekeeping on humanity's part: Have I done everything I can? Have I done enough? Did I do more today than yesterday? Am I good enough? As Luther himself experienced, these questions very quickly lead to despair, which includes both self-loathing and a hatred of God, who looms large as a terrible judge and impossible-to-please parent. The doctrine of original sin takes both these problems off the table: we are fully and utterly dependent on the salvific work of Jesus Christ; and we are fully and utterly unable to contribute to our salvation in even the smallest measure.

There is a delightful metaphor that emphasizes this reality, which, interestingly enough, also is found in Buddhism and Hinduism—and, given the animals involved in the metaphor, one might well conclude that it originated there. There are two ways of thinking about grace: "cat grace" (or "tiger grace") and "monkey grace." In the former, when faced with danger, the kitten does nothing; its mother picks it up from the ground and moves it to safety without any help from the kitten at all. In the latter, the baby monkey must cling to its mother as she jumps from branch to branch, otherwise it will fall off. Christian theology falls squarely on the side of human helplessness, the side of "cat grace."

Islam: The Human Capacity for Reason

This seems a fitting place to reiterate the Islamic teaching on sin that was discussed in the previous chapter on Islam, namely the fact that Islam has no doctrine of original sin. Instead, Islam holds that Adam and Eve were created with reason and the ability to both distinguish good and evil,

---

82. The Latin phrase is *facere quod in se est*, and comes from the Scholastic theologians of the Middle Ages.

and to choose the good. This ability was not lost in the fall. The story of the fall is told in two places in the Qur'an, but with a different ending than found in the Bible. In both 7:19-25, and 20:120-24, Adam and Eve are tempted by Satan (Iblis) to eat of the fruit of the tree of immortality. However, after eating the fruit (and covering their nakedness with leaves of the garden), they ask for God's forgiveness, and while God does turn them out of Paradise, God also forgives them, commanding them to live a life of faithfulness so that they will be rewarded on the Day of Judgment. In the same way, the "sons of Adam" are so commanded: resist temptation and obey God, and they, too, will be rewarded.

Islam emphasizes this freedom and this ability as one of its key teachings: on the Day of Judgment, each individual will be held accountable for his or her actions; and only the sin of *shirk*—associating some created thing with the One God—will not be forgiven. All other sins, Allah, who is considered endlessly merciful, can forgive: "God does not forgive that compeers be ascribed to Him, though He may forgive aught else if He please. And he who ascribes compeers to God is guilty of the gravest sin" (Qur'an 4:48). This is why the Five Pillars are so important for Islam: they are a way to order one's life around God, reminding oneself of God through the discipline of daily worship and obedience. This is also why Islam needs a prophet, who can call the people back to the right path when they stray and give them a model of faithfulness to follow, but not a savior, who must "right" the people him/herself, as they are incapable of returning to a faithful relationship with God on their own.

WE ARE JUSTIFIED AND FREED FOR LOVE

JUSTIFICATION: THE GIFT OF FAITH

Justification is the technical Christian term that refers to the human side of salvation, the ramifications, from a human perspective, of Jesus' salvific work: that is, justification is what salvation actually means for the human condition. It refers to being made right with God, being restored to right relationship with God. Alister McGrath observes that justification is at the heart of Christian theology because it describes the nature of the new relationship God has effected between God and humanity through the life, death, and resurrection of Jesus Christ. He writes:

> In the Christian doctrine of justification, we are concerned with the turning of the godless [hu]man against his godlessness; with his transformation from [hu]man *without* God to [hu]man *with* God, *for* God and *before* God; with his transition from *homo peccator* to *homo justus*. The doctrine defines the conditions under which [humans'] broken relationship with God may be restored, and the nature of that transition itself.[83]

As a doctrine, justification is associated predominantly with the theology of Martin Luther, who made it the cornerstone of his understanding of salvation, and also the center of his teachings on humanity and Christology. Carl Trueman writes: "It is a historical truism to say that Martin Luther is the theologian of justification. No one before or since in the history of the church is so closely associated with the doctrine as he is: it dominated his own thinking, it decisively influenced the direction of his own life, and it stands at the theological heart of the great rupture in the Western church between Protestants and Catholics."[84] The reason for this is that it provided the answer to the existential problem Luther had experienced in the Christian teaching of his time, which seemed to demand something of humanity—some work or payment—before salvation could be achieved. This idea made him cower under the wrath of an angry God, a terrible judge of a humanity enmeshed in its inescapable sinful condition. The recognition that God did all the work of justification freed Luther from this trap and enabled him to experience God as gracious, loving, and merciful; and salvation and even faith as a free gift from God.

The biblical locus for the concept of justification (and the source of Luther's theological breakthrough) is found in the writings of Paul, particularly in his letter to the Romans. In chapter three, Paul writes, "For we hold that a person is justified by faith apart from works prescribed by the law" (Rom. 3:28). Paul's emphasis here, which was seized and elaborated upon by Luther and the Reformers, is the fact that from start to finish, justification is a work of God, and humans can do absolutely nothing to prepare for it, participate in it, or earn it. Therefore, the phrase that actually best gets at the heart of what justification is about is "justified *by grace through faith*." This is much preferable over the shorthand version—"justified *by faith*"—because the latter suggests that

83. Alister E. McGrath, *Justitia Dei: A History of the Christian Doctrine of Justification*, vol. 1 (Cambridge: Cambridge University Press, 1986), 1–2.

84. Carl Trueman, "*Simul peccator et justus*: Martin Luther and Justification," in *Justification in Perspective*, ed. Bruce L. McCormack (Grand Rapids: Baker, 2006), 73.

the sinner is justified by her own faith; that is, it implies some sort of pact or contract with God: if I believe in you, then you will justify me. Obviously, this is deeply problematic, not only because it implies that justification is something humans do, but because it suggests that faith is also our own doing, rather than a gift from God.

Figure 6.2. The Harrowing of Hell: The Resurrected Jesus Christ Rescuing Adam and Eve, fresco at the Chora Church (Kariye Museum), Istanbul. May 2012.

By contrast, Luther presented a very different view of faith in his Small Catechism, in his explanation of the third article of the Creed. There he writes, "I believe that by my own understanding or strength I cannot believe in Jesus Christ, my Lord, or come to him."[85] In this understanding of faith, even our belief in Jesus Christ is a gift of the Holy Spirit, not something we are able to attain on our own. McGrath says it this way: "The phrase 'justification *by* grace *through* faith' brings out the meaning of the doctrine more clearly: the justification of the sinner is based upon the grace of God and is received through faith. [This doctrine] is thus an affirmation that God does everything necessary

85. Martin Luther, "The Small Catechism," in *The Book of Concord*, trans. and ed. Theodore G. Tappert (Philadelphia: Fortress Press, 1959), 355.

for salvation. Even faith itself is a gift of God, rather than a human action."[86] Luther states the same idea in different language in his Romans lectures. There he says, "the righteousness of God is brought to us without our merits and our works, while we are doing and looking for many other things rather than the righteousness of God. For who has ever sought, or would have sought, the incarnate Word, if He had not revealed Himself? Therefore He was found when He was not looked for."[87]

The central ramification of this teaching is that it ensures full and complete confidence in one's salvation, because it completely removes from the equation any aspect of human participation or cooperation. God does all, I do nothing: unworthy, unloving, ashamed, guilty—it doesn't matter. God saves us all, just as we are. Justification is the work of God through and through, and humans can neither contribute nor add to what God has done in Jesus Christ. All that is left is the joyful response by the believer, and the life of love, inspired by faith. This is what is typically called sanctification.

SANCTIFICATION: A LIFE OF LOVE

If Luther is the preeminent theologian of justification, surely John Wesley can lay claim to that title when it comes to sanctification, at least in a contemporary North American context. If justification refers to being made right with God—being forgiven and restored, sanctification refers to being made holy, the process of growth in the Christian life through the inspiration of the Holy Spirit.

Not much has been said up to this point about the Holy Spirit, but here is where She really comes to the fore. Certainly, as noted above, the Holy Spirit works to bring a person to faith. Again, to cite Luther's Small Catechism: "I believe that by my own understanding or strength I cannot believe in Jesus Christ, my Lord, or come to him *but instead the Holy Spirit has called me through the gospel, enlightened me with his gifts, made me holy, and kept me in the truth faith, just as he calls, gathers, enlightens, and makes holy the whole Christian church on earth and keeps it with Jesus Christ in the one common, true faith.*"[88] But once faith is kindled, the work of the Spirit is not over—rather, it has just begun; and in faith the Spirit continues to work, conforming us to Christ in word and deed, inspiring a deeper relationship with God and a greater love of our

86. Alister McGrath, *Christian Theology: An Introduction*, 5th ed. (Malden, MA: Wiley/Blackwell, 2011), 360.

87. Martin Luther, *Lectures on Romans*, in *Luther's Works*, vol. 25, trans. Walter G. Tillmanns and Jacob A. O. Preus (St. Louis: Concordia, 1972), 253.

88. Martin Luther, "The Small Catechism," 355, my italics.

neighbor. This "growth in grace" as sanctification is sometimes called—as long as "growth" doesn't imply a perfectly straight ascending line—is a lifelong process, a divine activity in which humans *can* participate (unlike justification), albeit weakly, in fits and starts most of the time.

Wesley used a variety of terms to describe this growth, this "journey into holiness and true righteousness," including "perfection in love, sanctification, or the restoration of the image of God."[89] He formulated what are called the "General Rules"—still found in the United Methodist *Book of Discipline*—as a way to facilitate this growth, structured around three basic guidelines: "It is therefore expected of all who continue therein that they should continue to evidence their desire of salvation, 'First: By doing no harm, by avoiding evil of every kind . . .'; 'Secondly: By . . . doing good of every possible sort, and, as far as possible, to all . . .'; 'Thirdly: By attending upon all the ordinances of God.'"[90]

Wesley had great optimism regarding the capabilities of humans to follow these rules—and, of course, great confidence in the work of the Holy Spirit, so much so that he went so far as to teach what is called the "doctrine of *entire* sanctification." This refers to a state of being in which God is able to "root out sin so thoroughly *in this life* that one could enter into and manifest to others a state of perfect love of God and neighbor."[91] This state emphasizes not only the work of the Holy Spirit and the inner transformation of the human being through grace, but also the work of the person herself, actively participating in the means of grace, which include both word and sacrament and also prayer, thereby manifesting the fruits of the Spirit: "love, joy, peace, long-suffering, gentleness, goodness, fidelity, meekness, temperance."[92]

There has been some debate about what exactly Wesley meant by *entire* sanctification—as might be imagined, across the spectrum of Christian denominations, confidence in an individual's ability to manifest *perfect* love of God and neighbor is by no means universal: surely he didn't mean *perfect*, did he? In fact, it seems that he did: *perfection* may be a provocative choice of words, but it is scriptural, and thus Wesley was determined to maintain it. (See

89. Rebekah L. Miles, "Happiness, Holiness, and the Moral Life in John Wesley," in *The Cambridge Companion to John Wesley*, ed. Randy L. Maddox and Jason E. Vickers (New York: Cambridge University Press, 2010), 210.

90. *The Book of Discipline of the United Methodist Church, 2012,* (Nashville: United Methodist Publishing House, 2012), 52.

91. Sarah H. Lancaster, "Current Debates over Wesley's Legacy Among His Progeny," in *The Cambridge Companion to John Wesley*, 309.

92. As quoted in Jason E. Vickers, "Wesley's Theological Emphases," in *The Cambridge Companion to John Wesley* 202–3.

Matt. 5:48, Matt. 19:21, 2 Cor. 7:1, 2 Cor. 13:9, Heb. 6:1, and 1 John 2:5, for example.) However, at the same time, love is the emphasis here, not sinlessness, even though he also did not hesitate to use that term.[93]

The point of Wesley's discourse, then, is that one should spend one's time and energy seeking to love God and serve the neighbor, not staring at one's navel, attempting to tally one's own sins. In other words, the focus of Christian perfection is outward, not inward; it is for the sake of the other and the glory of God, not for one's own personal merit or reward. "To be sure, Wesley sometimes spoke of entire sanctification in terms of freedom from sinful thoughts. Yet he regarded entire sanctification or Christian perfection has having above all to do with the filling of the human heart with love for God and neighbor and the governing of all subsequent thoughts, words, and deeds, by that love."[94] It is this emphasis on love that continually takes center stage for Wesley: he said that perfection is "loving God with all our heart and serving Him with all our strength. Nor did I ever say or mean any *more* by perfection than *thus* loving and serving God. . . . Entire sanctification, or Christian perfection, is neither more nor less than pure love—love expelling sin and governing both the heart and life of a child of God."[95]

Sanctification, then, answers the "What now?" question that accompanies justification. While some might think that justification is the culmination of the Christian faith, in actuality, justification is instead the beginning: the foundation for a transformed life of love, a life that shows forth the glory of God in service and care for the neighbor. It is a life that testifies to the deep connection between one's relationship to God and one's relationships in the human family, relationships where we see Christ in the face of each other, and embody the heart and hands of Christ in word and service for the sake of the other. Justification and sanctification go hand in hand, then, and are inseparable—just like faith and love.

93. Ibid., 80–81.

94. Ibid., 205.

95. As quoted in W. E. Sangster, *The Path to Perfection: An Examination and Restatement of John Wesley's Doctrine of Christian Perfection* (London: Hodder & Stoughton, 1943), 77.

Figure 6.3. A stock image of Avalokiteshvara, showing his multiple arms, eyes, and heads, which enable him to view and rescue scores of sentient beings in suffering.

Buddhism: The Bodhisattva Vow

As described in the previous chapter on Buddhism, around the first century ce, sutras appeared that claimed to be the authentic discourses of the Buddha.[96] In the schools of Mahayana Buddhism that developed around these sutras, certain Buddhist doctrines were elevated, expanded upon, and refined. So, for example, given the Buddhist doctrine that all enlightened beings should be motivated by compassion to guide others to enlightenment, early Mahayanists asked, "Then shouldn't they prolong their lives indefinitely, until all living beings, everywhere, can attain enlightenment and escape from samsara?"[97] The positive answer that this question presupposed led to what is called the bodhisattva vow. These new sutras of the Buddha were seen as extolling a new path, a path claimed to be superior to the path of the arhat. This path was called the bodhisattva path, and it differed from that of the arhat in that the disciple took a vow to postpone his (or sometimes her) attainment of final nirvana in order to devote his many lifetimes to helping others attain awakening. The bodhisattva path begins with the arousal of one's own awakened mind and then develops through the practice of specific perfections that are designed to benefit all living beings.[98] Therefore, a bodhisattva (literally, "enlightenment-being" or "a being headed for Buddhahood") is one who has vowed to attain enlightenment for the sake of all living beings. Thus one of the main characteristics of the bodhisattva path is compassion; the bodhisattva does not seek purification and *nirvana* for him or herself, but instead seeks to accumulate merit over countless lifetimes that can be used to help others attain awakening. That is, instead of abandoning the world of living beings to the fate of endless cycles of *samsara*, bodhisattvas choose to remain in the world of suffering in order to rescue living beings from this "ocean of sorrow." Thus as Donald Lopez writes, "With these great powers, advanced bodhisattvas are not only models to emulate but saviors to beseech."[99] In Mahayana belief, there is a plurality of bodhisattvas, including the beginners who have only just made the bodhisattva vow and also the vast array of celestial bodhisattvas who appear in response to the invocation of believers. Shakyamuni Buddha remains the paradigmatic figure in this pantheon, but he is only one among others. The most well-known of

96. This section is modified from a previously published article; see Kristin Johnston Largen, "Liberation, Salvation, Enlightenment: An Exercise in Comparative Soteriology," *Dialog* 45, no. 3 (Fall 2006): 267–68.

97. Strong, *The Experience of Buddhism*, 133.

98. Richard H. Robinson and Willard L Johnson, *The Buddhist Religion* (Belmont, CA: Wadsworth, 1997), 99.

99. Lopez Jr., *The Story of Buddhism*, 80.

the bodhisattvas are what are sometimes called "savior" bodhisattvas, or "celestial" bodhisattvas, of whom Avalokiteshvara is perhaps the preeminent example. These celestial beings dwell in distant "Buddha-fields" where they respond to the cries of living beings in distress, and intervene to help them. Avalokiteshvara, whose name means "the lord who looks down upon," is thought to be the very embodiment of compassion. Often he is depicted with 1,000 arms, and on each of his 1,000 palms rests an eye, representing his ability to see all and help all who are in need. In addition, he often is shown with multiple heads, piled on top of each other and also facing out on all sides, because it is said that his head split open from pain when he surveyed the world of suffering. One of the most famous scripture writings devoted to him has been incorporated as a chapter in the Lotus Sutra, although in some countries it still circulates independently as well. Let me quote a section of that chapter in full, as it describes very well both the compassion and the saving power of Avalokiteshvara:

> The systemic visual and auditory recollection of the bodhisattva Avalokiteshvara will, without fail, result in this world in the elimination of all the sufferings and sorrows of living beings. If an evil-minded fiend, intent on killing you, throws you in a pit of coals, recall Avalokiteshvara, and the fire will be extinguished as though it were sprayed with water. If someone throws you into the depths of the ocean, the abode of nagas, monsters, and demonic beings, recall Avalokiteshvara, the king of the waters, and you will never drown. If an evil-minded fiend, intent on killing you, tosses you off the top of Mount Meru, recall Avalokiteshvara, and you will be upheld in midair like the sun. . . . Seeing beings oppressed by hundreds of sorrows and afflicted by many sufferings, he looks down upon the world, including the gods, and protects it. . . . He, Avalokiteshvara, has perfected all qualities, and he looks upon all being with pity and loving kindness.[100]

This text makes clear that if Avalokiteshvara is called to mind, or called upon, he will assuredly come to one's aid, taking whatever form is needed for living beings to be saved. He becomes a rich man, a householder, a laywoman, a young girl—even a dragon or a nonhuman being. In every

100. Ibid., 182–83.

instance, he takes the form of whatever being will most effectively and expediently teach enlightenment to those sentient beings in need. In a different expression of this same idea, perhaps the most well-known Buddhist mantra, *om mani padme hum*, is an invocation to him, calling on him for assistance and deliverance. This is only one example of the way in which celestial bodhisattvas function in Buddhism to assist sentient beings in the path of liberation from suffering.

LOVE AND JUSTICE FOR ALL: A BRIDGE TO INTERRELIGIOUS DIALOGUE

The emphasis on love and justice can create a pathway for interreligious dialogue. While a majority of dialogues between religions—both in person and in print—focus on doctrinal issues, including specific beliefs and practices, there is a growing emphasis on dialogue that emphasizes shared commitments to works of love and justice. In these dialogues, finding common ground around ideas of God, understandings of prayer, or a shared view of salvation is far less important than finding a way to mobilize religious communities to act together to combat poverty, injustice, and environmental degradation. This is not a new idea, of course, but with increased global communication and awareness—particularly of places where the rainforest is being depleted, endangered animals are becoming extinct, glaciers are melting, women are sexually exploited and denied education, and children are dying of disease and malnutrition—many religious leaders are taking a much more active role to combat these evils, relying on the life-giving teachings of their own traditions to encourage interreligious work. In their book *The Myth of Christian Uniqueness*, editors John Hick and Paul Knitter gather different pluralist thinkers under three different headings, which they call "bridges" to dialogue: "The Historico-Cultural Bridge: Relativity," "The Theologico-Mystical Bridge: Mystery," and "The Ethico-Practical Bridge: Justice."[101] It is this latter bridge that is relevant here, where the motivation for interreligious dialogue is "the confrontation with sufferings of humanity and the need to put an end to such outrages."[102]

So, for example, Marjorie Hewitt Suchocki argues that "[a] feminist perspective, therefore, suggests that . . . [j]ustice is thus to be the fundamental

101. *The Myth of Christian Uniqueness: Toward a Pluralistic Theology of Religions*, ed. John Hick and Paul F. Knitter (Maryknoll, NY: Orbis, 1992).

102. Ibid., xi.

criterion of value and the focus of dialogue and action among religions."[103] Aloysius Pieris finds connection between the core liberative experiences of Buddhism (gnosis, or liberative knowledge) and Christianity (agape, or redemptive love), arguing that both are needed in "the struggle against forced poverty" that must be shared by both faith traditions.[104] Finally, Paul Knitter argues that "[a] purely Christian theology of liberation . . . suffers the dangerous limitation of inbreeding, of drawing on only one vision of the kingdom."[105] Therefore, common ground for dialogue can and should be found in "*the preferential option for the poor and the nonperson*—that is, the option to work with and for the *victims* of this world."[106]

For Christian theologians in this camp, Jesus' statement that "Whoever is not against us is for us" (Mark 9:40) can be applied here, with the argument that those who are working to eradicate poverty, end the trafficking of children, and protect vulnerable animal populations are doing Christ's work—even if they don't do it in Christ's name—and Christians can and should work alongside them. Surely the Holy Spirit can work in non-Christians just as well as in Christians for the sake of the last and the least in the world, and surely we don't have to come to a consensus on every theological detail before we can agree to embrace a shared vision of love and justice that crosses religious boundaries.

INTERRELIGIOUS QUESTIONS FOR FURTHER DISCUSSION

1. How is the concept of the inherent Buddha nature similar to the idea of inherent goodness in humanity? How is it different?
2. How do the concepts of *darshan* and *puja* challenge traditional Christian worship practices? Are there any similarities? Is there anything Christians can learn from these practices?
3. How does the "chosenness" of Judaism relate to God's salvific will for all?
4. How are Sufis similar to Christian mystics? What is the role of the mystical tradition in Christianity? What does it have to teach Christian theology as a whole?

103. Marjorie Hewitt Suchocki, "In Search of Justice: Religious Pluralism from a Feminist Perspective," in *The Myth of Christian Uniqueness*, 149.

104. Aloysius Pieris, S.J., "The Buddha and the Christ: Mediators of Liberation," in *The Myth of Christian Uniqueness*, 162–75.

105. Paul Knitter, "Toward a Liberation Theology of Religions," in *The Myth of Christian Uniqueness*, 180.

106. Ibid., author's italics, 185.

5. How are the differing understandings of sin in Islam and Christianity illustrative of larger differences between the faith traditions? What can Christians learn from Islam on this point?
6. How might the concept of the bodhisattva vow helpfully inform a Christian understanding of sanctification?

7

A Wild and Wonderful World

REHABILITATING A CHRISTIAN DOCTRINE OF CREATION

In 1967, the journal *Science* published an article by Lynn White, titled "The Historical Roots of Our Ecological Crisis." In the course of his essay, White emphasized how Christianity and what he called "Christian axioms" continue to dominate Western thinking. And he asked the question, "What did Christians tell people about their relations with the environment?"[1] In his view, the answer is not a positive one, at least where creation is concerned. White decried the anthropomorphism of Christianity, which, he argued, "not only established *problem* a dualism of [hu]man and nature but also insisted that it is God's will that [humans] exploit nature for his proper ends."[2] In addition, Christianity, in its zeal to purge any vestiges of "pagan animism" in the cultures into which it was brought, destroyed any sense of a living spirit present in the natural world, leading to a sense that humans are "superior to nature, contemptuous of it, willing to use it for our slightest whim."[3]

At this point, the reader might assume that White ended his article by repudiating and rejecting Christianity altogether: if it has been the cause of such problems, certainly it would be best to move beyond it altogether. However, that is not the conclusion White drew. Instead, White argued for a *solution* rehabilitation of Christianity, believing that since the "roots of our trouble are so largely religious, the remedy must also be essentially religious, whether we call it that or not. We must rethink and refeel our nature and destiny."[4]

I begin this chapter with this short summary of what is now an almost fifty-year-old article because several points that White makes continue to be relevant

---

1. Lynn White, "The Historical Roots of Our Ecological Crisis," *Science* 155 (March 10, 1967): 4, http://www.uvm.edu/~gflomenh/ENV-NGO-PA395/articles/Lynn-White.pdf

2. Ibid.

3. Ibid.

4. Ibid., 6.

for a contemporary Christian understanding of creation. First, the recognition that Christianity has, indeed, contributed to the human-centered exploitative attitude toward creation, which in turn has led to the willful neglect and abuse of the environment. Second, the understanding that the environmental crisis is, indeed, a theological problem and requires theological resources to effectively combat and change it. Finally, the belief that there are within the Christian tradition resources that can be brought to bear upon this crisis with positive results. All three of these insights shape the reflections in this chapter, in which I seek to tell a different story about the relationship humanity—and God—has with the environment, a story that I would call a twenty-first-century ecologically grounded theology of creation.

In telling this story, this chapter unfolds as follows. First, I explore the "wonderfulness" of creation from a variety of perspectives, including God's ongoing creative activity, panentheism, and theological aesthetics. Second, I examine the "wildness" of creation, including discussions of science and theology, and theodicy. As in the previous two chapters, this Christian doctrine of creation is interposed by relevant doctrines and practices from different religious traditions; and questions for further exploration conclude the chapter.

A WONDERFUL WORLD

WHAT'S IN A NAME? "CREATION" VS. "NATURE"

Naming the universe "creation" is not a neutral act. It is, in fact, a theological assertion of hope, faith, relationship, and divine presence—a word that contains within it a particular understanding not only of the cosmos (humanity included) but also of God and God's activity. The most obvious reason for this is that first and foremost, of course, the word "creation" implies—no, actually demands—a "creator." Therefore, when Christians use language of "creation," they also are declaring God's existence: but what kind of God, and what kind of creation? These questions have been answered differently throughout the Christian tradition, but from today's vantage point, the following affirmations seem to be most consistent with both fresh theological insights from around the globe, and new information about the world from the various scientific disciplines.

First, the language of creation indicates that something of God can be known from our observation of, and interaction with, the world as a whole. This already has been described in the previous chapter on the doctrine of God, using the language of "general revelation" (as opposed to "special revelation"—the revelation of God in Jesus Christ), and the idea of the "two books" of divine revelation: understanding the book of scripture and the book of nature as two complementary sources for "reading" God's self-disclosure.

Second, the language of creation emphasizes the world's radical dependence on God: without God, the world would not exist—not only from the beginning of time, but from moment to moment. Creation is not eternal, creation is not divine; instead, the world and its creatures rely on the life-giving power of God for their sustenance and fecundity, in ways both grand and prosaic. Third, the language of creation also asserts the creative nature of God. God was not compelled in any way to create the universe: instead, creation is a result of God's loving freedom and grace; and the kind of world God created—in all its diversity, complexity, and mystery—reflects something of God's own complex and mysterious nature.

Finally, while we can no longer think about an "order" in creation the way our forebears in the faith once did (more about that to follow), we can continue to affirm that creation as a whole has meaning and purpose, a *telos* that is unfolding from the heart and mind of God, even when we cannot discern it. What this means is that even though chance does play a role in the events of creation, even though randomness and uncertainty are a part of daily life, all is not simply haphazard and arbitrary. Instead, God has infused the entire cosmos with significance, and calls to the universe from the future, drawing the whole world into the kingdom of God where, in the eschaton, creation will realize its fullness in perfection.

[margin notes: World is dependent on G; creative nature of God; creation has a telos]

Islam: Allah the Creator

Do Christians and Muslims worship the same God? This question is not so easily answered, and support can be mounted for both negative and affirmative responses. On the negative side, first and foremost are the differing views each religion has regarding Jesus Christ. As already noted, while Muslims revere Jesus as a great prophet, they are adamant in rejecting his divinity. This difference is bound up with other theological differences as well—including different understandings of the "how" of salvation and human responsibility in one's relationship to God. In addition, the fact that Muslims and Christians do not share sacred scripture is another point of contention. On the positive side, however, is the fact that Muslims and Christians are cousins—descended from sons of Abraham, and that both are considered "people of the book," with many shared ancestors and shared stories. In light of this common ancestry, it should come as no surprise that when we examine how Muslims view God and creation, looking specifically at the witness in the Qur'an, we find many similarities between Islam and Christianity.

First and foremost, the Qur'an is absolutely clear that Allah is the sole creator of the universe: Allah is the single maker, sustainer, provider, and controller. "God is the creator of everything. He is One, the omnipotent" (Qur'an 13:16). Further, in Islam, it also is taught that God created *ex nihilo*, purely from God's will and God's word: God is "Creator of the heavens and the earth from nothingness, He has only to say when He wills a thing: 'Be,' and it is" (Qur'an 2:117).

Related to creation, the Qur'an shares many images with the Bible. For example: "It is God who raised the skies without support, as you can see, then assumed His throne, and enthralled the sun and the moon (so that) each runs to a predetermined course. . . . It is He who stretched the earth. . . . He covers up the day with the night" (Qur'an 13:2-3); "Blessed is He who placed in the heavens constellations of stars, and placed a burning lamp in it and the luminous moon" (Qur'an 25:61); "It is He who sends down waters from the skies, and brings out of it every thing that grows . . ." (Qur'an 6:99); and "God created every moving thing from water: One crawls on its belly, one walks on two legs, another moves on four. God creates whatsoever He will" (Qur'an 24:45).

In addition, the Qur'an testifies that all creation is *muslim*—that is, submitted to Allah's will:

> So, a rock is perfectly the rock that Allah commands it to be, the tree is exactly what Allah commands it to be, and wild animals such as the deer, the camel or the tiger are all exactly as Allah wishes them to be. Everything in creation is obedient to Allah in this way, no matter whether it is non-living like the air, the earth or the oceans, or living, like the animals, the plants, the bacteria and the fungi. It makes no difference whether something is microscopic or immense. The particles of atoms and the massive galaxies of outer space are all obedient.[5]

All creatures worship and obey Allah simply being what they have been created to be; and in so doing, they witness to Allah's unity and greatness: "The sun and the moon revolve to a computation; and the grasses and

---

5. "Science within Islam: Learning How to Care for Our World," by Yunus Negus, in *Islam and Ecology*, ed. Fazlun Khalid with Joanne O'Brien (London: Cassell, 1992), 37.

the trees bow (to Him) in adoration" (Qur'an 55:6); and "All that is in the heavens and the earth sings the praises of God the King, the Holy, Omnipotent, the Wise" (Qur'an 62:1). Perhaps this is what Muhammad meant when he said, "The whole of this earth is a mosque,"[6] a place of vibrant worship of God, an acknowledgment of the Creator by His creation.

Thus it is said that in Islam, nature is "a sign and a trust given to humans,"[7] by which they are able to learn about God: "Do you not see the birds held high between the heavens and the earth? Nothing holds them (aloft) but God. There are verily signs in this for those who believe" (Qur'an 16:79). For many Muslims then, science is a way of "deciphering the signs of God in the cosmic book of the universe. Natural sciences discover the Divine codes built into the cosmos by its Creator, and in doing so, help the believer marvel at the wonders of God's creation."[8]

Finally, there is a strong current of determinism in the Qur'an that emphasizes that Allah controls every event that happens and that Allah is responsible for all the workings of the world: nothing escapes His eye, and nothing happens without His command. For example: "It is He who created you from clay then determined a term (of life) for you and a term (is fixed) within Him" (Qur'an 6:2); "If God sends you harm, there is no one but He who can take it away; and if He bring you good, surely He has power over every thing" (Qur'an 6:17); "To God leads the right path, though some deviate. If He willed He could guide you all to the right way" (Qur'an 16:9); and finally, "When God intends misfortune for a people no one can avert it, and no saviour will they have apart from Him" (Qur'an 13:11).

CREATION'S INHERENT GOODNESS

As was described in the chapter on humanity, not only humans were created good but also creation itself, although this "goodness" has been interpreted very differently in the course of Christian history. More specifically, for centuries, the goodness of creation has been categorized as "instrumental," that is, creation has been seen as "good" insofar as, and only to the degree that, it is "good" for

6. As quoted in Negus, "Science within Islam,"38.

7. "Islam and Modern Science: Questions at the Interface," by Muzaffar Iqbal, in *God, Life, and the Cosmos: Christian and Islamic Perspectives*, ed. Ted Peters, Muzaffar Iqbal, and Syed Nomanul Haq (Burlington, VT: Ashgate, 2002), 17.

8. "Three Views of Science in the Islamic World," by Ibrahim Kalin, in *God, Life, and the Cosmos*, ed. Peters, Iqbal, and Haq, 48.

instrumental value

humanity. In other words, instrumental goodness locates the value of something in relationship to something—or someone—else; it does not have value just as it is, but only as it is useful for another purpose. So, for example, a computer in and of itself does not have value (besides the monetary value a society affixes to it): in the case of a fire, no one would expect a firefighter to risk her life saving a computer. Computers are only valuable insofar as they support human flourishing and make our lives better, easier, more productive, more connected, etc. This is what is meant by instrumental value; and, unfortunately, this is the way creation has for too long been viewed.

A main reason for this can be found in the creation account in Genesis—particularly the language of humans having "dominion" over the other facets of creation. This language has resulted in Christians judging the rest of the created world as existing solely for our benefit: there for the taking, using up, and discarding as we see fit. Consequently, for centuries, there has been no check—theological or otherwise—on human desire, consumption, and exploitation of the natural world; this has had dire consequences that we are only now beginning to understand and experience.

A Christian doctrine of the inherent, or intrinsic, value of creation can *inherent or intrinsic value* go a long way in transforming this attitude of calculated self-interest. Intrinsic value—as opposed to instrumental value—points to the inherent worth of something, the claim that it has value just because it is what it is, not because it can do or provide something for someone else. Humans, obviously, are almost universally regarded as having intrinsic value, which means that it is not considered morally justifiable to experiment on them, use them as pawns in warfare, or buy and sell them, regardless of how significant or substantial the results might be. (This is not to say, however, that all humans always have been, or are, accorded that value: the number of people worldwide still held in slavery, still trafficked, still exploited testify to that fact.) Intrinsic value, then, creates an obligation on behalf of the individual; in relationship with that individual, whether direct or indirect, I have an obligation to treat that individual as a moral patient—that is, someone whom I have the responsibility of treating with care, respect, and ethical concern.

This also enables us to look again at the creation account in Genesis with fresh eyes. Given that Genesis records that God blessed every aspect of the nonhuman creation with the same designation of "goodness" that God blessed the human creation, there is certainly justification within the Christian tradition to advocate a doctrine of intrinsic goodness for the whole of creation—and all its creatures—not just for humanity. From this theological vantage point, Christians find themselves in a much stronger position to connect the well-being of humanity to the well-being of creation as a whole, to embed human existence within the larger web of created life, and to appreciate all the ways in which God is present and at work in the nonhuman creation. It allows Christians to recapture a more holistic vision not only of God's creative work, but also of God's redemptive love, and the cosmic vision of the restoration and reconciliation of the entire universe, in which no corner of creation will be "left behind."[9] This is the beginning, end, and middle of the Christian story of God's history with the world.

RAMIFICATIONS FOR THE RELATIONSHIP BETWEEN HUMANITY AND THE REST OF CREATION

Upholding the goodness of creation affects the way we view the relationship between humanity and the rest of creation. One way to think about this is replacing a mindset of anthropocentrism with what is sometimes called "ecocentrism." As the etymology of the first word suggests, "anthropocentrism" puts humanity at the top rung of the ladder, the sun around which the rest of creation orbits. It insists that humans are the only creatures that have intrinsic value, and that the entire rest of the cosmos was created solely for the well-being and support of humanity. Therefore, animals, plants, and the environment as a whole do not have any moral claim on us, nor is it incumbent upon humanity to take steps to preserve creation any more than is needed for human flourishing. This means that when asking about the viability and wisdom of drilling for oil in Arctic waters, using primates for testing experimental drugs, or regulating fishing practices, the primary—or even only—consideration should be the effects on humanity: In what ways do such practices nurture and further human welfare, and in what ways do they hinder it?

Ecocentrism starts with a different premise. Where anthropocentrism sets humans above and apart from the rest of creation, ecocentrism enmeshes them in what is often viewed as a "web" of creation, where all beings are closely connected to each other, and no one species is located in a privileged position. Ecocentrism emphasizes that "humanity must be understood within the context of the whole of creation (not isolated from it), both in terms of human connectedness with this larger social and natural environment and in terms of the distinctiveness of human being in these relationships."[10]

---

9. This phrase refers to a popular series of novels by Tim LaHaye and Jerry B. Jenkins, based on a "rapture" theology, an eschatological vision in which in the end times, true Christians are taken to heaven and the rest are left behind on earth to suffer the reign of the Antichrist and God's judgment.

10. *Constructive Christian Theology in the Worldwide Church*, ed. William R. Barr (Grand Rapids: Eerdmans, 1997), 191.

I want to emphasize that the affirmation of humanity as intertwined with all of creation does not carry with it an insistence that all beings are "equal," or that it is incumbent upon humans to accord to mosquitoes the same value that they accord blue whales. However, it does recognize that these animals do have their own integrity, their own purpose, and their own right to survive, reproduce, and even thrive; and humans are responsible for taking the needs of all creatures—and creation itself—into consideration when making decisions that affect the whole world. One well-known example that is relevant here is the tunnel that was cut into a giant sequoia (the Wawona tree) in Yosemite National Park in the 1880s, eventually attracting many tourists, particularly those who wanted to drive through it. When it finally fell in 1969, it was over 2,000 years old, and some speculated that the tunnel had hastened its demise. From an ecocentric perspective, one must ask the question whether such a tunnel violated the integrity of the tree, particularly if such an action contributed to its death. In a similar vein, and perhaps even more pointedly, ecocentrism demands that humans ask hard questions around animal testing, logging, oil drilling, and trophy hunting—just to name a few examples—questions that take into account not only the human costs and benefits, but also the costs to the whole family of creation.

Buddhism: The Relationship between Humans and Animals

It is fair to say that Buddhism has a somewhat ambivalent understanding of animals in general, and their relationship to human beings. Certainly, from the earliest times, animals were seen as "lower" than human beings; and rebirth in an animal form was considered a punishment, not a reward. In general, in their present existence animals are not seen as being able to progress on the path to enlightenment; and the animal world is considered a place of particularly entrenched suffering, as animals do not possess the capacity for wisdom and self-reflection. In addition, negative characteristics are often portrayed using animals; for example, at the center of the "wheel of life"—a common symbol of the cyclical existence of samsara—there are three animals, each of which represents one of three poisons of existence: a pig, which stands for ignorance; a snake, which stands for aversion; and a bird, which stands for attachment.

Yet, at the same time, animals also are considered sentient beings, who like ourselves and all others caught in the round of rebirth (*samsara*) possess within themselves Buddha-nature and the potential for enlightenment. Thus many Buddhists think it important to treat animals with care and respect. The Buddhist interpretation of *ahimsa* (nonharming), which is found in other Indic religions as well, includes animals in its teachings: the precept against "taking life" includes animal life (leading to a vegetarian diet for many Buddhists); and the practice of "right livelihood" includes the prohibition against slaughtering animals for a living. Added incentive for these practices is found in the teaching of rebirth: "There is not a single being, wandering in the chain of lives in endless and beginningless samsara, that has not been your mother or your sister. An individual, born as a dog, may afterward become your father. . . . One's own flesh and the flesh of others is the same flesh."[11] Indeed, in the large collection of *Jataka* tales, similar in some ways to Aesop's fables, there are many stories about the Buddha being born into an animal form—a lizard, a deer, etc.—and in that form revealing some truth about the nature of existence.

Buddhist communities today continue the centuries-old practice of purchasing, then setting free, captive animals; often, the practice coincides with the celebration of the Buddha's birthday. This practice has a long history in the tradition, and can be found as far back as eighth-century China, where a decree from 759 established over eighty ponds solely for the release and protection of fish.[12] Donald Lopez notes that the *locus classicus* for the practice comes from the following story in the *Sutra of Golden Light*. The story goes that in a previous life, the Buddha lived as a man named Jalavahana. One day, he came across a pond that was drying up, in which 10,000 fish were dying. Using twenty elephants, he ferried water to the pond in order to replenish it and save the fish. Even that was not enough, however: he also waded into the pond and pronounced the Buddha's name, and preached a short sermon on Buddhist teaching. This caused the fish to be reborn in one of the heavenly realms when they died.[13] This story illustrates the Buddhist belief that one should not only rescue animals physically, but also tend to their spiritual needs, seeking to facilitate a positive rebirth for them as well.

11. Stephanie Kaza, "Western Buddhist Motivations for Vegetarianism," in *Worldviews: Environment Culture Religion* 9, no. 3 (2005): 396–97.

12. Donald S. Lopez Jr., *The Story of Buddhism: A Concise Guide to Its History and Teachings* (San Francisco: HarperSanFrancisco, 2001), 197.

13. Ibid., 198.

CREATIO EX NIHILO, CREATIO CONTINUA: GOD'S CREATIVE WORK

In the course of the Christian tradition, there have been two primary ways of describing God's creative activity. The first is *creatio ex nihilo*, and the second is *creatio continua*. Each of these descriptors offers important insights for understanding what it means for Christians to call God "creator"; thus I describe each of these in turn.

CREATIO EX NIHILO

There are very few doctrines in the long and complex history of the Christian tradition that can be said—without too much overstatement—to be unanimously held; and so when we come across one of these, we do well to take note. *Creatio ex nihilo* means "creation out of nothing," and from the earliest church fathers to today's diverse collection of global theologians, this is one of those near-universals that has withstood the tests of time and context. While the phrase first appeared in a commentary on Genesis by second-century theologian Theophilus of Antioch, it was Irenaeus who really promulgated it—and after him, Tertullian and Augustine.[14] There are several reasons why this doctrine has had such broad, deep, longstanding support within the Christian community. Of them, three are the most important: first, it accentuates God's absolute, sole sovereignty over the universe; second, it emphasizes the dependence of the world on God for its very existence; and third, it underscores not only the goodness of creation, but its purposefulness and meaningfulness.

First, the assertion that God created all that exists out of sheer emptiness stands at the heart of the creedal claim, "I believe in God the Father almighty, maker of heaven and earth." This belief roundly rejects any dualistic notion of creation: there is no timeless "something" out of which God created—no abiding "matter" or force that is somehow "coeternal" with God, or assisted in any way in God's creative work. God alone is sovereign over all that is, and God alone has power over nothingness and annihilation: God alone is able to call into being what is from what is not. In short, "The *creatio ex nihilo* perspective first of all affirms that God alone is the source of all that is, and God's creative activity is free and unconditioned."[15] God did not create the universe

14. Sjoerd L. Bonting, *Creation and Double Chaos: Science and Theology in Discussion* (Minneapolis: Fortress Press, 2005), 68–69. It is worth noting that Bonting himself argues against the doctrine of *creatio ex nihilo*, favoring a doctrine of creation out of chaos, which he calls "chaos theology."

15. Robert John Russell, "T=O: Is It Theologically Significant?" in *Religion & Science: History, Method, Dialogue*, ed. W. Mark Richardson and Wesley J. Wildman (New York: Routledge, 1996), 203.

out of some external compulsion, or some inner lack or deficiency; instead, God created the universe freely, out of God's superabundant love and generosity.

Second, this doctrine affirms that the entire creation is dependent upon God for its very being, and cannot and could not exist—either at the beginning of time or at any moment within time—without the creative will and power of God. This means, obviously, that the world is not God—the world itself is not divine or infinite. The relationship between God and creation, while intimate and intertwined, is not one of equals or partners: "*Creatio ex nihilo* also affirms that the world is an autonomous and distinct reality because it was created by the free resolve and decree of God. As a creation by God, and not God's own self, the world is contingent, finite, temporal, and relative; only God is necessary, infinite, eternal, and absolute."[16] What's more, this dependence is enduring and ongoing, as true today as it was 13.75 billion years ago. God not only created the world out of nothing, but continually holds it in God's hands, preserving it from falling back into nothingness moment to moment, day to day, year to year. As Langdon Gilkey writes, "The world is not self-sufficient, but dependent on God as its Creator and its continual preserver."[17]

Finally, the doctrine of *creatio ex nihilo* emphasizes not only the goodness of creation itself, but what's more, the purpose and meaning within creation. Because creation has its origins in the perfect will and desire of a perfectly good and true God, creation in its fullness is not haphazard, fickle, or futile. Even though for both individuals and communities the world can be a dangerous, unpredictable place, Christian doctrine holds that we are not, in fact, stuck in a twisted funhouse, full of dead ends, distorted mirrors, and heart-stopping surprises lurking behind every doorway: "In Christian belief, we are not born into an arbitrary, chaotic world, nor are we thrust into an existence that necessarily involves suffering and meaninglessness."[18] Instead, Christians argue that God's eye is on the sparrow, God is continually bringing good out of evil, and ultimately, God is preparing a place for us at journey's end. From start to finish, all of creation is under God's loving dominion, working out its destiny under the grace and guidance of an ever-present God. While certainly we will experience both chaos and suffering in our lives, because God created the world in wisdom and love, the world does have intention and sense at its core—even if not for each one of us individually at all times and places.

16. Ibid., 203.

17. Langdon Gilkey, *Maker of Heaven and Earth: A Study of the Christian Doctrine of Creation* (Garden City, NY: Doubleday, 1959), 131.

18. Ibid., 178.

Lastly, it is worth noting that this doctrine of *creatio ex nihilo* has interesting and important ramifications for scientists, and for a theological perspective on scientific research. Robert John Russell writes that "[s]ince God creates freely, the world need not be at all, and it need not be the way it is. Hence for us to know the world, we must experiment; we cannot discover the way nature is by reason alone. Moreover, since the world is not divine, it is not sacrilegious to experiment with nature. Thus we both (morally) can and (epistemologically) must experiment with nature to gain knowledge."[19] A caveat is perhaps required here, regarding the language "experiment with nature." It goes without saying that in the same way that extreme caution is taken when using human subjects in experiments (we, too, are a part of "nature"), so also great caution and respect should be taken in any experiments involving creation, particularly with animals. Having said that, however, the sentiment Russell espouses should encourage Christians to seek wisdom from science, and engage scientific theories with eagerness and openness. If it is true that all that exists has its origins in God, we can freely and without hesitation explore all aspects of creation, searching its mysteries, confident that what we will find will help us better appreciate, understand, and care for all God has made, giving glory always to the One from whom all life, in all its forms, flows.

CREATIO CONTINUA

In contrast, but also in complement to all that was said above, the doctrine of *creatio continua* emphasizes God's continuing relationship with the world, God's continuing involvement and providential care, and the *living* creative power of God. It emphasizes that God's continuing work is not over—it is not in the past, receding further and further in the rearview mirror as life progresses. Instead, God's creative activity is present for us in the here and now, and even at work in our future, preparing a way and a place for us that we cannot now even imagine, let alone foresee. In this way, the doctrine of *creatio continua* preserves and celebrates God's freedom to do "a new thing" every day, in every moment—both now and in the future. God's work is not over, God's engagement with the world is not finished, and God continues to inspire and transform creation with God's life-giving, creative presence.

Another important reason for the Christian community to highlight this way of describing God's creative work is that it dovetails nicely with scientific understandings of the world. For example, John Polkinghorne describes two conditions that must apply to any account Christians give of God's action in the

---

19. Russell, "T=O: Is It Theologically Significant?" 203.

world. First, this action "must be continuous and not fitful, correctly referred to as 'interaction' rather than 'intervention.' There can be nothing capricious or occasional in God's activity."[20] This means that a theological articulation of God's relationship should maintain and support the understanding of the universe revealed to us through the sciences, rather than subvert it. Therefore, instead of focusing on the work of God as manifest in this or that discrete "miraculous" activity—the man with terminal cancer who suddenly finds himself in remission, the infertile woman who suddenly finds herself pregnant, the hurricane whose path suddenly veers from its expected trajectory—Christian theology can and should emphasize the ongoing "miraculous" work of God, revealed in the changing of the seasons, the vast migrations of animals on wing, foot, and fin, and the subtle evolution of animal species. Certainly, this does not mean that God *cannot* intervene in creation in phenomenal, extraordinary ways: no Christian theologian would dare to constrict the possibility of God working in any way God chooses. However, the point here is that such one-of-a kind, unusual, inexplicable activity is not the normal way in which God reveals God's loving care and presence in creation. God does not pop in and out of creation, like "Q" in *Star Trek: The Next Generation*, acting here for good and there for ill, depending on the capricious whim of the moment. Instead, God's gracious, loving activity is constant, continuous, and dependable.

Second, Polkinghorne writes that God's action in the world "will always be contained within the grain of the created order. The laws of nature are not constraints externally imposed upon God; rather they are, in their regularity, expressions of the faithful will of the Creator. God is their ordainer and does not work against them. . . ."[21] This statement points to the inherent harmony that exists between divine agency and creation's own agency, between God's dynamic activity and the dynamic ebb and flow of the forces of nature, the lives and deaths of creatures, and the planetary orbits. This is the reason the psalmist writes of "fire and hail, snow and fog, tempestuous wind, doing God's will" (Ps. 148:8), of how God has set "the moon and the stars" in their courses (Ps. 8:8), and that the heavens declare the righteousness of God (Ps. 97:6).

God and the world are not opposed in their workings; instead, the world itself actively participates in God's creative activity, as God works in, through, and with it to further God's ends for creation. This does not mean creation is perfect, or that every individual event that happens is "God's will"—as though God were manipulating each occurrence with a single purpose in mind.

20. John Polkinghorne, "Chaos Theory and Divine Action," in *Religion & Science*, ed. Richardson and Wildman, 244.

21. Ibid., 244–45.

Instead, as Polkinghorne notes, it means that because God is the author of creation, God is not only the one who knit together the sinews of the human being, but also the one who established the delicate gravitational balance that daily delights surfers, the one who binds electrons to the nucleus of an atom, and the one who girded the earth in wind belts. The laws of nature are a manifestation of God's ongoing creative activity, and therefore they both reflect and contribute to that activity.

There is one more important ramification of this understanding of God's ongoing creative work. If it is true that the world itself is active in God's creative work, how much more, then, are humans active participants in this divine labor, in that humans have the ability to recognize God's artistry in creation and willingly consent to contribute to it in some small way. Particularly apt here is the description of human beings as "created co-creators." Philip Hefner developed this idea in his book *The Human Factor: Evolution, Culture, and Religion* (among other places). There, he states his proposal as follows:

> Human beings are God's created co-creators whose purpose is to be the agency, acting in freedom, to birth the future that is most wholesome for the nature that has birthed us—the nature that is not only our own genetic heritage, but also the entire human community and the evolutionary and ecological reality in which and to which we belong. Exercising this agency is said to be God's will for humans.[22]

What is significant here is the deep connection this idea presumes between God, humanity, and the rest of the natural world; more specifically, the belief that God works through humanity for the sake of the world, and also that humanity is created not simply to fulfill its own needs, but for the sake of the larger flourishing of the entire cosmos.

Hefner himself makes this explicit, with several auxiliary hypotheses he attaches to this proposal, including one that recognizes that any meaning and purpose one might posit for humanity can only be found located within and connected to meaning and purpose posited for nature as a whole. He writes, "Both the creation and the human being have purposes for their existence, and the two are intertwined within the larger notion of God's destiny for the entire creation."[23] Another hypothesis suggests that human beings receive knowledge

---

22. Philip Hefner, *The Human Factor: Evolution, Culture, and Religion* (Minneapolis: Fortress Press, 1993), 27.

23. Ibid., 39.

and grace—including divine knowledge and divine grace—through, rather than apart from, nature.[24] Both hypotheses emphasize that God, humanity, and creation are interwoven, interrelated, and interpenetrating with each influencing the others, though not equally, of course, and each in some sense dependent on the others, though again, from God's side, this interdependency is freely chosen, and the limits it creates freely accepted.

Judaism: Tikkun Olam

The Jewish teaching of *tikkun olam* has become much better known in the past few decades—far beyond the bounds of Judaism itself—and it is gaining currency as an important theological metaphor for addressing the plethora of serious environmental crises facing creation as well. It has been used as a motivator to seek peace between nations, to empower communities to work together to address poverty and injustice, and to take action to combat environmental pollution, despoliation, and habitat loss.

Tikkun olam means "repairing/healing/perfecting the world," and the phrase has a long history in Jewish tradition. Jonathan Sacks notes that "*tikkun olam*" first appears in the Mishnah, in the context of specific issues of jurisprudence, like slavery, for example, that need to be rectified in order to avoid negative consequences, not only for individuals, but for society as a whole.[25] Further, he goes on to say that the phrase (*le-takken olam*) also is found in a well-known and oft-used Jewish prayer, the *Alenu* (the word means "it is our duty," or "it is incumbent upon us"[26]), which is the last prayer of the daily liturgy. It reads in part, "Therefore it is our hope, O Lord our God, that we may soon see the glory of Your power, to remove abominations from the earth so that idols are utterly cut off, *to perfect the world* under the sovereignty of the Almighty. Then all humanity will call on Your name. . . ."[27]

However, it is its definition and description in the context of the Lurianic kabbalistic teaching of *zimzum*, which will be discussed below, that have given it the meaning most often used today. According to Isaac Luria, in the course of creating the universe, God sent forth God's presence in rays of light, which proved to be too strong for the vessels intended

---

24. Ibid., 264–65.

25. Jonathan Sacks, *To Heal a Fractured World: The Ethics of Responsibility* (New York: Schocken, 2005), 75.

26. http://www.jewishencyclopedia.com/articles/1112-alenu.

27. Sacks, *To Heal a Fractured World*, 75–76, my italics.

to contain it. They shattered, and the fragments of light were scattered throughout creation. It is thus part of the task of humanity to collect these fragments of light, thereby repairing the brokenness in creation, and, in the process, "restoring something of lost harmony to the cosmos."[28]

Sacks argues that what is unique and important in Luria's interpretation is that it bridges the gap between "historical" and "messianic" time; that is, it explains how we get from "here" to "there": "here" being the world of strife and brokenness we experience now; and "there" being the eschatological vision of a perfected and cosmically restored universe. Sacks writes that in Luria's narrative, "it is *a redemption of small steps*, act by act, day by day. Each act mends a fracture of the world. The way from here to there, like the journey of the Israelites through the wilderness takes time. There are setbacks on the way—sins, rebellions, false turns. A journey of a few days takes 40 years. But there are no short cuts, no miraculous leaps."[29] In this way, step by step, day by day, year by year, humanity and creation as a whole move closer to the future God intends for the world. The idea of *tikkun olam* reminds us that we may not be able to do it all, but we each can do a little, and together, those little acts add up and make a difference, particularly when viewed as contributing to God's own ongoing work in creation. Abraham Heschel said that it was God's desire to have "humanity as a partner in the drama of continuous creation. By whatever we do, by every act we carry out, we either advance or obstruct the drama of redemption."[30]

At this point, one word of clarification is necessary. Sacks makes clear that, in Kabbalah itself, these "small steps" are not understood to be acts of mercy and justice in the world—like feeding the hungry and protecting the rainforests. Instead, in Kabbalah, the necessary "steps" are those of prayer and spiritual study. Thus Sacks concludes that "Lurianic kabbalah is at best a metaphor, not a prescription," for social and environmental justice. Yet at the same time, it is a metaphor worth preserving, for two reasons. First, "It suggests that our acts make a difference. They repair fractures in the world. They restore a lost order."[31] Second, they empower humanity to continue the struggle against sin and evil, even when malevolent powers

28. Ibid., 75.

29. Ibid., 77.

30. As quoted in Mark L. Winer, "*Tikkun olam:* A Jewish Theology of 'Repairing the World,'" *Theology* 111 (November/December 2008): 436.

31. Sacks, *To Heal a Fractured World*, 78.

seem overwhelming: "Lurianic kabbalah is not afraid to look at catastrophe without concluding that the world is irreparable, evil endemic. . . . Out of broken fragments, it shapes a mosaic of hope."[32]

PANENTHEISM

The relationship between God and the universe can be described using a variety of models that convey both differentiation and connection. At either end of the spectrum are descriptions that are both unhelpful and unfaithful to God's self-revelation; they can be best understood by envisioning two circles, one representing God, the other, the cosmos. At one end is a deist model, where the circles are entirely autonomous and self-enclosed, neither touching nor overlapping at any point. In this model, God is entirely separate and unrelated to creation, having completely distanced Godself after God's initial creative work. At the other end is a pantheistic model, where the circles are so perfectly superimposed one atop the other that there is, in effect, only one circle. In this model, the entire being of God is exhausted within the bounds of creation: God is collapsed into the world, as it were. Neither of these models do justice to God's loving, ongoing engagement with creation.

Thankfully, there is a range of much better models between these extremes; and of them, one of the most creative and constructive is called *panentheism*—note the "en" in the middle: two small letters that constitute a world of difference between this model and one with which it is sometimes confused, pantheism. In this model, the smaller circle of the universe is completely enveloped by the larger divine circle, suggesting full penetration and participation in every aspect of the cosmos by the Divine: no facet of creation is "out of touch" with God, literally. Elizabeth Johnson describes panentheism this way: "Panentheism envisions a relationship whereby everything abides *in* God, who in turn encompasses everything, being '*above all and through all and in all*' (Eph. 4:6). What results is a mutual abiding for which the pregnant female body provides a good metaphor."[33]

Panentheism, then, seeks to reimage Divine transcendence as immanence, as it were: preserving the mystery of God while at the same time emphasizing that God is not located in some far-away heaven, but rather at all times and places closer to us than we are to ourselves. In this way, not only are we able

32. Ibid.

33. Elizabeth Johnson, C.S.J., *Quest for the Living God: Mapping Frontiers in the Theology of God* (New York: Continuum, 2008), 188.

to experience the sacramental character of all creation, every creature—"bodies alive with the breath of God"[34]—but we also gain a much richer understanding and appreciation for what Christian theology means when it asserts that in God "we live, move and have our being." A panentheistic model of the relationship between God and creation makes possible a world in which "[w]e might see ourselves and everything else as the living body of God,"[35] appreciating in new ways the value of human bodies, animal bodies, and the canyons, mountains, and oceans that comprise the body of planet earth.

DIFFERENT MODELS OF PANENTHEISM

As there are multiple versions of panentheism,[36] there also are multiple models that seek to concretely describe and envision what panentheism looks like, thereby illuminating its important theological ramifications. Let me share briefly four of those models: Sallie McFague and the world as God's body; Niels Henrik Gregersen and "deep incarnation"; Jürgen Moltmann and his interpretation of *zimzum*; and Elizabeth Johnson's understanding of *kabod*—God's glory.

The World as God's Body

Sallie McFague, one of the late twentieth century's most prominent ecotheologians, suggests the metaphor in which the entire universe is seen as the "body" of God. She does not mean this literally, of course—as though God were a mind or a spirit who "has" a body, but instead, she suggests viewing the earth as "part of the body of God, not as separate from God (who dwells elsewhere) but as the visible reality of the invisible God."[37] This is language typically used for Jesus, of course, and McFague does not mean to either relativize or trivialize the incarnation. Instead, she sees the incarnation as the paradigm through which we can understand God's "taking flesh" and "dwelling among us" much more broadly. This metaphor comes out of her dual emphasis on the goodness of bodies in general and on God's abiding, loving presence in creation. Both of these concerns lead her to endorse a panentheistic view of the world, noting that this model emphasizes the belief that "[e]verything that is is *in* God and God is *in* all things and yet God is not identical with the universe,

---

34. Sallie McFague, *The Body of God: An Ecological Theology* (Minneapolis: Fortress Press, 1993), 132.

35. Ibid.

36. See, for example Niels Henrik Gregersen's chapter, "Three Varieties of Panentheism," in *In Whom We Live and Move and Have Our Being: Panentheistic Reflections on God's Presence in a Scientific World*, ed. Philip Clayton and Arthur Peacocke (Grand Rapids: Eerdmans, 2004), 19–35.

37. Sallie McFague, *Body of God*, 102.

for the universe is dependent on God in a way that God is not dependent on the universe."[38]

What's more, it gives Christians a means for rejecting language that suggests God is either indifferent to the tragedies of life, or worse, that God is behind them, using them as some twisted pedagogical or punitive tool. She writes, "If the world is God's body, then nothing happens to the world that does not also happen to God. If we live and move and have our being in God, then, God though asymmetrically, lives in us as well."[39] God cares passionately about creation, and suffers—and rejoices—alongside it. Thus this model allows McFague to argue for a greater interdependence among all life, a greater awareness of God's sacramental presence throughout the whole creation, a need to recognize our own limits as human beings, and the importance of the body—human bodies and the body of creation—in any understanding of salvation.

Jesus as Earth and Grass

Picking up on this emphasis on bodies, it seems appropriate to note here the irony that was mentioned in an earlier chapter: one would hardly guess, given all the negative language toward the body within Christianity as a whole, that Christianity is the religion *par excellence* of divine incarnation. Unique among the world's religions, Christianity asserts that God really and truly became human, entering physically into the human experience and taking suffering, sin, and even death into the very being of God for the sake of the world. And, what Christian theology is coming to recognize more and more, is the fact that God being made human has cosmic significance, as it embeds God in all aspects of the physical world—not only in all humans, but in all animals, all places, all rivers, all mountains.

Niels Henrik Gregersen describes this very well in his articulation of the concept of "deep incarnation," his way of describing what he calls a "soteriological" panentheistic relationship of God to creation, soteriological because "[i]n the incarnate Christ God is conjoining the full gamut of material existence in order for the material world to be conjoined with God."[40] He writes, "My proposal is that the divine *logos* . . . has assumed not only humanity, but the whole malleable matrix of materiality. By becoming 'flesh' in Jesus, God's eternal *logos* entered into all dimensions of God's world of creation."[41]

---

38. Ibid., 149.
39. Ibid., 176.
40. Private email correspondence, January 24, 2012.

This means that God's presence cannot be limited to one specific place or time, nor can any specific place or time be privileged. Instead, Jesus' particularity turns out to be radically inclusive, with universal ramifications for the entire creation: "The flesh that is assumed in Jesus Christ, is not only the particular man Jesus, but the entire realm of humanity, living creatures and earthly soil."[42] Either the incarnation has meaning for the whole world, or it has no meaning at all.

> Incarnation signifies coming-into-flesh, so that God, the Creator, and the world of the flesh are conjoined in Jesus Christ. God connects with all vulnerable creatures, with the sparrows in their flight as well as in their fall (cf. Mt. 10:29), indeed, with all the grass that comes into being one day and fades the next day. In Christ, God is conjoining all creatures and enters into the biological tissue of creation itself in order to share the fate of biological existence. God becomes Jesus, and in him God becomes human, and (by implication) foxes and sparrows, grass and soil.[43]

The basic point is clear: in Jesus, "God joins the web of life, becomes part of Earth's biology . . . God becomes flesh, clay, Earth."[44]

Zimzum

Another metaphor for thinking about God's ongoing, indwelling presence in the world can be found in the work of Jürgen Moltmann, particularly in his book *God in Creation*. There, Moltmann elaborates on the Jewish kabbalist doctrine of *zimzum* (which Moltmann spells "*zimsum*," and will be discussed in more detail shortly). Moltmann uses this concept, which points to the idea that "[i]t is only a withdrawal by God into [Godself] that can free the space into which God can act creatively,"[45] to connect God's creative work with God's redemptive work in the incarnation, particularly as it is described in the

---

41. Niels Henrik Gregersen, "Deep Incarnation: The Logos Became Flesh," in *Transformative Theological Perspectives*, ed. Karen L. Bloomquist (Minneapolis: Lutheran University Press, 2009), 168–69.

42. Niels Henrik Gregersen, "The Extended Body of Christ: Three Dimensions of Deep Incarnation," in *Deep Incarnation: On the Scope of Christology*, ed. Niels Henrik Gregersen (Minneapolis: Fortress Press, 2013).

43. Ibid., 174.

44. http://seasonofcreation.com/wp-content/uploads/2010/04/a-theology-of-deep-incarnation-and-reconciliation.pdf.

45. Jürgen Moltmann, *God in Creation: A New Theology of Creation and the Spirit of God*, trans. Margaret Kohl (Minneapolis: Fortress Press, 1993), 86.

Christ hymn of Philippians 2. For Moltmann, then, one of the ramifications of the creative metaphor of *zimzum*, at least from a Christian perspective, is that "God's creative love is grounded in [God's] humble, self-humiliating love. This self-restricting love is the beginning of that self-emptying of God, which Philippians 2 sees as the divine mystery of the Messiah. Even in order to create heaven and earth, God emptied himself [*sic*] of his all-plenishing omnipotence, and as Creator took upon himself the form of a servant."[46] In this way, even though creation happens in some sense "outside" God, in another sense, all creation remains "inside" God, since God creates the very space for the cosmos to exist from within Godself. This, too, then, is a metaphor for a panentheistic understanding of God's relationship to the world.

God's Glory

In closing this section on panentheism, I want to return to the theology of Elizabeth Johnson, particularly her description of *kabod*, that is, God's "glory." She is speaking here specifically of the concept of the *kabod YHWH*, found in the Hebrew scriptures as one important way of describing the divine presence in the world. She writes, "the *kabod YHWH* is a light-filled metaphor meaning the weighty radiance of divine presence in the world, the heavy, plump, fat brightness of God's immanence drawing near and passing by to enlighten, warm and set things right."[47] She goes on to note how God's presence is never directly perceived—even Moses only catches a glimpse of God's backside—but is only revealed in and through the natural world, and its creatures and its events: "The world shares in the weighty radiance of God: the starry heavens sing of it, other natural creatures reveal it in flashes of speed, methods of feeding, and all their intricate, mysterious workings (Job 38–41)."[48]

For Johnson, not only does this powerful, glorious indwelling presence of God reveal a delightful, creative "ability to accessorize," manifest in a world full of marvelous wonders, it also reveals a God who is continually working at the heart of all things for healing, restoration, and freedom. "Participating in the glory of God, our whole planet is a beautiful showing forth of divine goodness and generosity. By being simply and thoroughly its magnificent self, it bodies forth the glory of God that empowers it, being as it were an icon."[49]

46. Ibid., 88.

47. Elizabeth Johnson, C.S.J., "Heaven and Earth Are Filled with Your Glory: Atheism and Ecological Spirituality," in *Finding God in All Things: Essays in Honor of Michael J. Buckley, S.J.*, ed. Michael J. Himes and Stephen J. Pope (New York: Crossroad, 1996), 88.

48. Ibid., 89.

49. Ibid., 93.

This panentheistic vision of God is heavy on hope and promise, describing a God involved in every aspect of creation, from the inside, from within, sharing with it God's own life, light, and goodness.

Judaism: The Kabbalist Doctrine of Zimzum

Kabbalah in general is difficult to explain, as it is less a clear, coherent system of thought and practice and much more "a multiplicity of different approaches, widely separated from one another and sometimes completely contradictory."[50] Thus in this short space, only the barest introduction can be offered. That said, however, there are some general principles and teachings that are widely shared. In general, the term "Kabbalah" is "the most traditional and commonly used term for the esoteric teachings of Judaism and for Jewish mysticism, especially the forms in which it assumed in the Middle Ages from the 12th century onward."[51] The word itself comes from the Hebrew root *kbl*, and it refers to "received tradition," or that which is handed down by tradition.[52] Kabbalah includes both mystical and magical elements, aspects of theosophy and theurgy, and it is concerned primarily with a comprehension of God and God's purposes for creation that is beyond rational study.

Because of this, there is within Kabbalah an aspect of the esoteric, which resists public communication of its teachings, preferring direct transmission from teacher to initiate. Thus many practitioners of Kabbalah—though not all—reject any notion of historical development. Instead, they emphasize the eternal nature of the profound wisdom it contains, believing that it is revealed again and again when humans have forgotten it. An example of this is the accepted tradition that "the Kabbalah was the esoteric part of the oral Law given to Moses at Sinai."[53] This tradition of oral—and often secret—transmission is one of the reasons why Kabbalah is very difficult to systematize: from its original roots in the mix of Persian, Jewish, and Greek ideas present in first-century Palestine, it spread over the centuries throughout Europe (and beyond) not only through oral transmission, but also through the circulation of various texts and commentaries. The most influential popular text of Kabbalah is the *Zohar* (*Sefer ha-Zohar*), written in the thirteenth century by Moses de Leon,

50. Gershom Scholem, *Kabbalah* (Jerusalem: Keter, 1974), 87.

51. Ibid., 3.

52. Ibid.

53. Ibid., 5.

although it purports to have been written centuries earlier. It contains Torah commentary and mystical reflection on the nature of God.

The doctrine of creation in Kabbalah is typically described using the language of emanation. Kabbalists believe that God in Godself, who is called *Ein-Sof*, which means "infinite," is complete apart from creation and entirely inaccessible to humanity. It is said that "*Ein-Sof* is the absolute perfection in which there are no distinctions and no differentiations. . . . It does not reveal itself in a way that makes knowledge of its nature possible, and it is not accessible even to the innermost thought (*hirhur ha-lev*) of the contemplative."[54] Therefore, the basic, pressing question was how to get from God to creation: how to make the leap from the completely ineffable, unknowable, infinite, limitless Divine Essence to the mundane world of form and matter. What is clear is that there was no compulsion on the side of the Divine: the move from hiddenness to manifestation is simply a mystery.

The text that describes how this occurred is called the *Sefer Yezirah*, the "book of creation." It begins with a declaration that God "created the world by means of '32 secret paths of wisdom'"; these paths are the ten "*Sefirot beli mah*" and the "22 elemental letters" that comprise the Hebrew alphabet.[55] The *Sefirot* in particular warrant further explanation. It is disputed among different kabbalists about whether or not the ten *Sefirot* are actually identical to God and share the divine essence, or whether they are merely God's vessels or tools through which God accomplishes God's work. In any case, what is agreed upon is that the *Sefirot* emanate from *Ein-Sof* one after another—"as if one candle were lit from another without the Emanator being diminished in any way."[56] Each one contains within itself various archetypes of different created beings, and each thing that exists comes into being through the activity of these different *Sefirot*. They each have different names and exist in a particular order: the first is *Keter Elyon* ("supreme crown"), then comes *Hokhmah* ("wisdom"), then *Binah* ("intelligence"), down through *Malkhut* ("kingdom"), sometimes called *Atarah* ("diadem").

One of the main points of difference among different kabbalist systems relates to the first step—that is, the first move from ineffability to outward expression. One such explanation—the one that concerns us here—posits

54. Ibid., 89.
55. Ibid., 23.
56. Ibid., 102.

that the first move of the Divine was actually not a step outward, but a step inward, a withdrawal of *Ein-Sof* into itself in order to "make room" for something other than the Divine to exist. This is the heart of the doctrine of *zimzum* mentioned previously, which means "contraction." Isaac Luria (sixteenth century), the founder of the Lurianic school of Kabbalah, is credited with developing this idea into a full-blown cosmological principle. Basically, it argues that because of God's infinity, there is no "space" for anything else to exist; therefore, before God can create anything, God must first withdraw into Godself—a divine contraction of God's own being—in order to make possible "something which is not *Ein-Sof* to exist."[57] There are different ways of explaining both this process of contraction and the subsequent creation that filled the empty space. One version says that "as a result of the act of divine contraction an empty vacuum was formed in the midst of *Ein-Sof* into which emanated a ray of light that filled this space with ten *Sefirot*."[58]

Interestingly enough, the doctrine of *zimzum* also became one way to explain the presence of evil in the world: "The metaphysical root of evil is inherent in the very privation that the act of *zimzum* involves, and the whole development of created beings depends on their being given an opportunity to perfect themselves according to their merits and to separate the power of evil from the power of good."[59] The idea of God's self-contraction and the subsequent creation of that which is not God, that which is removed from God, contains inherently within itself aspects of darkness (that which is not light), evil (that which is not good), and fragmentation (that which is not perfect and whole). Humans, then, live in this complicated world of light and darkness, good and evil, seeking restoration, *tikkun*.

GOD THE BEAUTIFUL: THEOLOGICAL AESTHETICS

Talk of God's life, light, and goodness lends itself naturally to talk of God's beauty, a topic that is much underdeveloped—though gaining interest—in most contemporary theological discussions. I argue that a brief mention of it here is particularly warranted, given how the experience of God in the beauty

57. Ibid., 129.
58. Ibid., 131.
59. Ibid., 135.

of creation is such an important aspect of many people's experience of and relationship with the Divine.

The term "aesthetics," used to refer to "the philosophy and science of the beautiful," is relatively recent, coined by Alexander G. Baumgarten in 1735.[60] However, as a subject of theological and philosophical reflection, the quest for "beauty" has been around for millennia—some would argue for as long as there have been human beings to reflect on the deeper meaning of the world around them. Alejandro García-Rivera describes aesthetics as the discipline that asks the question *"what moves the human heart"*;[61] and more specifically, he points to *theological* aesthetics as the recognition of and explicit reflection on the religious dimension of this question. Gesa Thiessen elaborates on this point: ". . . theological aesthetics is concerned with questions about God and issues in theology in the light of and perceived through sense knowledge (sensation, feeling, imagination), through beauty, and the arts."[62] Typically, theological aesthetics focuses specifically on products of human creativity and imagination, but I would argue that if it is appropriate to reflect on the knowledge of God that comes through human artistry, how much more is it both possible and necessary to reflect on the knowledge of God that comes through God's own artistry in creation.

There is an additional reason for this reflection. A deeper understanding and appreciation of theological aesthetics is a particularly desirable topic of theological reflection for Protestants, who have emphasized a theology of the word of God perhaps to the detriment of other means through which God might reveal Godself. Discussing this specific opposition, Karl Rahner writes:

> If theology is not identified *a priori* with verbal theology, but is understood as [humans'] total self-expression insofar as this is borne by God's self-communication, then religious phenomena in the arts are themselves a moment within theology taken in its totality. In practice, theology is rarely understood in this total way. But why should a person not think that when he hears a Bach oratorio, he comes into contact in a very unique way with God's revelation about the human not only by the word it employs, but by the music itself. . . . If theology is simply and arbitrarily defined as being identical with verbal theology, then of course we cannot say that. But then

---

60. Alejandro García-Rivera, *The Community of the Beautiful: A Theological Aesthetics* (Collegeville, MN: Liturgical Press, 1999), 9.

61. Ibid.

62. *Theological Aesthetics: A Reader*, ed. Gesa Elsbeth Thiessen (Grand Rapids: Eerdmans, 2005), 1.

we would have to ask whether such a reduction of theology to verbal theology does justice to the value and uniqueness of these arts, and whether it does not unjustifiably limit the capacity of the arts to be used by God in his revelation.[63]

If this is true of music, art, and other human creative activities, how much more is this true when we look at God's creative activity in the natural world? If God can and does use human creative activity to reveal something of God's nature and purpose, how much more does God reveal Godself through God's ongoing activity in creation? Thus the claim of theological aesthetics in relationship to creation is simple: ". . . the beauty of creation makes us glimpse the beauty of God."[64]

Theological aesthetics, then, is particularly relevant when discussing a doctrine of creation, as it affirms the knowledge and experience of God through the kind of sensory experiences humans often have while present with nature. Further, it affirms that God is not only the source of that which enlightens our minds and guides our moral compass, but also is the source of that which causes us to gasp in wonder and takes our breath away. That is, God is not only the fountain of the true and the good, but also the fount of all beauty. This means that beauty is not merely a superficial diversion, a pastime for the rich and indolent, but rather that beauty and its pursuit have a divine origin and are at the core of life itself. Thiessen says it this way:

> Beauty is not an extra, it is essential to all existence. Truth or goodness without beauty become dull, lifeless, boring, formalistic and cold. It is beauty—sensuous and spiritual, spiritual in the sensuous, and sensuous in the spiritual—which excites and nourishes human feeling, desire, thought and imagination. It is the splendor of beauty that makes the true and the good whole. The magnitude of beauty in nature and in all human creation, wherever it is experienced, gives us a glimpse of the beauty of God, therein lies its saving power. In this way beauty becomes a way to God and a manifestation of God at the same time.[65]

---

63. Karl Rahner, from "Theology and the Arts," as quoted in *Theological Aesthetics: A Reader*, ed. Thiessen, 219.

64. *Theological Aesthetics: A Reader*, ed. Thiessen, 63.

65. Ibid., 6.

Applying this to our understanding of creation, it is important to note that one of the ways the beauty of God has been perceived in nature is through the categories of harmony and wholeness. So, theologians since at least Augustine looked to the harmonious workings of the parts of creation as a means of understanding God's nature and will for the world. Let me offer just a few examples spanning several centuries of the Christian tradition. In book thirteen of *Confessions*, Augustine writes:

> And you, God, "saw all that you had made, and it was very good" (Gen. 1:31). To us also who see them, they are all very good indeed. . . . Seven times I have counted scripture saying you saw that what you made is good. But on the eighth occasion when you saw all that you had made, it says they were not merely good but "very good"—as if taking everything at once into account. For individual items were only "good" but everything taken together was both "good" and "very good." This truth is also declared by the beauty of bodies. A body composed of its constituent parts, all of which are beautiful, is far more beautiful as a whole than those parts taken separately; the whole is made of their well-ordered harmony, though individually the constituent parts are also beautiful.[66]

A similar emphasis can be seen in the Middle Ages, with theologians like John Scotus Eriugena, who, in *Periphyseon*, described the divine beauty of creation this way:

> Furthermore, the beauty of the whole established universe consists of a marvelous harmony of like and unlike in which the diverse genera and various species and the different orders of substances and accidents are composed into an ineffable unity. For as instrumental melody is made up of a variety of qualities and quantities of sounds which when they are heard individually and separately are distinguished from one another by widely differing proportions of tension or relaxation, but when they are attuned to each other in accordance with the fixed and rational rules of the art of music give forth through each piece of music a natural sweetness, so the harmony of the universe is established in accordance with the

---

66. Augustine, *Confessions*, book XIII, trans. Henry Chadwick (Oxford: Oxford University Press, 1998), chapter 28, paragraph 43, p. 299.

uniform will of its Creator out of the diverse subdivisions of its one nature which when regarded individually clash with one another.[67]

In the period following the Enlightenment, one of the most gushing theologians of beauty is eighteenth-century Calvinist theologian Jonathan Edwards—somewhat of a surprise to those who know Edwards best from his dour reflections on God's election and judgment. He, too, recognizes the beautiful harmony of nature, but at the same time, he emphasizes what might be called a "moral" aspect of beauty, describing the way in which "spiritual beauties"—grace, goodness, calmness, etc.—are reflected in corporeal beauties, particularly the "suitableness" and "agreeableness" of the different components of the natural world. He writes:

> The beauty of the world consists wholly of sweet mutual consents, either within itself or with the supreme being. As to the corporeal world, though there are many other sorts of consents, yet the sweetest and most charming beauty of it is its resemblance of spiritual beauties. . . . So there is a great suitableness between the objects of different senses, as between sounds, colours, and smells; as between colours of the woods and flowers and the smells and the singing of birds. . . . The gentle motions of waves, of [the] lily, etc., as it is agreeable to others things that represent calmness, gentleness, and benevolence, etc. the fields and woods seem to rejoice, and how joyful do the birds seem to be in it. How much a resemblance is there of every grace in the field covered with plants and flowers when the sun shines serenely and undisturbedly upon them . . . how lovely is the green of the face of the earth in all manner of colours, in flowers, the colour of the skies, and lovely tinctures of the morning and evening.[68]

Moving into the contemporary theological scene of the twentieth and twenty-first centuries, the name most associated with theological aesthetics is Hans Urs von Balthasar. A complex, creative thinker, Balthasar pushed the bounds of theological reflection in original, constructive ways, engaging not only the theological tradition but also philosophy, literature, and drama. Always,

67. John Scotus Eriugena, from *Periphyseon* as quoted in *Theological Aesthetics: A Reader*, ed. Thiessen, 72.

68. Jonathan Edwards, from *Images or Shadows of Divine Things*, as quoted in *Theological Aesthetics: A Reader*, ed. Thiessen, 171–72.

however, beauty was at the heart of his work, particularly as understood as *doxa* and *kabod*—God's "glory." Thus it rightly can be said that "[o]ne of the central concerns of Balthasar's theology is to recover the conviction that God is the supreme Beauty."[69] It is beauty, rather than truth or goodness, then, that is the focus of Balthasar's theological project, detailed in his multivolume masterpiece *Herrlichkeit* (*The Glory of the Lord*); and Balthasar himself stated the reason for this: ". . . God does not come primarily as a teacher for us ('true'), as a useful 'redeemer' for us ('good'), but for *himself*, to display and to radiate the splendor of his eternal triune love in that 'disinterestedness' which true love has in common with true beauty. For the glory of God the world was created; through it and for its sake the world is also redeemed."[70]

Note his use of "the world" here. While it is true that Balthasar himself did not in any comprehensive way link divine beauty to a doctrine of creation as such—focusing instead on human creatures, rather than the universe as whole—nonetheless, for Balthasar, "the world is a theophany of God's glory,"[71] showing forth the beauty of God and participating in God's final redemption for all that God has made.[72] Incidentally, similar aesthetic commitments are behind the Eastern Orthodox traditions of iconology and iconography, where icons are viewed as visible manifestations of the gospel, and the meditative practice of beholding beauty becomes a window onto the Divine.

However, all this is not to say that God is revealed, found, and sought only in the beautiful parts of creation, as though God rejects, ignores, or condemns the broken places of ugliness, brutality, and devastation. Indeed, Christian theology asserts strongly that God not only resides in those places, but is revealed there as well—but in a different way, seen through a different theological lens. More about this will be said later in the chapter, as we consider the insights and challenges regarding a doctrine of creation explored through issues of science and theology.

---

69. John O'Donnell, S.J., *Hans Urs von Balthasar* (Collegeville, MN: Liturgical Press, 1992), 18.

70. As quoted in *The Analogy of Beauty: The Theology of Hans Urs von Balthasar*, ed. John Riches (Edinburgh: T. & T. Clark, 1986), 213.

71. O'Donnell, S.J., *Hans Urs von Balthasar* , 32.

72. See, for example, Celia Deane-Drummond, "The Breadth of Glory: A Trinitarian Eschatology for the Earth through Critical Engagement with Hans Urs von Balthasar," *International Journal of Systematic Theology* 12, no. 1 (January 2010).

Figure 7.1. Nanzen-ji Temple, Kyoto. April 2012.

Buddhism: Buddhist Aesthetics and the Zen Temple

One of the most well-known aspects of Zen Buddhism in the West is its particular aesthetic, which is expressed through art forms such as flower arranging, calligraphy, and gardens, particularly rock gardens. Typically, what we might call a "Zen aesthetic" is described using four ideas: "harmony (*wa*), reverence (*kei*), purity (*sei*), and tranquility (*sabi/wabi*)."[73] Together, these ideas facilitate both an awareness of the emptiness of all things and the awareness of a thing as it is, in all its loveliness and its transience. As a part of this aesthetic, the experience of nature "just as it is" is of particular importance, as a realization of the harmonious relationship between humanity and nature can lead to enlightenment: "In nature revealed as such, the human being realizes his own selflessness. . . ."[74] Thus the promoting of such a relationship, particularly through the experience

73. James A. Kirk, "The Attitude Toward Nature in Zen Buddhism," *Iliff Review* 32, no. 2 (Spring 1975): 25–26.

74. Ueda Shizuteru, "The Zen Buddhist Experience of the Truly Beautiful," trans. John C. Maraldo, in *Eastern Buddhist* 22, no. 1 (Spring 1989): 25.

of seeing the simplicity of nature in its pure being, is a key part of a Zen aesthetic.

Not surprisingly, the architecture and layout of a Zen temple reflect well these aesthetic commitments: "Zen, and its philosophy of direct experience, freedom from attachment, acceptance, impermanence, openness, celebration of the ordinary, simplicity . . . naturalness, reverence for nature, and mindfulness, is symbolized to varying degrees by the temples and their entry paths."[75] In practice, what this means is that Zen temples have what can be called porous boundaries between inside and outside, between walls and space, between the natural and the human-made. Typically, walkways are open on at least one side, and sometimes two; rooms often have one or two sides open to enclosed gardens; and even between the rooms themselves there are only sliding paper walls or screens, most of which are decorated with nature scenes in which animals and plants predominate. All of this is quite intentional: "A harmonious relationship with nature is communicated through the form and materials of the temple, and a blurring of the edge between habitation and nature."[76] In a Zen temple, one can always smell the rain, watch the sun move across the sky, and see the waning of the moonlight in the early hours of dawn. In a Zen temple, and a Zen temple complex especially, the buildings and their gardens—including walls, paths, and foliage, seek to convey a harmony and balance that reflect the harmony of the universe as a whole. This peaceful, serene, uncluttered landscape visually reinforces an important tenet of Buddhism that emphasizes ". . . rocks and stones, large and small, are the Buddha's own possessions,"[77] themselves able to "expound the true teachings. . . ." In short, in a Zen temple, "As well as hearing the cosmos as a sermon, one can see, or read, the natural word as scripture."[78]

And, in the twenty-first-century context in which we find ourselves, this aesthetic and religious commitment has important practical and even soteriological ramifications:

75. Thomas Barrie, *Spiritual Path, Sacred Place: Myth, Ritual, and Meaning in Architecture* (Boston: Shambhala, 1996), 191.

76. Barrie, *Spiritual Path, Sacred Place*, 209.

77. As quoted in François Berthier, *Reading Zen in the Rocks: The Japanese Dry Landscape Garden* (Chicago: University of Chicago Press, 2000), 5–6.

78. Ibid.

Japanese Buddhism adds pedagogic and soteric dimensions by inviting us to regard rocks and other natural phenomena as sources of wisdom and companions on the path to deeper understanding. But nowadays the earth is as much in need of saving as are its human inhabitants—and is especially in need of being saved *from* its human inhabitants. To this extent there may be practical, not just aesthetic, lessons to be learned from our relations with rocks, and compelling reasons to attend to what Goethe calls "the mute nearness of great, soft-voiced nature."[79]

A WILD WORLD

COMPLEXITY, CHANCE, AND UNPREDICTABILITY

At this point in the chapter, a shift must be made that does not call into question anything that was said above, but seeks to balance it with the recognition that not all is rainbows and butterflies in creation, that life does not always—if ever—proceed according to a discernible divine plan, and that contrary to what well-meaning Christians sometimes profess, not everything happens for a reason. Instead, more and more, we are discovering that creation in itself—and that includes human existence, too—is messy, uncomfortably unpredictable, and enigmatic. There doesn't seem to be any unfolding of a master plot, any clear progression to an enlightened future, or any knowable manual that provides a definitive set of guidelines that explain the workings of the universe. Thus Christians are left asking the difficult question of what they are to make of the world; and, more importantly theologically, where is God in all the complexity and dynamism involved in the various processes—micro and macrocosmic—that sustain and drive the cosmos today?

SCIENCE AND THEOLOGY

Facing these questions, Christian theologians find themselves—willingly or not—engaging science: scientific theories, scientific experiments, and the insights science brings about the nature of the universe. Thus it is important to begin this section with some reflection on the ongoing engagement between

---

79. Ibid., 142–43.

theology and science, particularly because this is a place of much misunderstanding and misinformation.

Wesley Wildman writes that "[t]he relationship between science and religion is fascinating partly because it compactly expresses a kind of schizophrenic anxiety within the contemporary West generally: *How can we think and act scientifically and theologically, critically and worshipfully, technologically and ethically at the same time?*"[80] The result of this anxiety has been that many Christians are not sure what they are supposed to think about science; and, on the other side, many scientists are not sure what they are supposed to think about religion. Still today, many Christians have the idea that science is hostile to religion in general and Christianity in particular, and that all scientists are atheists. Both assumptions are patently false. At the same time, many scientists have the idea that Christianity is hostile to science, and that all Christians are scientific luddites. Again, both assumptions are patently false. Instead, Christianity and science have much to learn from each other; and in particular, Christianity can be helpfully informed by the wisdom of science as it seeks to ever more clearly and faithfully speak about the work of God in the world, and God's presence in creation.

Thus the first thing that must be done is to correct the idea that science and theology are ideological foes, and have always been at war: the metaphor of warfare between the two is both unhelpful and inaccurate. In fact, at least from the time of Aristotle science was considered part of philosophical and theological reflection on the cosmos and its Creator. This connection continued through the Middle Ages, when, in the writings of Thomas Aquinas among others, "Aristotelian cosmology and Christian theology were merged to form the *medieval picture of the universe*."[81] Even in the seventeenth century, European scientists still operated primarily within a Christian theological framework: "It has long been recognized that natural philosophers such as Robert Boyle and Isaac Newton saw the study of nature as a religious duty. Knowledge of God's power and wisdom could be inferred from the intelligence seemingly displayed in the designs of nature."[82] Indeed, "For Newton, as for Boyle and Descartes, there were *laws* of nature only because there had been a Legislator."[83]

80. Wesley J. Wildman, "The Quest for Harmony," in *Religion & Science*, ed. Richardson and Wildman, 41–42, author's italics.

81. Ian G. Barbour, *Religion and Science: Historical and Contemporary Issues* (San Francisco: HarperSanFrancisco, 1990), 5, author's italics.

82. John Hedley Brooke, "Science and Theology in the Enlightenment," in *Religion & Science*, ed. Richardson and Wildman, 8.

83. Brooke, "Science and Theology in the Enlightenment," 9.

Thus it is far more accurate and helpful to think about a range of ways in which theologians and scientists have positioned themselves in relationship to one another. Ian Barbour describes four different ways of relating science and religion—all of which have been employed over the centuries, and all of which are still with us today: *conflict*, of which the historical case of Galileo is a classic example; *independence*, which establishes separate "turf" for each and insists that scientists and theologians play only in their own sandboxes; *dialogue*, in which general areas of conversation are raised and discussed by each group; and finally, *integration*, where specific scientific theories are integrated into specific theological doctrines.[84]

For a twenty-first-century theology—particularly when considering a doctrine of creation—it matters greatly as to which way is favored by Christian theologians. As Ted Peters and Martinez Hewlett note:

> . . . a misunderstanding about our faith might create an unnecessary deafness to a divine call to study God's creation through the eyes of the microscope and telescope. What is at stake is the understanding that the world God has made is complex and magnificent; and science provides the lenses through which we can view the fingerprints and footprints left by God's history with our beautiful world.[85]

Christians have no need to fear science or reject it. Instead, it can be embraced as a dialogue partner in the difficult but necessary task of articulating the ongoing relationship God has with creation, and understanding our place and role in that relationship.

"ORDER" IN THE TWENTY-FIRST CENTURY

One thing is clear: we can no longer think about an "ordered" world in the way we once did. Barbour describes clearly the way in which the picture of the universe is much different today from both medieval and Newtonian views. He notes that up through the time of Isaac Newton, nature was seen as stable, with its fundamental parts fixed; events could be explained and even predicted—either on the basis of divine purpose or mechanical causes—and humans were seen as the apex of creation (particularly human reason).[86]

---

84. Barbour, *Religion and Science: Historical and Contemporary Issues*, 77ff.

85. Ted Peters and Martinez Hewlett, *Can You Believe in God and Evolution? A Guide for the Perplexed* (Nashville: Abingdon, 2006), 3.

86. Barbour, *Religion and Science: Historical and Contemporary Issues*, 281–83.

However, in the twenty-first century, the world looks very different. It is clear that at its core, nature is not "stable," but rather constantly in flux—"evolutionary, dynamic, and emergent"[87]—and fundamentally unpredictable; and, instead of humans being at the top of some evolutionary ladder, we find ourselves embedded in a complicated cosmic relational web that has no "top" at all.

We have quantum physics to thank for many of these changes, two of which warrant special mention here. First, physics replaces certainty with indeterminacy, recognizing that we can predict probabilities for events, but we cannot predict the outcome of any specific event in its entirety. For example, we can predict the typical path of a certain type of hurricane, but we cannot predict with perfect accuracy the specific path any one particular hurricane will take. This is best exemplified in the Heisenberg uncertainty principle, which states that the accuracy with which we can determine the position of an electron is inversely related to the accuracy with which we can determine its momentum, and vice versa. That is, the closer we come to fixing one, the farther away we get from fixing the other. This fact led Heisenberg to posit indeterminacy as "*an objective feature of nature* and not a limit of human knowledge."[88] Thus quantum physics locates the source of unpredictability not in human limitations, but in the very workings of the cosmos itself.

Second, physics posits the inaccessibility of objectivity; that is, one cannot talk about any object in itself, instead, we can only talk about the object as it exists in relationship with the subject observing it. Niels Bohr in particular described this phenomenon using what he called the Complementarity Principle, arguing that it is not possible to describe or theorize about an experiment in and of itself; instead, one must include the interaction between the experiment and the experimenter: no one is merely a spectator; instead, she is always part of the experiment. The consequence is that "it is now clear that we, as human knowers, do not have a purchase on physical reality *as it is in itself*. What we know about it, particularly at the quantum level, is inextricably convolved with *our* observation of it."[89] Both of these discoveries together—along with the discovery of quarks and Einstein's theory of relativity—have resulted in a very different picture of the universe from what we had inherited from Newton and others. Thus today, if we want to talk about "order" in the universe at all, we must recognize that it is an order-in-flux:

87. Ibid., 283.

88. Ibid., 172.

89. William R. Stoeger, "Key Developments in Physics," in *Religion & Science*, ed. Richardson and Wildman, 186.

an order that cannot be definitively stated or predicted, an order that cannot be definitely known or defined, and an order that possesses within itself the capacity for change.

SPECIFIC EXAMPLES FROM SCIENCE

The following three examples of scientific theories and practices serve both to challenge and enhance a Christian understanding of creation. Thus they require further reflection and consideration, as they all have a history of a mixed reception by Christians.

Big Bang Theory

The "big bang" refers to the dominant theory in contemporary cosmology that describes the origins of the universe. It postulates a singularity (something infinitely hot and dense, and infinitesimally small) that occurred roughly 13 billion years ago—no one knows why or how it appeared—from which the universe has been expanding ever since. There are those Christians who welcome the big bang theory, as it seems to offer a concrete way to explain the "how" of God's initial creative work, particularly as odds are very slim that life as we know it could have developed from such a beginning. Thus some Christians argue that ". . . the universe has been 'fine-tuned' from the start for the subsequent construction of stars, planets, life and mind. . . . We find a single blast (the Big Bang) fine-tuned to produce a world that produces us when any of a thousand other imaginable blasts would have yielded nothing."[90] However, at the same time, many are wary, wanting to avoid a "god of the gaps" position, in which God is evoked only in those places where there are "gaps" in scientific knowledge. For this reason, many Christians and scientists alike emphasize that the big bang theory "does not 'prove' the existence of God . . . instead, some scientists will only say that monotheism is 'consistent with' or 'complementary to' this cosmology, not that it is a conclusion 'commanded by it.'"[91]

Evolution

Charles Darwin published his *On the Origin of Species* in 1859, following his experience serving as naturalist on the HMS *Beagle* in its voyage around the world. As is well known, it was his observation of small variations among species, particularly finches on the Galápagos Islands, that sparked his theory

---

90. Holmes Rolston III, "Science, Religion, and the Future," in *Religion & Science*, ed. Richardson and Wildman, 63.

91. Ibid.

of natural selection. From this observation, he theorized that, because of competition within a species, those with the most beneficial variations would survive, while others would die before they could reproduce. Thus over time, those advantaged individuals would be able to reproduce more rapidly and successfully, and in this way, that variation would be perpetuated through the species as a whole; this is the process by which evolution would occur. While in this first publication, Darwin said nothing about humankind, he did discuss the application of his theory to humans in a later book, *The Descent of Man* (1871).

While many Christians continue to feel their faith is threatened by theories of evolution, many others argue that evolution creates opportunities for fresh, constructive understandings of God's work in the world. For example, Philip Hefner sees in a theory of evolution positive ways to embed humanity more deeply within the marvelous, dynamic creative processes at work throughout the whole of the cosmos. He writes:

> *Bricolage*—constructing new things from the materials at hand—is evident throughout the biosphere. Whether we note the formation of jawbones from antecedent gill slits or the triune structure of the human brain that contains within itself the neurological ancestry of reptiles and ancient mammals, it is stunningly clear that human being is a segment of a process that can be related reasonably, on the basis of empirical observation, to the whole of nature.[92]

Genetics

Genetics is the study of genes, including their variations and the process of inheritance, and, in many cases the way in which they manifest themselves in human life—both individually and communally. As a modern discipline, it can be traced back to Gregor Mendel, a monk who noted the way specific characteristics were passed from one plant to another. Today we know that genes are found in DNA (deoxyribonucleic acid), and the way they manifest themselves in any one individual results in that person having specific traits—eye color, height, and sometimes a genetic predisposition to disease: cystic fibrosis, childhood leukemia, and Down syndrome. For obvious reasons, then, scientists have taken a great interest in attempting to learn all they can about how genes work—and, more controversially, how to manipulate them to create a healthier, happier human being.

---

92. Hefner, *The Human Factor*, 65.

There are many misconceptions about genetics, which have resulted in negative views of the entire enterprise by many in the Christian community. The crux of the problem can be summed up in the phrase "playing God," which can surface in Christian discussions. Audrey Chapman notes that this phrase "has come to be used as a shorthand for concerns that it is inappropriate for humans to change the way other living organisms or human beings are constituted. The term conveys the view that engaging in genetic engineering amounts to usurping the creative prerogative of God."[93] Ted Peters, in his book of the same name, spells out three different theological concerns to which "playing God" can refer: "*learning God's awesome secrets*"; "the actual wielding of *power over life and death*"; and "the use of science to *alter life and influence human evolution.*"[94] It is this last concern that is chiefly pressing, particularly in light of research being done to determine whether or not certain genes indicate a propensity to violence that would perhaps mitigate one's responsibility for one's actions; whether or not there is a "gay gene" that would result in a biological cause for homosexuality; and whether or not genetically engineered animals can and should be created and patented.[95] However, at the same time that many theologians wrestle with these issues, they also affirm the God-given abilities and intellect humans possess, and our call to use these abilities to participate in God's creative work in the world, for the sake of the whole creation.

THEODICY AND A THEOLOGY OF THE CROSS

Undoubtedly, one of the most challenging issues Christian theologians must face—particularly in discussions of a doctrine of creation—is the existence of evil, and the numberless, ruinous experiences of suffering that permeate all aspects of creation. The name for this issue is "theodicy," which comes from the two Greek words *theos*, meaning God, and *dike*, which means justice. Thus "theodicy" refers to the theological challenge of demonstrating the justice of God even in the face of overwhelming anguish in the cosmos. In David Hume's formulation, the problem is stated along these lines: If God is able to eradicate evil, but chooses not to, God is not all-loving; if God is not able, then God is not all-powerful. If God is both all-loving and all-powerful, then why does evil exist?[96] It's a compelling question, to say the least.

---

93. Audrey Chapman, "Understanding the Religious Implications of the Genetics Revolution," in *God, Life, and the Cosmos*, ed. Peters, Iqbal, and Haq, 310.

94. Ted Peters, *Playing God: Genetic Determinism and Human Freedom* (New York: Routledge, 1997), 10–11.

95. Peters discusses all of these examples in *Playing God*, chapters 3–5.

Obviously, then, the problem of theodicy raises all sorts of delicate and difficult questions about understanding and explaining God's action in the world, and the nature of God's relationship with creation as a whole; and many of the so-called "solutions" leave us in a worse place than where we began. For example, looking at human suffering in particular, it is clear that a loving God is not well defended by the suggestion that God visits suffering intentionally upon us, in order to "test" our faith—as though the only paradigm we have for understanding God's relationship to humanity is that of Job. Nor is a loving God well served by the idea that God punishes the wicked with suffering, particularly when "the wicked" so often exactly correspond with those whose behavior we deem un-Christian—as though God were a church or a pastor's personal bodyguard, roughing up the riffraff against whom she preaches.

Nor is a powerful God supported by the insistence that God has a master plan, of which every single event is a necessary part; yet, for some inexplicable reason, that "plan" unavoidably includes rape, sadistic cruelty, child soldiers, and child brides. Here one cannot help but endorse the view of Ivan Karamazov who "returns his ticket" to protest a world in which the torture and death of even one tiny creature is required to ensure harmony for the rest.[97] Finally, a powerful God is not served by the insistence on the pervasive agency of "the devil," which, unless viewed metaphorically, seems to imply a cosmic boxing match between two divine adversaries, where Satan far too often wins the round.

When it comes to creation itself, the issues are equally problematic. First, we might even ask what is meant by the category of "natural evil." Is a hurricane evil? Hardly in and of itself, even though the consequences of its existence and movements may well be experienced as evil by humans and animals. Aside from global warming and other environmental phenomena that can be linked to sinful human behavior, the same thing could be said about drought, flooding, and snowstorms. Creation in and of itself is hardly "evil" simply because the earth rotates and revolves around the sun, and air currents combine with ocean currents, and seasons come and go.

Yet at the same time, certainly at the very least we can talk about natural evil existing within the animal kingdom, insofar as we connect evil to suffering.

96. "Is [God] willing to prevent evil, but not able? then he is impotent. Is he able, but not willing? then he is malevolent. Is he both able and willing? whence then is evil?" David Hume, *Principal Writings on Religion including Dialogues Concerning Natural Religion and the Natural History of Religion*, ed. J. C. A. Gaskin (Oxford: Oxford University Press, 1993), 100.

97. Fyodor Dostoevsky, *The Brothers Karamazov*, trans. Richard Pevear and Larissa Volokhonsky (New York: Farrar, Straus & Giroux, 1990), 245.

It is clear that the predator-prey relationship causes suffering—at least for the impala and the rabbit; and it also is clear that isolation, abuse, boredom, and neglect cause suffering, particularly for those animals with more complex brains. And, what of Holmes Rolston's famous example of the "extra" pelican chick, the second white pelican chick hatched a few days after the first, which, assuming the first survives, typically is maltreated and starved by the first until it either falls out of the nest or wanders away, unwelcome to return?[98] Finally, what about the loss of the dodo, the Japanese sea lion, and the perilous existence of the Javan rhinoceros—whose current global population is under fifty individuals and fading fast? Should it not be described as evil when an entire species goes out of existence? These examples and others lead theologians like Christopher Southgate to describe the problem of "evolutionary theodicy," which includes both "the suffering of creatures and the extinction of species."[99]

In light of all this, one way to solve the problem of the experience of evil in the world is to posit what John Polkinghorne calls a "detached, single-action view of divine agency."[100] Basically, this is the view in which one acknowledges only God's one overarching act of creating and holding the universe together, rather than particular, discrete acts within it: God acts generally and universally, but not individually or specifically. The upside here, of course, is that, again in Polkinghorne's words, "if God does nothing in particular, then God cannot be blamed for anything in particular either. To put it bluntly, such a God is off the hook of the Holocaust."[101] However, it is clear that this vaguely deistic conception of God hardly resembles the God who delivered the Israelites out of Egypt, entered into a covenant with Abraham, and fed Elijah in the wilderness. As Keith Ward said so well, "It often seems that we can neither stand the thought of God acting often (since that would infringe our freedom), nor the thought of [God] acting rarely (since that makes him responsible for our suffering)."[102]

While all of this might tempt a theologian to throw up her hands, there remain a few key insights that can and should be said in the face of evil, which, while they do not provide a definitive answer, do helpfully nuance the problem. First and foremost is the fact that, as every parent, every child, every partner has

98. Holmes Rolston III, *Science and Religion: A Critical Survey* (Philadelphia: Temple University Press, 1987), 138. He notes that these "second chicks" have only a one-in-ten chance of fledging.

99. Christopher Southgate, *The Groaning of Creation: God, Evolution, and the Problem of Evil* (Louisville: Westminster John Knox, 2008), 9.

100. John Polkinghorne, "Chaos Theory and Divine Action," 243.

101. Ibid., 243.

102. As quoted in Polkinghorne, "Chaos Theory and Divine Action," 244.

experienced, suffering is an unavoidable part of life: of change and growth, of challenges, of losses and disappointments, of missed opportunities, of goodbyes and regrets. There is simply no way to avoid all suffering if one lives out one's life in fullness—and this is true for many animal species as well. Thus, Migliore writes, "To wish the world were immune from *every* form of struggle and *every* form of suffering would be to wish not to have been created at all. To insist that believers should be immune from the limits and risks of all creaturely existence would be petty and self-indulgent."[103]

Second, the fact is we must consider not simply individual suffering, but the inevitable relational suffering that exists with families, societies, and even globally. Given the deep relationality that networks all existence together in complex systems of engagement, we influence each other—and are influenced by each other—in ways we often do not even see, let alone consider. The choices each of us make about consumption, procreation, travel, and occupation affect vast networks of people, animals, and even the world itself in ways we will never know. How does one get at the "evil" in such an intricate web, without destroying the web altogether? Austin Farrer says it this way:

> Poor, limping world, why does not your kind Creator pull the thorn out of your paw? But what sort of a thorn is this? And if it were pulled out, how much of the paw would remain? How much, indeed, of the creation? What would a physical universe be like, from which all mutual interference of systems was eliminated? It would be no physical universe at all.[104]

Finally, there is free will to contend with, and, as every parent, every child, every partner has experienced, individuals (and societies, and nations, for that matter) must be able to make their own decisions in order to fully realize their humanity, and that includes making bad decisions, the consequences of which can cause terrible suffering not only to themselves but to others as well. We would not be human without free will—creation would not be creation without freedom—and an unavoidable result of this freedom is actions taken in ignorance, spite, or spontaneity, all of which can have disastrous outcomes.

Yet, none of these insights speak directly to the issue of God and God's justice. For that, I would argue that the most compelling answer to questions

103. Daniel Migliore, *Faith Seeking Understanding: An Introduction to Christian Theology*, 2nd ed. (Grand Rapids: Eerdmans, 2004), 119.

104. Austin Farrer, *Love Almighty and Ills Unlimited: An Essay on Providence and Evil* (London: Collins, 1962), 51.

of theodicy is, in fact, less an answer than a response—a cry of faith that pierces the darkness of evil and suffering with a ray of light and hope. This response is the conviction that the God of passionate love for God's creation is also a God of *com-passio*, compassionate suffering with creation; and it is here that we see the flipside of the beauty of God. Christian theology confesses a God who came into the world in the form of a helpless infant, born in a backward town to a poor no-name couple, and died ignominiously just a few decades later, abandoned and betrayed by his friends, tortured as a criminal on a cross. God may well be present and reveal Godself in the beautiful, but the crucified God of love and compassion also—and ultimately—is revealed in the ugly, the painful, and the suffering. This is where God most clearly shows God's face.

This conviction is the linchpin of a theology of the cross, articulated by Luther most clearly in his Heidelberg Disputation from 1518. There, in his discussion of a "theologian of the cross," he makes clear that the very understanding of who God is and what God has done for us in Jesus Christ is dependent upon acknowledging the fullness of God's self-disclosure on the cross. To this end, thesis 20 reads: "That person deserves to be called a theologian, however, who comprehends the visible and manifest things of God through suffering and the cross." This challenge from Luther serves as a constant reminder that Christian theology must seek God where God chooses to be found: in and among the hurting, the despairing, the lost and the outcast.

Gerhard Forde writes that "God refuses to be seen in any other way" except on the cross. Thus, "What is vital here is absolute concentration on the rejected, crucified Jesus."[105] This is how Luther can say "the cross alone is our theology":[106] in Jesus, God chooses to dwell in suffering with the despised, the exploited, and the ignored, making a home with the suffering. Thus Gilkey writes that "the whole message of the Christian Gospel is ultimately based on the assertion that the evils and sufferings that oppress [humans'] lives are so real and so significant to God that He wills to share them and bear them for [people]."[107] Not even just for all people, but for all creation—all humans and all creatures—God is "the fellow sufferer who understands";[108] and in this way, "God's suffering presence is just that, presence of the most profoundly attentive and loving sort, a solidarity that at some deep level takes away the aloneness of the suffering creature's experience."[109]

105. Gerhard O. Forde, *On Being a Theologian of the Cross: Reflections on Luther's Heidelberg Disputation, 1518* (Grand Rapids: Eerdmans, 1997), 79–80.

106. As quoted in Forde, *On Being a Theologian of the Cross*, 81.

107. Gilkey, *Maker of Heaven and Earth*, 181.

108. Quoted in Southgate, *The Groaning of Creation*, 52.

Figure 7.2. Shiva as Nataraja

Hinduism: Shiva, God of Destruction and Creation

As mentioned earlier, Hinduism operates with a cyclical understanding of time, in which each eon of creation and preservation is followed by a movement of destruction—necessary to create the space for the next iteration of the cycle. The particular deity most closely associated with the destruction part of the cycle is the god Shiva; in the *Trimurti*, he is responsible for destruction, while Brahma initiates creation, and Vishnu preserves and maintains the universe during any particular epoch. To Western ears, "destruction" has singularly negative implications; however, in the Hindu context, destruction is just the other face of creation. "To destroy, therefore, is practically to recreate, and Death stands at the gates of Life."[110] Shiva, therefore, is at least as much creator as he is destroyer,

109. Ibid.
110. E. Osborn Martin, *The Gods of India* (Delhi: Indological Book House, 1972), 167.

as Shiva's destructive activity is, in some sense, the first act (or at least the prologue) of creation, even as it is simultaneously the last act of creation. The image of Shiva that best embodies this creative tension is the *Nataraja*, which, in Sanskrit, means "king of the dance."

In this image, Shiva is framed in a circle of flames, which represents the fleeting, phenomenal world. Only the right foot is planted, resting not on the ground but on a figure of a dwarf called *apasmara*, who represents malice and ignorance, whom Shiva subdues. His left foot is lifted up, symbolizing his ability to receive the petitions of his devotees and give them his grace in return. In one hand he carries a drum, called the *damaru*, which stands for the primal sound of creation. In another hand, he carries the fire that destroys the world. A third hand is shown with a raised palm, which is a calming gesture of blessing, while the fourth hand is pointing downward at his foot, indicating where the devotee can take refuge. In this image, then, we see the dynamic interplay of both creation and destruction, and Shiva's ability to both reconcile and hold them in tension. In his matted hair there are snakes, and around his neck he wears a string of skulls, both of which symbolize his rejection of worldly values and embracing of death.

The dancing itself warrants further explication. Stella Kramrisch describes it as follows:

> Nataraja dances the cosmos into existence, upholds its existence, and dances it out of existence. The Lord veils existence with illusion so that it is seen as real, and, dancing, he removes the veil. The raised leg of the dancer shows the liberating freedom of his dance, the drum raised by the right hand sounds the note of creation, the flame in the left hand flickers in the change brought about by destruction, the right hand grants freedom from fear, the fear of repeated births and deaths, and assures the maintenance of life. The dancer's foot is firmly planted on the infant shape of the demon Amnesia, the Apasmara Purusa, and accentuates the vertical, cosmic axis of the god's body. The movement of the dancer around this axis, self-enclosed in balanced gyration, is encircled by flames.[111]

111. Stella Kramrisch, *The Presence of Siva* (Princeton: Princeton University Press, 1981), 440.

This description points to the soteriological aspects of the dance, which are of central importance. Ananda Coomaraswamy notes that ". . . the purpose of the dance is to release the countless souls of [humans] from the snare of illusion. . . ."[112] This means that, in addition to everything else, Shiva dances to enlighten believers, to show them the true nature of creation, and liberate them from illusion. All of the various aspects of the dance serve this one purpose.

ESCHATOLOGY AND LAST THINGS

At the close of this chapter and the close of the book, it is appropriate to give the last word to eschatology, to the ultimate Christian hope for the future: a vision of the kingdom of God—breaking in upon us now in glimpses and hints—that embraces and transforms the whole universe, and all God's creatures. God is not done yet, we are all still together underway, and there is much still to do. Yet, the promise Christians cling to is that we have read the final chapter, and we know how this story ends. God is not only in and with God's creation here and now, working on us and through us from above and below, around and about, deep within all life itself, but God also beckons from beyond, drawing us to Godself in the future, where God is preparing a place for us with no tears, no groaning, and no brokenness. Completion awaits; perfection awaits; Sabbath awaits; and perhaps we will wake one day to find that the whole lifetime of the entire cosmos was embraced in those first few verses of Genesis after all:

> Could we think of the creation week of seven days as inclusive of the entire history of the creation from big bang to whatever will become of the universe in the future? Could evolutionary history constitute one small episode in the divine epic of creation. . . . Could we see ourselves standing between the initial moment when God opened his divine mouth to say, "Let there be . . ." and the final moment when God declares that, "behold, it is very good"? Could we still be looking forward to the Sabbath day, to God's first day of rest yet in the future?[113]

I fervently hope so, for if so, so much good yet awaits us: so much as yet unrevealed and undiscovered; so much yet to astound and amaze. None of us

112. Ananda K. Coomaraswamy, *The Dance of Shiva* (New York: Noonday, 1957), 77.
113. Peters and Hewlett, *Can You Believe in God and Evolution?*, 85.

is yet what we will be, and the earth is still in the process of becoming, but through it all, Christians trust with Julian of Norwich that somehow, in some way, at the end of all days, when we see God face to face, by God's grace, "all shall be well, and all shall be well, and all manner of things shall be well."

INTERRELIGIOUS QUESTIONS FOR FURTHER DISCUSSION

1. What might encourage Christians to affirm that Christians and Muslims worship the same God? What might cause us to hesitate? What might be gained from such an affirmation?

2. What can Christians learn from the ways in which Buddhism describes the relationship between humans and animals? Is our salvation in any way interwoven with animals? If so, how?

3. What would it mean for Christians to adopt the practice of "healing the world"? How does that relate to an understanding of human sinfulness, and the vision found in Revelation of "a new heaven and a new earth"?

4. Can Christians think about God "limiting" Godself in creation? What does that mean for an understanding of God's fundamental attributes and ways of acting in the world?

5. Is there a specific "Christian aesthetic"? If so, what would it look like, and what ideas would it seek to promote?

6. Is God also a God of "destruction" in Christianity? If so, how can that be reconciled with God's love and mercy?

Index of Names and Subjects